The Doctrine of the Messiah
in Medieval Jewish Literature

The Doctrine of the Messiah

IN

Medieval Jewish Literature

By

JOSEPH SARACHEK, D.H.L.

Author of

"The History of the Anti-Maimonidean Controversy"

WIPF & STOCK · Eugene, Oregon

Wipf and Stock Publishers
199 W 8th Ave, Suite 3
Eugene, OR 97401

The Doctrine of the Messiah in Medieval Jewish Literature
By Sarachek, Joseph
ISBN 13: 978-1-60608-284-3
Publication date 12/22/2008
Previously published by Harmon Press, 1932

TABLE OF CONTENTS

ix

PREFACE

This volume does not purport to be a complete history of Messianism. Neither has the writer ventured to portray the many adventist movements that centered about glamorous Messianic personages. Should the reader notice the omission of some scholar who lived in the period treated, let him bear in mind the desirability of limiting a treatise of this kind for the greater ease of its publication and availability to the general reader. It was intended to offer the modern reader precise and authentic knowledge concerning the Jewish redeemer, his character, the time of the advent, the reestablishment of the Hebrew state, the millennium and resurrection. Possibly no other doctrine is laden with so much of legend and mystery, nor is any other teaching tinged with so much vagueness. If the author has helped to define and clarify the doctrine he will feel himself adequately repaid.

The scholars and thinkers whose views are presented flourished in the five centuries that began with that most eminent gaon, Saadia, and ended with Abrabanel, who survived the expulsion from Spain in 1492, by several years. Saadia, with whom the geonic era may be said to have closed, articulated in his systematic theology the religious faith and reflections of the Midrashic school. So too, Abrabanel, uninfluenced by the rationalism of Maimonides, Crescas, and others, enunciated the earlier geonic, traditional views. The savants of these five centuries made that period the heyday of intensive and varied Jewish learning. Judaism today is sustained largely by the momentum they gave to it. Their doctrine of the redemption is still the belief of the large mass of Jews today.

Significantly, the major portion of Jewish and Christian apologetic literature hinges upon the theory of the Messianic advent, which is the original point of difference between Jews and Christians, and has naturally been the subject of acrimonious and unceasing controversy. Christian theologians have written very profusely on the subject, since it involves the very foundation of their theology. They have ransacked the Bible, Talmud, Targumim, and Midrash diligently, and have performed pioneer work in collating all predictive and Messiological passages. Save in rare instances, all these studies were undertaken with a Christological bias. In comparison, Jewish Messianic literature is sparse. Whatever works by medieval authors appeared were purely defensive.

PREFACE

In recent years our religious literature has been enriched by the accession of scholarly books on the Messianic theme. Although they possess extraordinary value, they fall short because of their fragmentary and limited treatment. The present book is the first attempt made to offer a systematic and comprehensive exposition of the accredited Messianic dogma. The attention of the reader is drawn to several special features of this book: 1. The doctrinal affirmation of the belief. 2. Messianic exegesis, or the derivation of the many phases of the redemption from Scripture. 3. Messianic poetry. 4. Polemical aspect. 5. Resurrection.

The writer gladly acknowledges his indebtedness to all those whose cooperation and friendship have made this book possible. My esteemed teacher, Dr. Louis Ginzberg, Professor of Talmud at the Jewish Theological Seminary of America, has made me his lifelong debtor by suggesting the scope of this study and the technique for its development. He has given the manuscript constant supervision and painstaking attention. To Dr. Cyrus Adler, President of the Seminary and to Professor Alexander Marx, Professor of History and Librarian of the Seminary, I am thankful for reading parts of the manuscript. I also wish to record the debt to my colleague, Dr. Louis Finkelstein, Solomon Schechter Professor in Jewish Theology, who examined the manuscript and aided me with many splendid suggestions. I acknowledge, too, the valuable assistance of my wife whose discriminating criticism has been constantly helpful.

In conclusion, I tender my thanks to the officers, trustees and members of the Jewish Center of University Heights for all their goodness and kindness toward me.

JOSEPH SARACHEK.

January, 1932.
New York City.

Chapter I

INTRODUCTION

1—Importance of the Doctrine.

The purpose of this book is to give a systematic exposition of the standard Messianic doctrine of the Jews, to set forth what the leading synagogue authorities held concerning it, and to show what modifications it underwent at their hands, either in the way of broadening or exaggeration. The intense hold which the expectation of the Messiah had on medieval Jewry is evidenced by the fact that its intellectual and spiritual leaders introduced it into their philosophic works, their Halakic codes, their Bible commentaries, their poetry, and their abundant apologetic literature. The treatment of the doctrine by the Cabalists (mystics) is omitted intentionally, as the purpose of this work is to present the normal attitude of the Synagogue.

It is clear that the Messianic doctrine belongs to a different phase of Jewish theology than that which embraces the beliefs in God, immortality, and Providence. This doctrine is political rather than theological; more practical than speculative. It links itself to God, inasmuch as religion links all the earth and civilization to a Supreme Being, yet genetically it is a social and practical ideal. The belief in the Messiah can be traced from its vague and remote Biblical beginnings to its greatest fullness as a dogma of the Jewish authorities of the Middle Ages. A knowledge of sacred literature, of the tempestuous course of Hebrew history, and of human psychology will reveal its rise, its function, its power and its rationale.

THE DOCTRINE OF THE MESSIAH

The Messianic faith was a safety-valve to the Jewish people in every strained situation. They pinned their hope to a mighty and saintly liberator who would rescue them from the torture-chamber and lead them to a mansion shielded by their Heavenly Father. He would turn their darkness into light and their sorrow into joy. What was at first a passionate hope, evoked by crucial circumstances, gradually crystallized into a national belief and later into a theological dogma. As such it became of absorbing interest to the layman and the scholar. It was a favorite theme of the pious; it was imbibed by the young at home, taught in the academies, preached in the synagogue, and prayed for at every divine service; glamor was added to it by the poets and mystics. In response to the continuous clamor and poignant cry of Israel for deliverance, there grew up a wealth of adventist sentiment and detail, embodied in the legal, legendary, devotional, poetic and exegetical literature of Israel. And in the exquisite garden of Messianism, there sprouted also the weeds of false cults and charlatans.

In a broad sense one may consider that Messianism offered to Israel the philosophy of optimism as a solution of the problem of human evolution and destiny. The Jew explains the world as a moral order under divine guidance, and when hard pressed by difficulties he clings to an abounding faith in a brighter future. His historic attitude has ever been one of hope in the perfectibility of Israel and mankind.

Such reliance and trustfulness became the preservatives which permitted the Jew to survive despite physical weakness. We may say of the prophets and their followers, as Ahad Haam says of Maimonides: "He understood what they failed to understand—that a people cannot live on logic, that without a hope for the future even the Law, with all its logical principles would sink into oblivion, and

INTRODUCTION

that all the signs of history and all the proofs of scholasticism would not avail to save the Law—and its people—from death."[1]

2—*Origin, Hebraic not Foreign.*

The beginnings of the Jewish Messianic idea are quite obscure. Many scholars who follow the vogue of identifying the essential beliefs of Judaism with relics of primitive cults are baffled when they essay to trace the Messianic doctrine to its source. The hypothesis that it developed out of "floating myth material", current with most ancient peoples, is defended by Oesterley in a dissertation on "The Evolution of the Messianic Idea", in which he summarizes the views favoring a foreign origin. The evidence he offers is quite vague and inconclusive, while the "antecedents" which he promises, are in some instances not given and in others are too meagre to be taken seriously.

Very recently two books have been written to prove the pure Hebraic roots of the Messianic idea. Hölscher, in "Die Ursprünge der Judischen Eschatologie", rejects the legendary theory and assigns its inception to the overthrow of the first Commonwealth in 586 B. C. E., when the Jews, deprived completely of nationhood, yearned for the restoration.[2] According to him the first and finest expression of the longing and faith of the people is found in the sublime words of Deutero-Isaiah. Dürr, in "Ursprünge und Ausbau der Israelitisch-judischen Heilandserwartung", also combats the claim for an Egyptian or Babylonian origin.[3] He has searched the literature of those theosophic systems and concludes "that there can be no talk of a real (Messianic) prophecy" in them. They lack

[1]Ahad Ha-'am, Selected Essays translated by Leon Simon, p. 87.
[2]See Theologische Literaturzeitung, 1926, no. 16, p. 417.
[3]*Ibid.*, no. 18, p. 465.

— 3 —

the central figure of a king Messiah. Neither did the doctrine spring from a mythological notion of a final world-cataclysm. This author surmises that the messianic belief arose out of the all-essential faith of Israel that they are the chosen people, destined to become the world's regenerators and masters. The promise of God that Israel be a "kingdom of priests and a holy nation" was the germ which grew, in time, into a national conviction that they would some day enjoy spiritual primacy over the world.

Many Hebrew and Christian writers date the origins of Messianism as far back as the cradle of Hebrew history: in the divine assurances to Abraham that his progeny will be a source of blessing to all mankind. From the background of patriarchal struggle and ambition arose the aspiration for a future of conspicuous power, abundance, and tranquility. The combat between Jacob and Esau in their mother's womb and Esau's moral defeat in the loss of his birthright, nursed the faith that Israel would vie with other nations and ultimately triumph over them.

The Mosaic period contributed the oracles of Balaam, predicting the mastery of Israel over its adversaries, "in the end of days"; and other passages put the people's dispersion, repentance, and restoration in the same far-off period.

The enthronement of David, son of Jesse, in Jerusalem furnished the keystone as well as the most romantic element of Messianism. David was promised the throne in perpetuity for his descendants; his rule was the consummation of centuries of formative existence and of conflict with internal and foreign destructive forces. He was Israel's savior par excellence. His blessed state, however, did not prove durable. And, as time rolled on, the nation's halcyon days stood out as ideal in contrast with the impossible present.

INTRODUCTION

3—*Characteristics of Prophetic Messianism.*

Whether or not we regard the national anticipations and projections of pre-prophetic times as embryonic Messianic material, it is certain that in the literary prophets only do we find representations of a glorious future in the accredited Messianic sense. Under the kings, the hope of salvation received its historical impulse and began to play a dominating and conscious part in the life of the people. The prophets found motivation for their advocacy of a restored Israel and a transfigured world in the social and religious evils of their times, in the current political misfortunes, and in their inherited eschatological beliefs.

The doctrine of a Utopian future was a distinct creation of the prophets just as the one-God idea, the selection of Israel, the immutability of the Torah, and the moral laws were distinctly Mosaic. No doubt the prophets did not stand alone in their pronouncement of an ideal world. They were the spokesmen of a large proportion of the people, whose convictions they voiced. But the form in which the legacy has come down to us represents the richest and fairest optimism. The Messianic utterances stand out as a cluster of glittering jewels among the prophets' diatribes against the ungodly nations, their denunciations of social abuses, political short-sightedness, religious hypocrisy and their magnified praises of God.

That the future redemption will be miraculous is quite certain from the allusions of Is., 11:16, and Mic., 7:15, which put forth the Exodus as its pattern. Apparently the ancient strife between Israel and Egypt will be re-enacted in the more bloody and decisive conflict between Israel and the nations, in the end of days, so graphically described in Zech., 14:12, and Ezek., 38 and 39. Ezekiel specifically names Gog, of the land of Magog, who typifies Israel's archenemy in all later accounts of the redemp-

THE DOCTRINE OF THE MESSIAH

tion. That this prophet regarded Gog as the final enemy appears from 38:18. The Messiah does not participate in these wars. God alone will vanquish the adversary by extraordinary and super-natural means.

An essential element of the restoration is the home-bringing of dispersed Israel, buoyantly anticipated by the prophets. We note with interest Isaiah's poetic allusion to the blowing of the shofar to assemble the people, a detail which has been taken over by later Messianic legendry and is used also in connection with the summons to the resurrection.

A thorough reconstitution of the Hebrew state upon its own soil presupposes the healing of an ancient breach, the reunion of the two kingdoms eloquently preached by the major prophets. Their Utopian representations abound in glowing pictures of the soil's extraordinary luxuriance. Life's necessities will be freely supplied. The affirmation of the indestructibility of the Hebrew people, a basic concept, is poetically expressed by Jer., 31:35-37.

Israel's spiritual pre-eminence is set forth in many brilliant oracles, particularly in Isaiah, which breathe the purest idealism and universalism. Is., 2:1-4, predicts disarmament and a universal judicial tribunal. The notion rarely occurs that the Jews will exercise political or material control over the world. The national aspiration, as articulated by the prophets, is that the Jews may possess sovereign power within their own state, and forever be free from foreign molestation.

Internally the state will be blessed with political stability and spiritual perfection. God and His law will be accepted intuitively by all people. The sole influence exerted by Israel upon the world will be ethical and spiritual; the God of Israel will be universally worshipped. As a token of their submission Gentiles will make an annual pilgrimage to Jerusalem on the Feast of Tabernacles.

Zion, from which will radiate every salutary influence, is central in the spiritual headship of Israel. Isaiah, among others, conceives Zion as the spiritual capital of the world, distinguished for truth and holiness. Zion is the cornerstone of a sure foundation for a universal religion. In order to function eternally in the new era, it will be inaccessible to the violent and impervious to moral decline. The cruel fate meted out to the Gentiles by Zechariah and Ezekiel will overtake only the wicked among them, even as it will the undeserving Hebrews. On the positive side the brotherhood of nations is strongly anticipated.

The uniqueness and originality of the prophet's Utopia is seen then in its double character, national or political, and universal or ethical. These two strands are twined into one. Into the early and quite natural hope of the nation for a lofty destiny the seers infused certain broad humanitarian elements. They preached peace, rectitude, truth, monotheism, and brotherhood. Their projected future embraced not only the happiness and sanctification of God's chosen people, but also the perfection and bliss of all humanity.

4—The Prophetic Apocalypse.

The apocalypse, like prophetic Messianism, deals with the future. One scholar defines it as a "revelation of mysterious things, which lie beyond the ordinary range of human knowledge." The point of departure from the prophets to the apocalypse is not to be found in their substance but in their form; not in their goal but in their method. The apocalypse employs a mysterious setting; ecstatic moods, kaleidoscopic world movements, and angelology, stamp it as a distinctive branch of sacred literature. In a certain sense it represents a vulgarization of prophetism.

THE DOCTRINE OF THE MESSIAH

In prophetism the hope of a glorious future is to be realized through a slow but sure process of human development aided by faith, political events, reform, and the mercy of God. In the apocalypse the element of mystery enwraps the vision of the future and the oracles of the seer. Everything centers upon "the day of the Lord" with its sweeping world-wide judgment, and the devastation of nature and human life. Only God the Judge will survive, and his holy people. The coming of the golden age will be catastrophic. It will be "sudden and unpremeditated." Angels act as bearers of the mysteries and as the efficient performers of Messianic tasks. The former victims gloat over the ruthless cruelty with which they will treat their oppressors. Resurrection is also a part of the apocalyptic scheme.

A splendid illustration of Biblical apocalypse is the book of Daniel. Its depiction of the succession of nations and of the end is dramatic and mysterious. Israel, the nation of saints, will exercise world-wide dominion, when the four monarchies, represented as earthly and perishable (animal or mineral) have reached their end. They will be totally obliterated. Gabriel, Michael, and other celestials are introduced as participants in the future drama. Highly apocalyptic is Dan., 7:9-14, where God's throne of judgment is described, and the investiture of Israel as a nation of saints. The doctrine of resurrection, of eternal reward and punishment, becomes in Daniel part of the future age, as it is in the definite apocalypses. But Daniel registers an advanced stage in the formation of a mysterious future. It had been germinating in his predecessors. The priest-prophet Ezekiel had been called "the father of apocalypse," because of the wide use he made of symbolism and imagery. The first chapter—the "merkabah"—became the classic source and pattern of Jewish mysticism. His delineation of the final bloody wars

against the forces of Gog and Tubal and the savage manner in which they would be exterminated is a feature of
the apocalypse.

Zechariah, in many ways, discloses a kindred strain,
especially in the last chapter of his prophecies, where he
describes the catastrophic day of the Lord, with its extreme devastation of those who come to war against the
Holy Land. Is., 24-27, possesses the eschatological setting
and doctrines familiar in apocalyptic writings. In chapter 24 the writer portrays in dramatic word pictures
the dire disaster that will overwhelm the entire earth,
after which God will rule in Mount Zion.

We find in the prophets many parallels to the stereo-
typed features of rabbinic Messianism. But there are
several points in which they differ. Among these are:
first, the absence of the redeemer-concept,—the concept of one who will gather Israel, subdue her foes,
and restore the pristine order of things. In Scripture,
God is obviously credited with these performances. Whatever Davidic or ideal ruler is predicted, he is merely an
incident of the epoch, an essential improvement of the
revived state rather than a prime mover in the eschatological drama. In its technical significance the term Messiah does not occur in Scripture, but is employed for the
first time in the apocalyptic Book of Enoch. The rabbinic
use of the name Messiah as a legitimate successor to
David, in the restored state, marked the advance of tradition over Scriptures in the formulation of the doctrine.
During and after the Roman wars, the Messiah's advent
overshadowed every other aspect of the belief. Second,
the favorable changes in the future are not represented
in the prophets as unified parts of one scheme to be un-
rolled at the advent, but merely desirable events that are
destined to occur. Third, the Messiah son of Joseph, is
unknown to the prophets. Fourth, the practice of calculat-

ing the year of grace is characteristic of the Talmudic and medieval authorities, and occurs only once in Scripture—in Daniel, who actually essayed to discover the apocalyptic "end".

And last, it should be observed that the note of finality is not so clearly sounded in Biblical as in later Messiology. Much of the former refers to an indefinite future, whereas that of rabbinism is final. Although many prophecies reach into the far off future or dwell upon preternatural phenomena and idealizations, such, for example, as begin "in the end of days," "on that day," or "the day of the Lord," yet that future is within the seer's historical or normal perspective. The term "end" in post-canonical literature, however, as the year of wonders, technically means the close of the present order and the commencement of a changed world.

On the other hand, "the day of the Lord", an absorbing and central theme in Biblical eschatology, was dropped from later theology. Its place was taken by the rabbinic "end" or advent. In Scripture, the transition from the present to the ameliorated order hinges upon the catastrophic "day of the Lord", whereas in rabbinism it is made contingent upon the advent of the Anointed One. In general one may say that in the primary sources the future hope gravitated about the new-born era rather than about the Messianic person, and as has been pointedly observed, "the Messiah does not appear at the beginning, the foundation of the blissful age, but rather at its end and culmination."

The day of the Lord will not bring utter extermination. A doctrine basic in all religion is that repentance is an avenue of escape. The regeneration of Israel is emphatically set down as a prerequisite for national salvation. Closely connected with this teaching is the corollary that in the final days Israel will undergo a selective process, so that the deserving ones will be redeemed. This theme of a righteous remnant of the people runs like a thread through all later Messianic writings. The prophets Nah., 2:1, and Mal., 3:1, proclaim the coming of a herald in their vision of the deliverance, whose function it will be to announce the glad tidings of salvation. The apocalyptic appearance of the ubiquitous Elijah is definitely foretold by Malachi, at the close of his prophecies, "before the coming of the great and terrible day of the Lord."

5—*The Doctrine in the Talmud.*

The Biblical elements of the Messianic belief received fresh momentum from the fateful collision between Judea and Rome. The loss of temple and country, the scattering of the people, and the apparent extirpation of the legitimate Davidic line accentuated the inherited features of the Messianic idea and made room for new elements. According to a widespread tradition, Rome was the fourth and last empire that subdued Palestine. Consequently the people eagerly anticipated the accession of Israel to world power. They hugged the sentiment of the comforter: "As I brought all this calamity upon this people, so will I bring all the good of which I spake."

At every juncture in Israel's history, some righteous souls could divine the presence of a savior, a Messiah. To Isaiah, Hezekiah was the God-appointed one. Haggai and Zechariah saw him in the person of Zerubabel. R. Johanan b. Zakkai believed that the redemption was imminent, as can be seen from his dying request to his pupil, "to prepare a throne for Hezekiah, son of David, who is about to come."[4]

---

[4]San. 94a; Prof. Ginzberg, in Moore's Judaism III., pp. 201, 202, gives quite a different explanation for Johanan's statement. The political character of the hope appears from San. 96b where Messiah is called "bar naphli" with reference to Amos, 9:11. Ginzberg suggests a play on the Greek word "nephale", meaning cloud, and would connect it with Dan., 7:13.

THE DOCTRINE OF THE MESSIAH

Certain legal enactments of the tannaim are made to rest on the firm conviction that the vanished order would be restored forthwith.

Equally significant of the urgency and reality of the redemptist hope was the drama staged in 135 C. E. by Rabbi Akiba, who eagerly expected the fall of the Roman Empire and the accession of Israel to sovereign power. Akiba, too, centered his hopes on Bar Kochba, whom he hailed as the long awaited deliverer. Incidentally, the sage's championship of the ill-fated Bar Kochba, casts light on the traditional view of rabbinism, that the Messiah was to be purely human.

The great source for the standard sentiments and dicta concerning the advent of the Messiah and the hereafter is the Talmud. Yet despite the profuse material therein, we get no clear-cut delineation of the eschatological doctrines. This may be accounted for in several ways. First, because the Talmud is a compilation by scholars of different types and epochs; hence its variegated and fluctuating contents. Second, because in projecting an ideal future the imagination of a spiritually-minded people, stimulated by tormenting circumstances, soars freely. Last, the Messianic story belongs to the Agadah of the Talmud, which, unlike the Halakah, has no logical precision to follow and no norm toward which to strive. A large part of rabbinic Messiology is derived from Holy Writ by the exegetical method of the derash, an unreal and fictional interpretation. Although the notion of the advent was incorporated into the daily ritual and hence became part of Jewish authoritative belief, it was nevertheless treated as Agadah. The free manner of Agadah yielded a maze of grotesque representations. The more rational minded rabbis saw the illogical nature of the situation and decried all fantastic eschatological conceptions. Yet even those who indulged in conjectures realized that the principal thing was faith in the redemption, and not its derived embellishments.

Thus we cannot help but think that it was mere playfulness for the rabbis to set a dozen different periods for the duration of the Messianic state, ranging from 40 to 7000 years—or when they apply a dozen honorific names to the redeemer.

A pivotal question much mooted among the rabbis concerned the time of the end. "When will the Messiah come?" There were two general theories. On the one hand, the advent was conceived as depending upon Israel, on the other as controlled by God. In the former case it would come as a reward for the people's merits. As soon as Israel had duly repented, the redemption would occur. In the other case, it all depended upon God. He had ordained the year. When the year arrived the redemption would inevitably occur. A compromise between these two extreme views is the idea of compulsory repentance, according to which, if the predetermined end approaches and finds Israel unrepentant, God would set over them tyrants whose cruelty would force the nation to turn to the Lord in contrition. In this way the occurrence of the redemption would be ripe both as to time and the fitness of the people.

More specifically, the belief was current that salvation would come upon the fall of Rome. As the premise had been laid down that the "end" was an enigma, there was plenty of room for conjecture and calculation. Quite a number of statements indicate that the Messianic era would be ushered in at the beginning of the fifth chiliad or during that period.[5]

The most consistently treated and generally accepted theme was "The Birth Travails of the Messiah." This was to be a prelude to the unparalleled degeneracy and

---

[5] San. 97b.

helplessness of the world. Some of the scholars who pithily sketched the woeful days, had witnessed the destruction of the Temple in the year 70 and the revolution of 135. Their dismal description, evoked by the invader's tyranny, received color and force from their experiences. These pre-Messianic afflictions were regarded by the people as an indication of speedy redemption, and as a vehicle for their own moral improvement.

A noteworthy distinction between prophetic and rabbinic Messianism is the position accorded the Messiah. In the earlier belief more stress is placed upon the features of the renovated nation and ameliorated society than upon the great deliverer. In rabbinism everything centers about him. The very age is named after him. It is he who will initiate the great changes. This is particularly true of the later Talmudic period, the amoraic, Midrashic, and Geonic period. Unanimity prevails as to the functions and mortal nature of the redeemer. According to the prevailing Jewish opinion the Messiah will be born of the ancient royal line of David, upon this mundane sphere. He will vanquish foes, liberate Israel, and repossess Palestine; he will die and be succeeded by a direct descendant. According to another tradition the characterization in Is., 11:2, befits the Messiah. In tannaitic literature there is no trace of his pre-existent or supernatural character. A beraita to the effect that the name of the Messiah, together with six other things, was created before the world, gave rise to the vagary of his pre-mundane existence.[6] The grain of gold in the legend appears to mean that the Almighty foresaw the complete course of events on this earth and that he providentially appointed a savior to appear to Israel at the proper time. The alleged supernatural personality of the Messiah is adduced also from the rabbinic statement that the Messiah was one of nine,—among the

---

[6]Pes. 54a; comp. Ber. Rabba. 1:5; Bk. of Enoch, 48:31.

others being distinguished heathens and benefactors—to enter Paradise alive.[7] However, a statement of this sort does not imply the divinity or eternity of the redeemer any more than it would in the case of the others who are enumerated with him. It does mean that his reward is in Paradise as is that of the other righteous men. When the time for his heroic advent arrives, he will be resurrected along with many others. Rabbinic literature contains other curious legends of the Messiah's genealogy and his mundane whereabouts. The accredited and predominating view was of a matter of fact and mortal Messiah.

The notion of a suffering Messiah, the cornerstone of Christian Messiology, is not current in the Talmud, although some writers have discovered it in several passages. On this point Drummond remarks: "He (the Messiah) was indeed to be mortal like other men, but was to die in peace at the end of a triumphant and glorious reign. The possibility of reconciling the idea of the Messiah with the lowly and suffering life of Jesus was one of the most formidable obstacles which Christianity had to encounter in its controversy with Judaism. We may confidently say that within the period to which our inquiry is confined (apocryphal, Talmudic, and Targumic), although the Jews were not without the general notion that the afflictions of the pious atoned for the sins of the community, they had no expectation of a suffering and atoning Messiah."[8]

As for the two lesser lights in the scheme of redemption, Elijah and the Messiah son of Joseph, the former occupies a more important place. His apocalyptic appearance is promised by Malachi and he figures conspicuously in traditional eschatology. Elijah knows the intention of the Almighty and the secret of Israel's fate, and at the

---

[7]Derek Eretz Zuta, end of Ch. I.
[8]Drummond, The Jewish Messiah, p. 359. See however, San. 98a.

appointed time he will descend upon earth to assist the Messiah.[9] The Seder Olam, a semi-historical book of Talmudic times, says of him: "In the second year of the reign of Ahaziah, Elijah became hidden and was seen no more. When the King Messiah shall come he will be seen again; then hidden a second time; he will not be seen again until Gog and Magog appear on the scene.[10] To him is assigned the task of raising the dead. He is the supreme teacher who will disclose solutions to Halakic problems, settle controversies, and re-establish racial purity.[11] The Yalkut supplies a highly dramatic picture of his official announcement of the glad tidings. On the first day of his appearance he will stand on one of the mountain tops of Israel and lament the devastation of Palestine. With a resounding voice he will proclaim: "Good cometh to the world." On the second day he will likewise announce: "Peace cometh to the world." On the third day he will exclaim: "Salvation cometh to the world, saying unto Zion, thy King cometh."[12]

The Messiah son of Joseph is a mere figment of the imagination, an aberration from Biblical Messianism. The Talmud alludes to him only twice, but the later Targumim and Midrashim describe his meteoric appearance and mission with some detail. Both Messiahs will collaborate in the final redemption, as did Moses and Aaron in the Egyptian Exodus.

According to a plausible view the belief in an Ephraimitic Messiah arose from the attempt to separate the political function from the spiritual activity of the ideal deliverer. The cruel oppression accentuated the need of the warrior type of savior, so that the notion of a prelim-

[9]Ginzberg—Eine Unbekannte Sekte, p. 299-373, shows that Elijah was sometimes identified with the Messiah.
[10]Ch. 17.
[11]Eduyot 8:7 and end of Mishnah Sotah.
[12]Yalkut Shimeoni on Is. 52:7.

inary Messiah, who would conduct the military activities, inevitably arose. That type is vividly brought to mind by Akiba's idol, Bar Kochba, who laid no claim to wisdom, saintliness, royal descent, nor miraculous power. The exigency of the times required one like him to save the nation. Correlated with this theory is another, that upon the failure of Bar Kochba the people fell back on the consoling view that their fallen champion represented a secondary figure and that the principal and formidable Messiah would yet appear. It is possible also that the concept of an Ephraimitic redeemer sprang out of parallelism which the rabbis developed between the Exodus and the final redemption.[13] The conquest of Palestine was effected by Joshua son of Nun, an Ephraimite. Hence the final deliverance would not parallel the first one unless an Ephraimite assume leadership. But as no sectional leader could surpass or supplant the Messiah son of David, the legitimate heir, the Ephraimite was conceived as one who would attain only subordinate rank. Hence the two Messiahs represent the two kingdoms. The first one will gather up the scattered people, conquer the Holy Land, and then meet a tragic end.[14] Thereupon the son of David will succeed to rule over the new Israel, even as the prophets had predicted.

6—The Ideal Messianic Future.

A sharp line of demarcation is drawn in the Talmud between the Messianic state and the future world.[15] The former is the interregnum, the transition era of unknown duration between this imperfect world and the ideal world to come.

---

[13]See Ginzberg article "Anti-Christ" in Jew. Enc. Vol. 1 p. 627; also by the same author, "Eine Unbekannte Sekte," p. 336; Klausner, Raayon ha-Meshihi pp. 313ff.; see Journal of Theological Studies, V. 27, no. 106, Jan. 1926, for theories about the Ephraimite Messiah.

[14]Sukkah 52a.

[15]Shab. 63a, see also 113b.

THE DOCTRINE OF THE MESSIAH

The Messianic state is a humanitarian idea. It is the Hebraic version of a Utopia and will mark the amelioration of present day social conditions. The structure of civilization will remain the same, but qualitatively it will attain the acme of efficiency, goodness, and virtue. One gains the impression that the golden age will be the culmination of centuries of evolution, during which mankind will outgrow its animal nature and be transformed into a perfectly moral race. This liberal humanistic portrayal of the Messianic era conforms with the popular view of an ideal future. It will be as ideal as rectified human nature will allow it to be.

At that time Israel will be free from foreign domination. The view of Samuel, an early amora, that there would be no difference between the present and Messianic ages, except in the matter of subjection to the nations, is given wide currency in the Talmud.[16] Apparently it was the predominating view. Israel will be gathered together from all lands to Palestine. The borders of the Holy Land will be extended. It will be divided into thirteen sections, one for each tribe, including the tribe of Levi. Every family will be assured of economic independence and abundance of rich, varied, and arable soil.[17] Some scholars qualify the attributed perfection of Israel, saying that even then Israel will prosper, wax arrogant, and rebel.[18] The poor will never cease from the earth, and will continue to be a problem even in the new era. One scholar is quite certain that war implements will not be altogether discarded.

A necessary feature of the rejuvenated state must be the restitution of the Torah and the Temple in Palestine. The academies and synagogues which were banished to Babylon will be transferred to their original center. The

---

[16]Ber. 34b; San. 992; Shab. 63a and Pes. 68a.
[17]Baba Batra, 122a.
[18]Sifre Deut.; ed. Friedman p. 136a.

INTRODUCTION

accepted position was that the Torah is immutable, and
its integrity and lasting authority.are assured in various
passages. The extreme view found in the Midrashim, that
with the complete transformation of the present order the
Torah would be abrogated and a higher moral law promulgated, refers to the transcendental world to come.[19] The
Messianic age is a continuation of the present, and the
Torah will then be observed more assiduously and punc-
tiliously.

The status of Gentiles in the perfected society is not
uniformly and definitely stated in Talmudic literature.
The general belief is that when Israel becomes supreme,
the unrepentant Gentiles and the inveterate foes among
them will be extirpated; others will accept monotheism.
As a visible token of their acknowledgment they will practice some Jewish ordinances. Concerning the admission
of proselytes, we are informed that none will be received
in the better era, because their motive will be challenged.
Fear of divine vengeance, or eagerness to share in the new
blessings may prompt them to join the Hebrews.[20]

The status of the nations in the ideal future is indicated in several Agadic passages of the Talmud. Rome,
as the worst offender, will not be allowed to make amends.
Ishmael, a tanna of the early second century, says that
Egypt will in time to come proffer a gift to the Messiah,
who will be uncertain whether to accept it or not.[21] God
will then counsel him: "Accept it from them, for they
made a domicile for my children in their land." The
Ethiopians will wish to do likewise and will reason on the
principle of minori ad majus. If the Egyptians who enslaved the Hebrews were thus favored, how much better
is our position? God will then say to the Messiah, "Ac-

---

[19]Klausner, Die Messianische Vorstellungen. pp. 115ff.
[20]Yeb. 24b; Abodah Zarah 3b.
[21]Pes. 118b.

cept it (the gift) also from them." Thereupon the Ethiopians will also join the comradeship. Wicked Rome finally reasons: if these who are not of the same kindred as Israel were so gladly welcomed, how much better will we be received who are brothers to the Israelites? But God will enjoin Gabriel to reject Rome's gift and to rebuke her for her ferocity to Israel.

From this it appears that only Rome, of all the powers of the earth, will be utterly doomed. Rabbi Simlai, a third century amora, thus envisages the judgment scene.[22] God will take the Book of the Law unto His bosom and say: "Whoever has engaged in this Law, let him come here and receive his reward." Immediately all nations will swarm up in great confusion, but God will command them to come singly and in order. Rome will approach the celestial throne. When asked if it has studied Torah it will reply boastfully that it constructed roads, erected bridges, built bath houses, and accumulated treasures of gold and silver. "All these enterprises we did for the sake of Israel, that they might occupy themselves exclusively with the Torah." But the Almighty will rebuke them: "Ye imbeciles, what ye wrought, was for yourselves only. Is there one among you who can say something concerning the Law?" At this, Rome is affrighted and departs in deep dismay. Then Persia answers to the inquiry, "In what did you engage?" "We built bridges, subjected cities, waged wars. All this we did for Israel's sake, that they might be free to study the Torah." But the Almighty reproves them, saying: "You made bridges to levy toll and to impose taxes." They too leave in dismay. And why does Persia appear for judgment after hearing Rome condemned? Persia reasons that the latter destroyed the Temple, while she was instrumental in rebuilding it. Other

---

[22]Aboda Zara 2a.

nations also come voluntarily to trial and plead in their own defense but to no avail.

Parallel to the foregoing direct and normal conception of the golden age runs the hyperbolic portrayal of it. Dealing with the unknown future, it was easy for some to magnify the splendor of what was to come. Thus R. Gamaliel II, successor to Johanan b. Zakkai, transported by his imagination, dwells upon the supernatural wonders of the new state, the overfertility of its soil, and the fecundity of women. Women will bear children daily. Trees will give forth ripe fruit every day.[23] The soil will produce edible bread and woven garments. Wheat will grow tall like palm-trees and will have the fatness of an ox. The Holy One will bring a wind out of His storehouse which will blow over the wheat and furnish fine flour. A person will go into the field, take a handful and therewith nourish himself and his household. One grape will yield thirty measures of wine. A single grape will be a load for a wagon or a ship; the grape will be placed in a corner of the house and wine be drawn from it, as from a great barrel. Such abundance of food and ease of living will breed a race of giants.[24]

The Talmud creates an extravagant and fanciful Jerusalem, in line with the other marvels of the Messianic world.[25] It describes a feast which will be held for the righteous at the end of days. Gabriel will battle with the Leviathan, the sea-monster, and slaughter it. Wine has also been preserved since creation for the righteous.[26]

---

[23]Shab. 30b; Targum Jonathan Gen. 1:21 reads, "On the fifth day God created the great monsters of the water, Leviathan and its female, which are prepared for the day of consolation."

[24]Hag. 12a; San. 100a; see Apocalypse of Baruch, section III, chapters XX-XXXIV.

[25]Baba Batra 75b.

[26]San. 99a; Ber. 34b; Hag. 12b; Baba Batra 74b; For stories and literature on Leviathan and other eschatological creatures see Ginzberg, Legends of the Jews V., pp. 42-46; notes 123-127.

THE DOCTRINE OF THE MESSIAH

7—Resurrection.

Resurrection is to be regarded as part of the Messianic scheme. Although no positive statement appears as to when the miracle will occur, there is a strong presumption that the rabbis placed it either at the commencement or the termination of the Messianic epoch. This presumption is strengthened by the last mishna of the tractate Sota, where Elijah, a traditionally Messianic figure, is mentioned as the agent who will revive the dead. Another statement to this effect occurs elsewhere[27] and holds that the resurrection in this world effected by Elijah, Elisha, and Ezekiel was intended to show forth the magnitude and majesty of God; whereas the resurrection in the Messianic era would provide a reward for the righteous and God-fearing in the coming world.

The resurrection theme, of old a bone of contention between the Pharisees and Sadducees, is frequently and emphatically enunciated in the Talmud and kindred literature, and had become an approved dogma of Judaism by the first century. The tanna Eleazar ha-Kapar declared: "Those who are born are to die, and the dead are destined to live again."[28] The doctrine became liturgized in the tefilla (Eighteen Benedictions) and the early morning prayer.[29]

The certitude of the rabbis concerning the reanimation of the dead was no doubt inherited from earlier Judaism and based on the positive promises offered in Scripture.[30] Not content with these, however, the sages added further "proofs" which can hardly be accepted as valid, and are certainly unconvincing. These are exegetical inferences based on some suggestive characteristic of a word or thought, as the use of the future tense in Ex. 15:1, "Then

---

[27]Seder Olam Rabbah, ch. 5.
[28]Abot. 4:29.
[29]Ber. 60b.
[30]Deut. 32:39; Dan. 12:13; I Sam. 2:6; Is. 26:19.

Moses shall sing", (at the resurrection).[31] Of course, the
accepted translation is, "Then sang Moses."

The great motive behind this gigantic hope was purely
ethical; absolute justice required the judgment of body
and soul. In this world perfect recompense is not to be
had. Neither would it be fair to requite only the imperishable soul in the Hereafter. Hence there must be a
day when matter and spirit are joined together to receive
the bliss or doom decreed by God. In this compensatory
motive Judaism differs essentially from other theories
of human survival. The others are grounded on the
belief that matter is eternal. Therefore, the body, the
personality, remains immortal. The Jew, however, maintains that matter (corporeal and cosmic) had a beginning
and has an end. God in His goodness created life, and
may in His discretion end it. The final disposition of
human life for good or ill will be made by God at a trial
of the united body and soul. Resurrection, therefore, is
essential for the execution of the divine plan concerning
the final reward and destiny of the individual. This principle is illustrated by a conversation recorded in the
Talmud between a Roman Emperor and R. Judah the
Prince.[32] Said the emperor to the rabbi: "Body and soul
can absolve themselves from final judgment in the following manner. The body will declare the soul guilty, saying,
'From the day that it departed from me, I lay mute like
a stone in the sepulcher.' The soul on its side can declare:
'The body is guilty, for from the day that I parted from it,
I have been flying in the upper regions like a bird.' " To
this, the rabbi replied with the following analogy of a
king who had a beautiful garden with delectable,
newly-ripened fruits. "He placed in the garden two
keepers, one lame and the other blind. Said the lame one

---

[31]San. 91b.
[32]San. 91ab.

to the blind, 'I see beautiful fruit in the garden, carry me to them and we will eat them.' The lame man was carried on the back of the blind and they gathered the fruit and ate them. Later, the owner of the garden summoned them and asked, 'What has become of the precious fruit?' The lame keeper spoke up, 'Have I feet to go and get them?' And the blind one likewise protested, 'Have I eyes to see them?' What did the owner do? He placed the lame person on the blind one and judged them together. Even so, will the Holy One cast the soul back into the body, and judge them together."

8—*Nature of the Miracle.*

The possibility of resurrection as an actual physical phenomenon was studied by the rabbis, who adduced reason and observation to strengthen their faith in it.[33] They argued that if the body could come into being after non-existence, the presumption is very strong that a second person could arise from the one that existed. They offered analogies from the forms of animal life that result not from reproduction but from "spontaneous generation."[33a] The probability of the future re-existence of the departed was enhanced by the Scriptural accounts of the resuscitation performed by Elijah, Elisha, and Ezekiel.

A multiplicity of contradictory opinions as to whether resurrection will be universal or partial, fills rabbinical eschatology.

The notion that the miracle will be wrought only in the Holy Land also appears. This does not mean that it will be restricted to those who die there. People interred elsewhere will pass through subterranean channels to the holy spot, where they will arise to new life.[34]

---

[33]San. 91a.
[33a]*Ibid.* This was an accepted view in ancient times and even in the Middle Ages. Aristotle taught that good-sized animals are born from air, earth, heat and putrefaction.
[34]Ket. 111a.

The rebirth will not occur automatically, but by the design and instrumentality of the Almighty. According to another tradition, either the Messiah, Elijah, or perchance some other elect of God, will recall the dead.[35] The "dew of resurrection"—Is. 26:19—will refresh and arouse the interred. They will sprout forth from their sepulchers, in the same way that grass shoots up out of the earth.[36]

The quandary as to the form in which the dead will appear is discussed by the sagacious tanna, Rabbi Meir and Queen Cleopatra. "I know," said the queen, "that the dead will live again, for it says, 'They shall flourish out of the city like the grass of the earth', but when they rise up, will they rise naked or clothed?" The sage offered an analogy of the grain of wheat which is planted bare, but springs up out of the earth as a ripe product, wrapped with many coverings; how much more likely that the righteous will appear in their habiliments?[37] The prevailing opinion seems to be that the dead will arise in the same imperfect bodily condition as when they died, but after they have been restored to life they will be healed of their blemishes. The righteous persons who have been revived will not perish again, but will enjoy everlasting and saintly life in Jerusalem. The fate of the undeserving will be a second and permanent death.

9—The Future World.

The future world is a theological assumption; it transcends our experience and we can have only an inkling of what it will be. R. Johanan earnestly affirms that all good things foretold by the prophets related to the period of deliverance; but as for the days of the future—"No eye

---

[35]Mishnah Sotah, 9:15, Pes. 68a.
[36]San. 90b. Ps. 72:16.
[37]*Ibid.,* Comp. M. Wolf, Mohammedan Eschatology, p. 120. Aischa plays the part of Cleopatra and Mohammed of R. Meir.

hath seen it, save Thou, O God."[38] The belief in a future world results from the fevered faith of mystics who assume that the world to come will be one of supernal bliss and radiant joy, that God Himself will rule over it, and that only the chosen ones of the earth will be privileged to enter it.

In the world to come there will be no eating, drinking, procreation, jealousy, hate, rivalry, occupation. The righteous will sit with crowns and revel in the Divine Glory.[39] In other words, life beyond will express itself not in physical form but spiritually only. Pure happiness and bliss are not to be had on earth but in the future world. The present life is only an antechamber which leads into the glorious mansion beyond. In the opinion of R. Simon b. Yohai, eternal life in the world beyond is one of the three exceptional gifts bestowed upon Israel, the other two being the Torah and Palestine.

---

[38]San. 99b.
[39]Ber. 17a.

Chapter II

SAADIA

1—*Method.*

The writings of the saintly men considered in these pages were ardent attempts to present Judaism as a religion, perfect and supreme among the philosophies and faiths of mankind. As the authors varied in calibre and temperament so their writings differed in form and effectiveness. Several took cognizance of foreign systems of thought and, like Maimonides in his valuable book "Guide of the Perplexed", ventured to subordinate them to Judaism. Others placed their emphasis wholly on Judaism, ignored the claims of strange cultures, and produced inspiring expositions of Jewish theology, such as Bahya's "Duties of the Heart". A third group, however, avoided the beaten paths of the others and embarked upon the vast sea of philosophy, snatching occasionally a glimpse of the isles of Jewish opinion and thought. Solomon ibn Gabirol's "The Fountain of Life" is an example of this type.

Saadia ben Joseph (892-942), Gaon of Sura, belonged to the first group. He was the most eminent of those giants of post-Talmudic Judaism who flourished in the famous academies of Babylon, and through him Oriental Judaism attained its loftiest heights. Thanks to the learning of this progressive scholar, Judaism in the tenth century broadened its scope so as to include such studies as grammar, rhetoric, literary criticism, and philosophy and for the first time, perhaps, these studies were pursued and spread by a recognized Talmudic authority. Because of this, and since he recognized the value and functioning of the scientific method in Judaism, Saadia Gaon may rightly be called the pathfinder of enlightened Judaism in the Middle Ages.[1]

The truth of these claims is borne out by his epoch-making literary accomplishments. He translated the Bible into Arabic, a language then universally understood, for the instruction of Arabic-speaking Jews. By this achievement, the Scriptures were made accessible to the people. It ceased to be a book of mystery for the initiate only. It was no longer merely ancillary to the Talmud. This translation accommodated itself to the minds of the people and the trend of the times. Difficult and misunderstood passages were instructively clarified. Saadia also produced in Arabic a commentary to the Scriptures. In his grammatical and exegetical writings he laid the foundation for the future critical and objective study of the Bible. The characteristically medieval bent of his mind is clearly discernible in his *magnum opus*—"Book of Doctrines and Beliefs" written in Arabic, in which he examines and defends the doctrines of Judaism. His familiarity with foreign literature and science lent freshness and novelty to his presentation of Judaism.

Saadia possessed no sedate soul. His spirit was militant, and his personality and official career were no less remarkable than his original writings and points of view. His spirit was inflexible, his judgment stern and his conscience sensitive. He was a bitter opponent and a formidable controversialist. One of his chief claims to immortal fame is his valiant defense of rabbinic Judaism against the Karaites of his day. He wrote numerous refutations of the writings of Karaite teachers in which he met his detractors with their own weapons; grammar, science, logic, and common sense.

In brief, Saadia Gaon had two great intellectual interests, Judaism and secularism. Judaism represented a

---

[1]For the best study of Saadia, see Malter, Life and Works of Saadia Gaon, Philadelphia, 1921.

constant hereditary force. Its manifold expression, racial consciousness, favored theology, and sacred literature were his birthright possessions. Secularism was an acquired, environmental influence. It included the sciences, Greek and Arabic culture, and popular wisdom. These were products of the time and place which the intelligent person was expected to obtain because they were deemed proper, necessary and timely. In Saadia we can separate the two strands in his mental make-up. We see him first as a deep-dyed traditionalist; then as one sponsoring the need of reason in religion, employing philosophic method and terminology, and conversant with alien literature. Saadia fused his philosophy with Judaism, utilizing the former to serve and strengthen his Jewish principles. Although he claimed freedom of thought and the right to original inquiry, his conclusions were substantially in accord with orthodox Jewish doctrine. His Messianic conception particularly shows that he subordinated science to tradition, as he did the secular disposition of his mind to the ardent national desire of his racially conscious self. With the lapse of many centuries, Saadia has come to fit into the mold of rabbinism. Although his secular intellectualism still exercises a subtle charm over us we now think of him chiefly as a stalwart defender and ingenious cultivator of Jewish tradition.

In his chapter on Redemption in the Emunot, Saadia quotes only once from the Talmud to confirm his view on compulsory repentance. Otherwise, he utilizes the Scriptures wholly to build up a Messianic future. His principal religio-philosophic work is indeed a Biblical exposition, in ten chapters, of the following fundamental concepts of the Jewish creed: 1—Existence of God. 2—Unity of God. 3—Divine Commandments. 4—Free will. 5—Religious Merits and Demerits. 6—The Soul. 7—Resurrection. 8—Redemption. 9—Reward and Punishment in the Hereafter. 10—Ethics.

THE DOCTRINE OF THE MESSIAH

The gaon's complete reliance on Scripture may be explained, as due either to a desire to combat Karaism with its own weapons, or to reveal to the Jew the wealth of wisdom and inspiration in the Bible.

Karaism was a schismatic sect of Judaism, started in the middle of the eighth century by one, Anan ben David. It rapidly became popular and dangerous and clashed frequently with the parent faith. It rejected the oral law, the involved deliberations and decisions of the Talmudists and geonim. Its point of view, briefly stated, was that the Bible contained the full and original word of God and that it was sufficient as a guide for conduct and law.

In basing his theology and ethics on the "Written Law" and ignoring the Talmud, Saadia may have aimed to convince the Karaites that Judaism does not depend upon Talmudism, but that our rich and diversified faith is fully and implicitly contained in Scripture. He believed in the authenticity and integrity of the Bible. He believed firmly that it contained the promise and hope of redemption. He did not doubt that his explorations in the Scriptures had brought to light the sources and support of the Messianic belief. Whereas Maimonides was content merely to derive his Messianic belief from the Bible, Saadia placed his reliance completely upon the Bible and created the material as well as the spiritual fabric of the Messianic world out of its passages. In fact, Saadia depended on Scripture for every detail of the redemption. His literal interpretations made his views of the prospective era very fanciful and vulnerable. Although his basic ideas are reasonable, certain particulars reveal an attitude that favored a supernatural and transcendental future. In compliance with Midrashic views, he believed that some Jews would be transported to Palestine on the clouds, and that Jerusalem would become a city of supernatural wonders. The miracles connected with the Exodus did not challenge his faith, and consequently he did not doubt that as they had occurred then, they could occur again in the future deliverance.

The gaon incorporated the Messianic expectation into several prayers which, later became part of the liturgy. In a lengthy prayer for the eve of the Day of Atonement[2] the learned rabbi, in the first introspective part, beseeches God for personal blessings, while in the second section he implores God for Israel's deliverance. He bewails the excessive length of the exile, the affliction and the helplessness of the people, and entreats God to hasten the "end". He confesses that Israel's sins have caused her estrangement from God and her enslavement to the nations. He appeals to the Almighty on the grounds of mercy and goodness. He cites the ancient promises of God to save and sustain His chosen people. There is neither relief nor surcease from the yoke of despotism. Hence he moans, "We become weaker and weaker daily, and dwindle away with the passing of years." And he prays: "May it be Thy will, O Lord our God, and God of our Fathers, that an absolute end may come to the repentant of Thy people, the House of Israel, and end our dispersion and national mourning; a finality to the day of afflictions." And again: "Send forth the deliverer, that he may deliver us, and lead us, rejoicing to our soil with the light of Thy Shekina within us; and the vision of Thy prophets in our midst."

2—*Roots of the Messianic Idea.*

Saadia's views on resurrection and redemption, as contained in the seventh and eighth chapters[3] of his Emunot,

---

[2]Siddur Ozar ha-Tefillot, Wilna, 1914, pp. 1085-1090.

[3]These two chapters were reprinted separately in Mantua, 1556, and subsequently as the Book of Resurrection and Deliverance. See H. Malter's Saadia Gaon, pp. 363-369. References in this treatment are to the Bialystok edition of the Emunot v'Deot.

and in his Bible commentary, are presented in the following pages. Although he embraced the Midrashic concept of the Redemption, he adduced plausible and convincing reasons for so doing, a proof of his thorough scholasticism. It is true also, that the Messianic views of the geonim, as a class, coincided with those of Saadia, possibly the greatest gaon of them all. His intellectualism did not bar him from accepting the Messianic belief in all its details and picturesqueness. In general, one may say that Saadia Gaon extracts the belief in final redemption from three sources; the mercy of God, the predictions of the prophets, and the wonders of the Exodus.[4] A pious believer in Divine Providence, the gaon intuitively places his reliance upon the beneficent nature of the Almighty. He is just, fair, and will tolerate no wrong. He will not suffer Israel to perish. The distress of Israel, which is partly punitive and partly probationary, will be alleviated. He will bring salvation to his beloved. He who fashioned the world from nothing, and governs it now in all its magnitude can also save Israel. For at the time of salvation, the guilty will have paid the penalty for their wrongdoing, and will be pardoned, and the righteous, whose constancy has not been shaken by trials and tribulations, will receive their merited reward.

In addition to a dependence on God's might and mercy, we have the assurance of the prophets, His spokesmen.[5] In unequivocal terms they revealed the divine will and purpose. Their words are bounded by truth and righteousness, and their utterances and visions point unmistakably to Israel's redemption. The first to project the Messianic principle was Moses, who said: "The Lord thy God will turn thy captivity and have compassion upon thee, and

---

[4]*Ibid.*, p. 175.
[5]*Ibid.*

will return and gather thee from all the peoples"—Deut. 30:3; Deut. 32:40-43 also prefigures vengeance and restoration in the Messianic era. God will not prove false to His word. "He confirmeth the word of His servant, and performeth the counsel of His messengers; that saith of Jerusalem: "She shall be inhabited"; and of the cities of Judah: "They shall be built", and "I will raise up the waste places thereof."—Is. 44:26.

Zech. 8:7-8 points to the ingathering: "I will save My people from the east country, and from the west country; and I will bring them, and they shall dwell in the midst of Jerusalem; and they shall be My people and I will be their God, in truth and in righteousness." Sentiments of this kind are numerous.

The third source which re-enforced Saadia's Messianic belief was the divinely charged history of Israel, especially the Exodus. He offered the novel theory that the allusions to the Exodus throughout Scripture were to impress upon the nation the likelihood of a similar, but greater, event occurring in the future. He retained an ancient prevalent view, based on Mic. 7:15, that the liberation from Egypt would serve as a pattern for the ultimate redemption. "As in the days of thy coming forth out of the land of Egypt, will I show unto him marvelous things." The first Exodus was pre-ordained, and had been foretold to the patriarchs. It had also been attended by miracles, —the dividing of the Red Sea, the manna, the quail, the pillar of cloud, revelation, and the standing of the sun at mid-day. What has happened in the past can happen in the future. The ultimate deliverance will be a fulfillment of the divine promises made to the prophets, and will likewise be characterized by striking and supernatural events. Thus the gaon has a three-fold assurance of the Advent.

THE DOCTRINE OF THE MESSIAH

3—*Polemical.*

Saadia devotes a considerable part of his essay on redemption to the refutation of opinions at variance with his own. We can only surmise what effect his impatient and relentless attitude as a controversialist would have exerted had he lived in Christian countries and taken part in the inter-religious disputations on the Messianic belief forced upon Jews by their foes. The suavity of Nahmanides in the controversy of 1263 won him the friendship of the opposition. But lacking provocation, Saadia's polemical treatment of the doctrine is not exciting. He takes issue with those who explain the futuristic utterances of the prophets historically as applying to the rejuvenated second commonwealth. This was the vogue in some Karaite circles and among certain rabbis.[6] He also attacks the stand that the prophets made conditional promises only; that if Israel should prove worthy by faith and repentance, she would be delivered unto a state of independence, security and abundance; if not, the people would remain exiled and afflicted. Finally, he disproves the Christian contention that Jesus fulfilled the hope and prediction of Israel's seers.

a. Against Applying Predictions to Second Commonwealth.

To refute the first group, he offers fifteen convincing proofs that the promises in the Torah were not realized in the second commonwealth.[7] These fifteen proofs are divided into three categories.

1—Of the first five proofs, four are forced upon us by our own common sense; we would expect an ideal state

---

[6]Emunot VIII, p. 181; Saadia must allude to Karaites when he says "There are people who call themselves Jews." Jephet B. Ali, a Karaite, and the Rabbis Moses ibn Gikatilla, 11 Cent., Abraham ibn Daud, 12 Cent., and Hayyim Galipapa referred the prophecies to contemporaneous events. Albo discussed their views at length.

[7]*Ibid.* VIII, p. 182.

to be characterized by international peace, universal belief
in one God, security of Israel, harmlessness of the animal
kingdom, and the restoration of Sodom to its pristine
glory [8] But none of these moral factors are evident in
the second commonwealth.

2—The Bible also mentions five unusual situations
which may be taken as evidences of the Redemption.
These are the seven year conflagration of the forces and
armor of Gog and Magog;[9] the drying up of the Nile in
one place, and of the Euphrates in seven places;[10] the
dividing of the Mount of Olives;[11] the rebuilding of the
Temple;[12] and the issuing from the Temple of a stream
which will become a great river.[13]

3—Five other essential conditions still are awaited to
make the redemption decisive. The Israelites must return
from different isles of the sea but since they had not been
exiled by Nebuchadnezzar to any islands, this prediction[14]
could not have applied to the return from Babylon, and
must needs refer to a future salvation. No one must be
found in exile after the redemption[15]—however the number that returned from the Babylonian exile was only
42,350. Non-Jews will assist in the building of the
Temple;[16] but in the construction of the Temple under
Ezra, Gentiles actually hindered the work. The gates
of the city will be open day and night;[17] and Israel will
dominate the nations.[18] All this evidence is conclusively
against the possibility of identifying the restored state
under the Persian rule with the one visualized by the

---

[8]Ezek. 16:55; Shem. Rabbah 15:21 enumerates ten things, among them
Sodom, to be restored in the days to come.

[9]Ezek. 39:9-10.

[10]Is. 11:55.

[11]Zech. 14:4.

[12]Ezek. 47:1.

[13]Ezek. 47:1-12.

[14]Is. 11:12.

[15]Ezek. 34:11-16.

[16]Is. 61:5.

[17]Is. 60:11.

[18]Is. 60:12.

prophets as the fulfillment of their visions, and points instead to redemption from the present dispersion.[19]

b. Against Taking Predictions as Conditional.

The prophetic predictions of a glorious future were not made provisionally as in the Mosaic promises in which the conditional elements are very obvious, from the hypothetical language used. There, it is plainly stated that the blessings depend upon Israel's observance of the Law.[20] The spokesmen of later days, however, gave Israel positive assurances of salvation; they did not calculate on any other eventuality, but the certainty of a blessed future. Granted that the infidelity of Israel might entail punishment, and thus thwart the benign purposes of God, yet the punishment would not take the extreme form of annihilation, nor of a prolonged life-in-death struggle. God had already avowed that He would not suffer Israel to languish and wither away. At most He would chastise the people; but He would not divest them of their rehabilitating powers.

c. Against Christological Interpretations.

Lastly the gaon turns to the Christological interpretations of specific passages, and refutes them on the ground that neither the idealistic nor the ordinary aspects of the Messianic vision had been realized in the time of Jesus.[21] The world for instance, had not then, nor has it since, been converted to peace, monotheism, and moral living. In fact, social life has been constantly deteriorating. The seventy septenates (490 years) in Dan. 9:24,

---

[19]Emunot VIII, p. 182.
[20]Deut. 11:22; 7:12; 4:25; 8:19; Exod. 23:22.
[21]Emunot VIII, p. 184.

comprise the forty-nine years of Babylonian captivity, the 434 years of the second commonwealth, and the seven-year period of truce and strife culminating in the national calamity of 70 C. E. The "anointed one" of Dan. 9:26— "and the three score and two weeks shall an anointed one be cut off and be no more,"—does not mean Jesus. The word, Meshi-ah is nowhere in Holy Writ used as a proper name, but as a title of the authority of the high priest or king. In the Danielic passage it indicates the high priest. The death of this person will coincide with the destruction of the Temple. Jesus died many years before the Temple went up in flames. The Christian claim that its founder fulfilled the Messianic promises and that his new religion had divine sanction and integrity, is also dismissed on the ground, that he abolished the Torah and multiplied the being of God, as well as for other weighty reasons.[22]

According to Jephet b. Ali, a Karaite teacher contemporary with our author, Saadia referred Isaiah 53 to the prophets, or to Jeremiah, in particular.[23] Saadia interpreted the word "Shiloh", Gen. 49:10, as meaning "to whom the power is," namely, the Messiah.[24]

4—Time of the "End".

Since a redemption is inevitable, it is essential to determine its advent. Saadia maintains that its time is foretold in Daniel at the end of the fourth, or Roman, Empire. With Rome will collapse the Mohammedan state.

---

[22]*Ibid.* VIII, pp. 184-185—II, pp. 92-94.

[23]The 53rd chapter of Isaiah acc. to Jewish Interpreters. Driver and Neubauer, Vol. II, pp. 19 and 43. Abraham ibn Ezra also cites this explanation of Saadia, *Ibid.* I, p. 43.

[24]See *comm. ad hoc.* See also A. Posnanski "Schiloh", Leipzig, 1904, for the innumerable interpretations of the word.

THE DOCTRINE OF THE MESSIAH

The mysterious stone that shattered the dream statue of Nebuchadnezzar, symbolizes the Messianic power. As to the exact time when Israel's dispersion will terminate, there are two possible conclusions. One is the inevitable end, which God in His wisdom and mercy has predeter-mined and upon which the deliverance will follow swiftly.[25] The other is the premature termination, and depends upon the merit of Israel. If Israel repents, it will not have to wait for the "end" set by God. If, however, it remains steeped in sin, Israel will have to await the inevitable end.

In the latter case a vexing question is raised. Why, in the centuries of waiting for the "Anointed One", should the good suffer with the guilty? To this the gaon answers: nature and life are so fashioned by fate that calamities overwhelm even innocent children and babes; the deserv-ing together with the sinful. An earthquake or an inunda-tion has no regard for persons. Even in Egyptian serv-itude there were righteous people, such as Moses, Aaron, Miriam, and many others who together with the masses of Hebrews, bore the burden of suffering and abided patiently the happy season of deliverance.

In the midst of Saadia's messianic calculations we are refreshed by his opinions on the broader problem of Prov-idence in connection with Israel's sufferings and the fair-ness of God. What consolation can be offered Israel in her distressing situation? How shall anyone explain her infidelity in the midst of affliction? The gaon philoso-phizes in the style of a preacher and affirms that Israel's precarious position is in consonance with the known and inexorable law of nature that labor must precede fruition, that joy is the child of despair. His illustrations are vivid and convincing.[26] The imbecile makes sport when he sees

---

[25] *Ibid.*, p. 176; see San. 90a; Shem Rabbah 25:16.
[26] *Ibid.* I, Davidson, Saadia's Polemic against Hiwi Al-balkhi, N. Y. 1915, p. 79.

the farmer plow and sow his field, as if to say: "how can mere earth respond to man's efforts?" Yet it is obvious that the seed is vital and fertile, and the observer will be put to shame when he beholds the bountiful harvests which the soil has yielded. Saadia also illustrates his point from the domestic circle. The callous onlooker is often inclined to ridicule the parent who labors assiduously in behalf of his son; but when the son grows to manhood and has become a leader of men and affairs, a ruler, a general, a minister, a teacher, then it is obvious that the toils and hardships which the father had endured for his offspring were benevolent and essential. The principle of cause and effect which operates in the sphere of man and nature can be applied to the affairs of a nation. Israel, that sows in tears, will reap in joy. Its unhappy condition is indispensable, for it serves to prepare and educate Israel for a glorious future. The world, like the taunting observer, does not understand, and hence is derisive. It is amazed at our constancy, our trustfulness in the midst of trouble; but we know that good is in store for us, that in the end will be peace. It is the price we must pay for the ultimate blessings. God in His omniscience knows our trials and tribulations. He has forewarned us through the prophets of the woes that would betide us. He can and will save us.

Certain enigmatic expressions in the book of Daniel are employed by the gaon in order to fix the time for the inevitable "end" at 965 C. E.[27] Unlike some of the later authorities, Saadia asserted that Daniel knew "the year of wonders", communicated in the visions and couched in mysterious language.

Dan. 12:7—"And I heard the man clothed in linen, who was above the waters of the river, when he lifted up his right hand and his left hand unto heaven and swore by Him that liveth forever that it shall be for a time,

---

[27] *Ibid.*, p. 177 and Comm. on Daniel.

(mo'ed) times (moedim) and a half (v'hetsi) and when they have made an end of breaking in pieces the power of the holy people, all these things shall be finished."

The word mo'ed is not in the calculation. The datum is contained in the term "times" (moedim), comprising two periods: 480 years from the Exodus to the First Temple; plus 410 years of the duration of the Temple. One-half of this total 890, equals 445; adding 445 to 890 makes a total of 1335. This deduction tallies with Dan. 12:12—"Happy is he that waiteth and cometh to the 1335 days." Yomim, (days), Saadia translates "years" as in Lev. 25:29, where "yom" means year. Thus the time-limits of the other deliverances in the Bible are always given in years.[28]

In Dan. 12:11—"And from the time that the continual burnt-offering shall be taken away and the detestable thing that causeth appalment set up, there shall be 1290 days". Saadia understands the number to mean 1290 years.[29] These 1290 years are counted from the incident of "the removal of daily sacrifice" which happened 45 years after the erection of the Second Temple.

The third figure is in Dan. 8:14;—"And he said unto me: 'Unto 2300 evenings and mornings; then shall the sanctuary be victorious.'" Half of the 2300 evenings and mornings would reduce them to 1150 full days. But days mean years. Hence the end foretold in this verse is 1150 years, which are to commence 185 years after Daniel received the announcement. By giving a different *terminus a quo* for 1290 and 1150, Saadia is able to make their *terminus ad quem* coincide with the year 1335. Saadia's computation may thus be set down.

---

[28]See, Ezek. 29:13 and 4:5.
[29]Saadia finds significance in the fact that the total number of annual sacrifices amounted to 1290.

From Creation to Exodus[30]	2448
Interval to Solomon's Temple	480
Duration of Solomon's Temple	410
From destruction to first year of Darius	52
Year of Daniel's oracle	3390
End predicted	1335

4725—965 C. E.[31]

He wisely attempted to confute those who disbelieve in a definite end because of the three conflicting periods given in Daniel. An analogy to Daniel's figures exists in the divergent dates given for the deliverance from Egypt and from Babylon. In Gen. 15:13 redemption is assured at the end of 400 years. In Ex. 12:40 it is said to have taken place after 430 years. The actual servitude in Egypt lasted 210 years. The discrepancies arise from the fact that each datum is reckoned from a different starting point; either the birth of Isaac or the sojourn of Abraham. Regardless of these dates, when the auspicious hour arrived, the redemption occurred. So the conflicting periods in Daniel will undoubtedly terminate in one and the same year, the inevitable end set by God.

5—*Preliminaries to Final Redemption.*

a. Compulsory Repentance.

The redemption of course will not happen suddenly, like a bolt out of a clear sky. There are several pre-

---

[30]This chronology is found in the Seder Olam Rabba. The date 2448 is obtained (chs. 1-3) thus, from Adam to the Flood was 1656 years, thence to the birth of Isaac 392, thence to the Exodus 400, giving a total of 2448.

[31]See Emunot VIII, p. 178-179. This date was 32 years after Saadia wrote his Emunot. According to Dr. Posnanski, the 1335 years are to be counted from the third year of the reign of Cyrus, 367 B. C. Saadia's year for the Advent would be 968 C. E. In 965 the Messianic era would begin. For Saadia's date, see H. Malter, "Saadia's Computations" in D. Neumark's "Journal of Jewish Lore and Philosophy," 1919, p. 45-59; also S. Posnanski

liminary steps that lead up to the climax. Saadia intro-
duces into his Messianic theology the idea of compulsory
repentance. Israel will come to God either through love
and conviction or through force and affliction. If the inevitable end approaches and Israel has not yet made atonement, it will be necessary to crush the unregenerate spirit
of the nation and force it to seek God. The gaon builds
this thought out of the Talmudic opinion: "If Israel will
repent, they will be delivered, if not, God will place over
them a tyrannical ruler like Haman, and they will speedily
repent and be delivered."[32]   This enforced reformation
makes a setting for the birth-travails of the Messiah, the
woes of the pre-Messianic state, during which the legendary struggle will be fought between the Messiah ben
Joseph and Armilus over the possession of Palestine.

b. Woes of the Messiah.

A prelude of frightful oppression will come upon
Israel[33]. Consternation and grief will seize the people.
The death of the minor Messiah and the lamentation
over him are indicated, according to Saadia, in Zech.
12:10-14. In this he follows the Talmud.[34]   The nation,
Israel, will again be scattered, decimated and sifted. Many
will abandon the faith, and only a remnant that is genuine
and firm, will remain. This period will culminate in the
appearance of Elijah, the people's comforter, who will
deliver the survivors unto safety. Thus the entire tragic
prologue to the Messianic drama, with its recital of war
and woes, hinges upon Israel's unfitness to be redeemed.

"Die Berechnung des Erlosungsjahres bei Saadia", Berlin, 1901; also by
the same author in "Monatschrift für Geschichte und Wissenschaft des
Judenthums", Breslau, 1900, p. 400f.

[32]*Ibid.*, p. 179; San. 97B; Yerush. Taanit I-1.

[33]*Ibid.*, pp. 179-180 Saadia assigns the following passages to the Messianic woes; Dan. 12:1; Ezek. 20:34-38; Is. 24:16-23; Zech. 12:10; also
Zech. 14.

[34]Sukkah 52a.

c. Messiah ben Joseph.

The Messiah ben Joseph will be the conditional fore-
runner of the principal Messiah.[35] He may or may not
come. Saadia often qualifies him as belonging to the
northern tribes—to Joseph—the progeny of the matriarch
Rachel. In all probability he considers him the Messianic
representative of the Northern Kingdom. His gigantic
effort in behalf of Palestine and the cause of Israel may
in itself signify the healing of an old breach, the reconciliation of the North and South, the fusion of all tribes
into one powerful state. He will appear in Galilee and
proceed at the head of a small army of Hebrews to Jerusalem, which will then be in the possession of Rome.[36] He
will rout the enemy, but his rule will be short-lived.
Armilus, the Roman commander and anti-Messianic adversary, will wrest the Holy City from its erstwhile con-
queror, drive the Jews into the desert, and finally slay
the Messiah ben Joseph. Our author is the first trust-
worthy authority who mentions Armilus. In the apocalyptic Midrashim he is a conspicuous figure, portrayed as
a monstrosity with an origin and an influence that are
satanic.[37]

d. Wars of the Messiah.

The gaon subordinates the personality of the Messiah
to the great fact of Israel's liberation and the establishment of a millennium. He does not write at length about
the career or character of the Messiah. Perhaps his utter

[35]Emunot, pp. 179-180, the Ephraimite is mentioned in Targ. on Cant.
4:5; on Exod. 40:11 and frequently in Midrashim. See Yalkut on Is. 60.

[36]Obad. 1:21 and Jer. 49:20 are applied by Saadia to the war of the
son of Joseph against Rome.

[37]Armilus, the Romulus of Roman history, is mentioned in Targum on
Ps. 2:2; see art. by Ginzberg in J. E. II, p. 119; Bousset, "Der Anti-
Christ". Also the eschatological Midrash in Jellinek's Bet ha-Midrash; Mid.
va-Yosha I., p. 35; Otiot Meshiah II, p. 58 seq; Book of Zerubabel II,
p. 54 seq.

reliance on God and his desire to eliminate any human intermediator between the Almighty and the work of redemption accounts for this unusual fact. If Israel will repent, the mission of the minor prophet will be unnecessary, and the King Messiah will appear suddenly.[38] He will proceed to Jerusalem at the head of a Hebrew army, slay the Roman chief, and gain control of the Holy City. His rule will be marked by a display of benevolence and magnanimity.[39] No sooner will he revive and secure the Hebrew state than he will wage a frightful war against the fierce army of Gog.[40] The latter, roused by envy and fear, will battle with Israel in a final life and death struggle for world supremacy.[41] The armies of Gog will enlist the picked forces of different nations and will traverse many lands on their way to Palestine. A goodly number of these races will be won over to Judaism through their acceptance of the pure monotheistic faith.

Those who remain stubbornly antagonistic to Israel will be frightfully afflicted and decimated. They will be plagued in four ways: through fire, brimstone, fratricidal war, and physical decrepitude. The rest will be maimed and mutilated as an example to the world of the penalty exacted from the wicked.

6—*Resurrection.*

The first and most notable event after the crushing of Israel's enemies will be the resurrection of the dead. In the Emunot, this theme is treated before redemption, which shows that Saadia placed this grand miracle at the commencement of the new era. In this he deviates from

---

[38]Based on Mal. 3:1.

[39]The ornate language of Is. 61:1-4 describes the Messiah's beneficent rule.

[40]Saadia follows Ber. 7b; Aboda Zara 3b; Mid. Tehilim on Ps. 2.

[41]Saadia bases his views on Ezek. 38:10-23; Zeph. 3:9; Joel 4:1-17; Zech. 14:12; Is. 66:19.

the Talmudic scheme in which all miracles, among them, resurrection, will be enacted in a remote epoch, identified with the future world. Our author takes great pains to prove that the resurrection will occur on this earth during the fifth millennium, that is, within the normal course of time and events, and not in the future transcendental world.[42] What induced the gaon to insist on this view was his keen sense of justice. He was a rigorous moralist. He exemplified justice. Hence, resurrection, which spelled the final execution of God's judgment and decree, must necessarily take place at the turning point of Israel's career.

Four factors enter into a consideration of the possibility of resurrection.[43] They are nature, reason, Scripture, and tradition. Do the first two bar the miracle or invite us to believe in it? Do the latter two affirm or deny it? Nature, of course, is a primary factor in determining whether or not the dead will arise. Ordinary experience leads to the conclusion that the miracle is unnatural; that it violates the laws of human life. But this attitude is based on the wrong assumption that God does not control nature. If, however, we maintain that He created the world out of nothing, and that He has power to modify its course, then it is easily possible for the miracle to occur at the redemption.[44] Hence, belief in the re-existence of the dead is a corollary of our faith in the omnipotence of God. If one presumes to deny resurrection on the ground of its unnaturalness, one must also reject the miracles of the Bible, even creation, and ultimately God, Himself. Neither is resurrection a logical impossibility, like the return of yesterday, or the denial of a mathematical axiom. When the body decomposes, even

---

[42]Emunot, p. 162f.
[43]Ibid.
[44]The same rationalization is employed by Maimonides and the other theologians.

if burnt or devoured, its elements are not annihilated. The physical particles return to their primitive sources, and are conserved until they are summoned to assume their earlier articulate form. Hence resurrection is not inconceivable. Scripture plainly predicts the revival of those who slumber in the earth. Saadia cited the well known passages in Ezek., Ch. 37; Is. 26:19; Dan. 12:2; and Deut. 32:39. The restoring to life of the son of the Shunamite woman was an actual occurrence which bids us look forward to the repetition of the miracle on a grand scale at the redemption. He is opposed to those who expound these promises metaphorically.

No doubt there are words and verses in the Bible which, he believes, cannot be construed literally, and which permit other appropriate interpretations. But no such constraint rests upon us in explaining the afore-mentioned predictions. As for Ps. 78:39 and Job 14:12, and other verses which superficially point in the opposite direction, they do not cast doubt upon the doctrine, but state that during interment the dead are helpless and irrecoverable. The other authorities, notably Maimonides, explain anti-resurrection passages in a similar way. Finally, Jewish tradition, avers our author, substantiates the teachings of Scripture. He cites several opinions found in the Talmud regarding the details of the miracle, which show that this tenet was taken for granted, and, incidentally, that it will occur in this world. The gaon tells us that the promised reappearance of Elijah, a fore-runner of the redeemer who, we are informed, will bring about the miracle, involves the prophet's resurrection. Fifteen persons will be revived as principals at the final salvation. They are David, Methusaleh, Seth, Abraham, Isaac, Jacob, Moses, Jesse, Saul, Samuel, Amos, Zeph-aniah, Hezekiah, and Elijah.[45] He who denies resurrec-

---

[45]Sukkah 52a.

tion will himself not be revived.[46] The dead will rise up in their garments.[47] One who dies in the seven-year period of Gog's wars however, will not merit to live in the Messianic state and hence will be deprived of resurrection. The gaon clarifies the popular conception of resurrection by stating further details. Only the righteous or repentant will be eligible for revival.[48] The deformed or sick will arise in their ailing condition and will then be healed.[49] All the revived will eat, drink and marry. They will recognize each other and attach themselves to their family groups. There will be sufficient space for all the past generations. The revived will not die again, but their lives will be prolonged to reach unto the blissful world.[50] As to their passing into the spiritual existence of the future world, after their long material physical life in the Messianic state, Saadia explains that the people will gradually wean themselves away, and finally abstain altogether from things physical.[51] So Moses did when he deprived himself of satisfying nature's demands for stretches of forty days. There will be no danger of the revived violating God's laws. Only those who are certain not to fall into further error will be brought back to life. Even in the Messianic state the people will earn reward for doing good. Resurrection will open up new vistas of bliss and life. Those who are fortunate enough to be living during the "revival period" will continue to live for four or five thousand years.[52] The majesty of the rulers, saints, sages and the martyrs will be revealed before us in all its glory. Families will be

---

[46]San. 90a.
[47]Ibid.
[48]Emunot VII, pp. 171-173; Dan. 12:1; San. 92a.
[49]San. 91b.
[50]Ibid. 92a.
[51]For the change from corporeal to spiritual life in the future world see conflicting opinions in the essay on Crescas.
[52]Emunot VII, p. 173.

reunited and friendships will be restored. The mysteries of the after-life and the soul's experiences will become common knowledge. All in all, the miracle will be a great manifestation of the power of God.

7—Gathering of the Dispersed.

The future emancipation of the Jews will surpass in scope and in the grandeur of its triumphs and joys, any earlier deliverance. The core of the changed life of Israel will be the ingathering of the people to Palestine from all parts of the globe. The gaon's notion of the actual form of the return is quite naive. He is consistent in his literal understanding of the Bible, however fanciful the conclusion. He differs diametrically from Maimonides, who assumes the Bible to be figurative. So in the chapter on resurrection in Emunot, the gaon frowns upon any at-. tempts to read symbolic or esoteric meanings into Biblical words. These, then, are the facts of the return.[53] The rich non-Jews will transport the Jews of their lands to Palestine on swift steeds and magnificent litters. Those returning will be provided with costly conveniences which will be offered as gifts unto the Lord. The poor of the nations, in their enthusiasm, will carry the Jews on their backs and in their hands. Where it is necessary to cross water, the exiles will embark in seaworthy ships of gold and silver under the protective eyes of non-Jews. Those in Ethiopia will sail in boats of bulrushes instead of metallic ships to obviate the hazards in striking rocks, while those who may be dispersed in regions remote from human aid will be carried Zionward on a cloud.[54]

The multitudes who embrace Judaism will not be admitted to equality with the Hebrews.[55] The converts in

[53] Ibid., p. 181; the description is based on Is. 66:20; 49:22; 18:1-2; 18:7; 14:1-2; 61:5; Zeph. 3:10.
[54] Pesikta Rabbati ed. Friedman, p. 2a.
[55] Aristotle excluded slaves from equality in his ideal republic.

Palestine will be household servants, who will represent the elite among them. Others will be serfs and farm workers. The greater number will live in other parts of the world and will enjoy the prosperity, culture and freedom of their habitat. The entire world, however, will be united under Hebrew sovereignty and the nations will acknowledge one Supreme Ruler, the Creator of all life. As evidence of their perpetual devotion to this ideal, they will make an annual pilgrimage to the world's shrine, and there celebrate the harvest festival, Succoth.

8—The Restored State.

The Temple will be rebuilt in accordance with Ezekiel's detailed description, in dazzling magnificence.[56] It will be constructed of precious stones, and a halo of light, resplendent with God's glory, will fill the Temple area. A radiant shaft, more illuminating than the light of the sun, will extend from sky to earth and guide the pilgrims to the Holy Land.[57] A concomitant to the restored sanctity of Palestine will be the return of prophecy. Then all Israel, even children and servants, will be prophetically endowed.[58] Israel will be the prophet-nation unto all the earth, and will be sought by non-Jews to elucidate the obscure and to presage the future.

The Messianic regime will long endure. Saadia tersely states that they (Israel) will abide in this status during the entire duration of the world.[59] It will be utopian not only in the equitable organization of society but also in the quality of living. The Divine Glory will permeate every person with spiritual radiance. The moral law will

---

[56] Ezek. 40-42; Is. 60:3; 54:11-12.
[57] At creation, God hid the Messianic light under His Throne. It is one of ten things He will bring to the restored state. See Shem. Rabba 15:21.
[58] Joel 3:1-2.
[59] Emunot VIII, p. 181; "The days of salvation will be prolonged in the world."

be accepted generally and steadfastly. The decree of God will inhibit all evil propensities in man and will motivate him to do good. Then again, Israel's secure and happy position will place it beyond the reach of temptation and infidelity, and render it impervious to decay. Sickness will be eradicated. All material wants will be satisfied; all luxuries provided.[60] There will be no barren and deserted places, because every parcel of land will be utilized for a blessed purpose. So intense will be the satisfaction, the harmony and the joy of living in the Messianic state, that the earth will appear as though it had been transfigured into a new world. Thus Saadia metaphorically explains,[61] Is. 65:17—

> "For behold I create new heavens and a new earth;
> And the former things shall not be remembered,
> Nor come into mind."

---

[60]Ps. 144:12-15.
[61]Maimonides, of course, offers a similar explanation.

Chapter III

RASHI

1—*His Commentaries.*

Solomon ben Isaac, otherwise known as Rashi (born 1040), was the most celebrated figure in the rabbinical schools of France in the second half of the eleventh century. He was, also, an eye-witness to the spoliation of the Jewish communities of the Rhine country by the plundering hordes of the First Crusade (1096). He wrote no independent books on theology, law, history, or science, and therefore, unlike some of the other authorities in this series, he gave no systematic presentation of the Messianic ideal. The achievement which has earned for him the undiminishing admiration of the Jewish people, and immortal fame as the greatest Jewish commentator, is his commentaries on the Bible and, the Talmud. His is a running and terse exposition. He does not linger long enough to expound theories and doctrines. Hence, it is no simple task to build up a system of theology based on his commentary; nor is our present enterprise any less difficult. As we are to set forth a subordinate part of his theological views, the Messianic belief, we are compelled to collate the relevant comments on Scripture and offer them in logical form and sequence.

Before giving his views, it may be of interest to describe his commentary—since hermeneutics will determine the trend of his Messianic belief. He used two general methods: "Peshat" and "Derash". On the one hand, he explained the sacred text objectively according to grammar, chronology, and historic considerations. He candidly stated that his object was to elucidate each text on its own merits and to present a simple, unified interpretation of the Bible. Sometimes Rashi believed the Bible exaggerated and required a rational explanation, but with the same confidence he expounded parts of the Bible in the imaginative Midrashic style. He did not attempt to unshackle himself from the traditions and preconceptions of his predecessors, nor would it have been proper for him to do so. The Torah may have a varied significance. It is capable of elastic interpretation and need not be taken literally, at its face value. It is popular and pietistic, simple yet esoteric. But even as a Midrashist, Rashi did not blindly follow the rabbinic homilies. Often, where we would expect him to adopt a Midrashic point of view, he rejected it on the ground that even the Midrash must suit the context.

We certainly could not expect to find any alteration in the form of the ancient adventist belief in Rashi. The point of interest lies in his exegetical method, and one characteristic of this method which interests us, and by which we are able to understand his Messianic conceptions, is his prophetic interpretation of the Bible. In one instance Rashi appropriately discriminates between prayer and prognostication.[1] The idea is that Scripture contains much latent matter relating to the future, which must be deciphered. The Holy Book is the eye of the future. On the verse: "And God blessed the seventh day and hallowed it"—Gen. 2:3—he comments that the manna blessed and sanctified the seventh day. The mention of "Cush" and "Ashur" in Gen. 2:13-14 elicits the information that these two powers, not yet in existence, were here prognosticated. Ps. 14 forecasts the invasion of Nebuchadnezzar; and Ps. 53, a similar one, that of Titus. Rashi apparently believed firmly that the Bible presages the panorama of the future. This secret knowledge can be ascertained only by the mind

[1]Comm. on Ps. 15:11; Loshon *osid* v'eno loshon *tefilla*.

that is saturated with faith. To such a mind it will yield a harvest of eschatological ideas. Hence it is surprising to find that Rashi occasionally deviates from the traditions of Talmud and Agadah in not interpreting certain passages Messianically. The reason for this, no doubt, is the fact that Christian theologians took the Bible to be Christological, and in order not to expose themselves to criticism many Jewish exegetes waived their own Messianic explanations and expounded the text as allusions to the past.[2] For instance, on Ps. 2 Rashi comments: "Our masters apply this passage to the Messiah; but for its direct meaning, it is better to apply it to David." On the words "Thou art my son, this day have I begotten thee",—v. 7— Rashi formally states that the appellation "my son", is figurative, and refers to David, who was as precious to God as a son to his father. However, he dissents from tradition in construing Ps. 21 as Davidic instead of Messianic. Zech. 6:12: "Behold a man whose name is the Shoot", he identifies with Zerubabel and the entire section is referred to the second commonwealth.

Like Ibn Ezra, R. Solomon cited other views besides his own and expressed his preferences. Frequently he fitted alternative interpretations to the same passage. His uncertainty as to whether he should construe the text simply or Messianically is, at times, quite evident.

2—Messianic Exegesis.

Even in her darkest hours, Israel must have implicit faith in the Messianic future as real and possible. The black terror and devastation that came in the wake of the First Crusade did not extinguish the burning hope of salvation. In a penitential psalm which Rashi wrote for the Fast of Gedaliah, Israel pours forth her poignant grief before the Lord and prays for her restoration.

---

[2]M. Liber, *Rashi*, Jew. Pub. Soc., p. 119. See also for polemical tendency of the exegetes, L. I. Newman, *Jewish Influence on Christian Reform Movements*, pp. 325-6.

THE DOCTRINE OF THE MESSIAH

"Our ruin Thou didst long past see—
Is Thy fiery wrath still unappeased?
We sinned in days agone, we suffer now, our wounds are
    open,
Thy oath is quite accomplished, the curse fulfilled;
Though long we tarried, we seek Thee now, timid, anxious
    we, poor in deeds.
Before we perish, once more unto Thy children join
    Thyself,
A heavenly sign foretells Thy blessing shall descend upon
    us.
Brute force is shattered, and around about,
Thy affianced spouse, loving, yearning,
Calls on Thy faithfulness; she pleads with her eyes and
    asks, is she still Thine,
Is hers Thy love for aye?"[3]

God had told Abraham of the dispersion, and stands
ready to emancipate his descendants when the end arrives.
Whatever betide, Israel must persist in the sacred hope
of the advent. "My soul waiteth for the Lord, more than
watchmen for the morning, yea more than watchmen for
the morning"—Ps. 130:6. This exclamation points to the
constancy and buoyancy of the faithful who wait, even
after disappointments, for "end" after "end". For it all
lies with God. He will bring the *summum bonum,* the
greatest happiness to mankind, at the redemption.

Rashi designates the millennium by various names, referring to it as The World to Come, The Future, The
Future to Come, After the Sinners Have Perished.[4] Certain euphemistic words and phrases furnish him with a
clue to the Messianic import of a passage. "Layil"—night
—designates the darkness of dispersion. The word "boker"
—morning—symbolizes the dawn of the new day, the
morning of the millennium.[5] "It is morning to the night

---

[3]Liber, p. 178; this version is from Zunz's translation in his "Syn-
agogale Poesie", p. 181. The original piyyut is found only in one place,
the Seliha published in Prague in 1613. I am indebted to Prof. Davidson
for this information.
[4]Ps. 92:2; 93:1; 97:10; Ezek. 30:2; Is. 1:2.
[5]Ps. 46:6; 90:14; 92:1.

of trouble, sighing, and darkness." The word "simcha"—joy—wakes in him thoughts of supernal joy, the everlasting, celestial delight which will result from the redemption.[6]

Ps. 106:48, "from everlasting to everlasting—m'olom v'ad olom", and Ps. 61:5, "forever—olomim", connote two different worlds; the present world and the world to come. To Ps. 22:27, "Let the humble eat and be satisfied", Rashi adds "at the time of the deliverance in the days of the Messiah".

"Make us glad according to the days wherein Thou hast afflicted us"—Ps. 90:15—signifies "Rejoice us in the Messianic era in the same degree that we have suffered in the diaspora". "Thy light and Thy truth", in Ps. 43:3, means the King Messiah and Elijah. The caption to Ps. 9: "Al-Muth-labben", is given Messianic coloring and alludes to the period at which Israel will renew its vigor, and when the progeny of Esau will languish and disappear. The whole of Ps. 9 is understood messianically: the note of salvation is definitely sounded in the unshaken conviction that "The Lord will be a tower for the oppressed". Ps. 119:10 has reference to the eminence of Israel in the long awaited era.

The varied misfortunes and the final high destiny of Israel are sporadically mentioned in the Bible. The fourfold repetition of "how long" in Ps. 13:2-3 corresponds to the four subjugations in the last of which we now live. So also the triple recurrence of the question: "Why art thou cast down?" in Ps. 42:6, 12 and Ps. 43:5 relates to the three destructions of the Temple under Babylon, Greece, and Rome. The commentator finds reference everywhere to the Galut of his day.

In fact, the course and consummation of the world's history is portended in the Bible. The Messianic state will succeed the four mighty monarchies. Rashi, follow-

---

[6]Ps. 16:11.

ing rabbinic tradition,[7] finds a symbolization of this in the covenant which God made with Abraham—Gen. 15. The heifer, the she-goat, and the ram denote the materialistic and perishable empires, the undivided bird is Israel, which, though beset by the beasts, will not perish. At the appointed hour the Messiah will appear and free Israel.

This view is vividly presented in Daniel 2, in the story of the image. The head of gold represents the Babylonian empire; the breast and arms of silver, the Medo-Persian rule; the belly and thighs of brass, the Alexandrian empire; the iron legs and feet, part iron and part clay, represent sundered Rome; and "in the days of those kings", of the Romans, shall the divine power shatter the unholy empire; the Messianic state, which shall never be destroyed, will supplant it throughout the world.

The vision of the beasts in Daniel 7 is similarly explained. The lion stands for Babylon; the bear for Persia; the three ribs for its three kings—Cyrus, Artaxerxes, and Darius I; the leopard for Greece; the four wings are the four divisions of the empire; the frightful unnamed beast is Rome; the ten horns are the ten kings who held sway before Vespasian destroyed the Temple. The "one small horn" is Titus. "The one like unto a son of man" is King Messiah, who will overwhelm the heathen nations.[8] "Ancient of days" is God, who will sit in judgment.

In Rashi's comments, therefore, Rome stands out boldly as the antagonist of Israel. He regards the Roman empire, as the source and seat of all the pernicious power which will ultimately succumb to the onslaught of the Messiah.

The seventy weeks (490 years) in Dan. 9:24 mark the interval from the destruction under Zedekiah to the sec-

---

[7]Pirke R. Eliezer, XXVIII; Ber. Rabba XLIV; for a rational explanation of certain animal names given to the four world powers see Abr. Epstein, "M'Kadmonioth Hayahudim", Vienna, 1887.

[8]This is the Talmudic interpretation of "son of man" in San. 98a. See San. 38b for the application of "Ancient of days" to God.

ond destruction by Rome.[9] During the protracted years of
Roman oppression, Israel will expiate her sins and the
Temple will be cleansed again through the Messiah. The
seven hebdomads in 9:25 refer to the period from the
destruction of the first Temple to the proclamation of
Cyrus, "an anointed prince", at the return. Then will
follow sixty-two hebdomads, during which the second
temple will flourish only to end in disaster. "An anointed
one shall be cut off", in verse 25, refers to Agrippa.
Titus and his armies are implied in the phrase "people
of a prince", in verse 26. "His end shall be with a flood"
means that he will make a covenant with Israel for one
week and then break it.

He unearths references to Rome in the identical verses
in Ps. 60:11, and 108:11: "Who will bring me into the
fortified city? Who will lead me unto Edom?" "Fortified city", avers the commentator, is none other than
Rome. The second half of the sentence is taken as an
answer to the first half. The same God who led me
anciently unto Edom, will in the Messianic future bring
me into Rome. Other allusions to Rome are in the names
Magdiel and Iram,—Gen. 36:43—and in Num. 24:19: "And
out of Jacob shall one have dominion, and shall destroy
the remnant from *the city*."

3—*The Messiah.*

The advent of the Messiah is foretold in Gen. 49:10:
"Until Shiloh (Messiah) come",[10] and in the above quotation from Num. 24:19. On Mic. 5:1: "But thou, Beth-
lehem-Ephrathah, which are little to be among the
thousands of Judah, out of thee shall come forth unto

---

[9]Actually the time from the first destruction 586 B. C. E. to the second
destruction in 70 C. E. was 586+70, that is 656 years.

[10]In accord, with Targum Onkelos, Shiloh is taken to mean She'lo, to
whom the power belongs. The term is also divided into Shai-lo, to whom
presents will be offered by the nations, with allusion to Ps. 76:12; see
trans. of this passage in "The Holy Scriptures", Jew. Pub. Soc.

Me that is to be ruler in Israel", Rashi remarks that the Messiah ben David will be God-chosen, despite the taint in his family due to the intermarriage of Ruth the Moabitess and Boaz. Zech. 9:9 is unquestionably Messianic, because "we do not find a ruler such as is here described in the second commonwealth".

He finds other references to the Messiah in the following verses: Ps. 43:3: "O send out *Thy light* and *Thy truth;* let them lead me. Let them bring me unto Thy holy mountain, and to Thy dwelling-places." Ps. 72:8: "May he have dominion also from sea to sea, and from the River unto the ends of the earth." Ps. 89:52: "Wherewith Thine enemies have taunted the footsteps of Thine anointed." As a rule Rashi explains the Scriptural term *Meshi-ah* as does Saadia Gaon, i.e., as a person who occupies a position of honor and authority. In this verse, however, he identifies it with the redeemer.

The beast upon which the Messiah will ride when he enters the Holy City, is alluded to in Ex. 4:20 as having been ridden by Moses. It will be the same beast upon which Abraham led Isaac to the slaughter. Is. 11 describes the glorious personality and the flourishing career of the Messiah. He will be the recipient of gifts from mankind, who, by their offerings, will show their submission to him.[11]

Rashi mentions the Messiah b. Joseph in connection with Is. 11:13: "The envy also of Ephraim shall depart, and they that harass Judah shall be cut off. Ephraim shall not envy Judah, and Judah shall not vex Ephraim." He interprets the verse to mean that the Messiah b. David and the Messiah b. Joseph will not be envious of each other. He probably conceived them as representatives of the two kingdoms, and in their cooperation foresaw the reconciliation of all the tribes.

---

[11]Ps. 68:30.

4—*The End.*

Unlike other rabbinical authorities, Rashi does not deprecate calculations of the Messianic "end". Daniel had forewarned the people that men would indulge in fanciful calculations and that they would err. He professed that we do not know the secret year and that, at best, every calculation would be conjectural. Rashi deduces from Dan. 8:14 that the Messiah will arrive 2874 years after the Exodus, which would be 1352 C. E. The verse reads: "Unto 2300 evenings and mornings, then shall the sanctuary be victorious." The numerical value of *erev, boker* equals 574; adding this to 2300, we get 2874 years from the Exodus to the millennium. This figure coincides with the 1290 to be reckoned from six years before the second destruction, following which it is predicted in verse 11 that the temple will lie desolate. The following calculation gives the total for the terminal year, 2874.

```
Years in Egypt............210
Exodus to Solomon.........480
First Commonwealth .......410
Babylonian Exile .......... 70
Second Commonwealth ....420
                          ————
    Total .................... 1590
Present Dispersion acc. to Dan.
    12:11 .................... 1290
                              ————
                              2880
Temple sacrifice ceased before
    destruction ...............   6
                              ————
                2874 years from Exodus,
                or 1352 C. E.[12]
```

---

[12]Comp. Rashi, Comm. on San. 97b, where he deduces the year 1478 C. E. from Ps. 80:6; Nahmanides' year for the "end" is 1358, and this is also one of Abraham b. Hiyya's many conjectural "ends".

Rashi remarks that although Saadia's putative date has long passed, yet this failure should not prevent us from accepting other computed years. We do not know whether a date prophesied is correct or incorrect until it arrives.

The discrepancy between 1290 Dan. 12:11 and 1335 Dan. 12:12, is reconciled by making the first date refer to his birth and the second to his public appearance.

5—*Controversial: Isaiah.*

According to one of his biographers "Rashi does not make assaults upon Christianity; he contents himself with showing that a verse which the Church has adopted for its own ends, when rationally interpreted, has an entirely different meaning and application."[13] Rashi defends his interpretation of Is. 9:5 against Christian disputants, who see in the passage a prophecy and delineation of their savior. Rashi's comment is that the wicked ruler Ahaz will have a son unlike himself, "For a child is born unto us; and the government is upon his shoulders, and the Holy One, Blessed be He, Who is wonderful in counsel, a mighty God and eternal Father, shall call him by the name of Hezekiah, Prince of Peace."[14] The child whose birth is predicted is Hezekiah, who was one of the ideal rulers of Judah, his regime being characterized by peace, truth and godliness. The prediction is for immediate fulfillment, as is obvious from the word "henceforth", whereas, "he (Jesus) did not come until 300 years later".[14a] In his hope the prophet envisages the new ruler as the prince

---

[13]Liber, p. 118.

[14]See Hazofeh M'eretz Hagar, Budapest, 1911, p. 81 on Is. 9:5, where the writer shows that the earliest traditional interpretations applied the appellations of Is. 9:5 to Hezekiah or to the Messiah and not to God. The medieval Jewish explanation was directed against Christians who took the verse as proof of divinity of Jesus.

[14a]This is acc. to the 2nd rabbinical edition of the Bible, Venice, 1524. Rashi here possibly has in mind the tradition of an early Jesus who appeared 200 years before the destruction. The language of Rashi in later rabbinic editions on the verse in question is corrupt.

of peace. The expression "forever", does not mean eternity, but the whole life-time of Hezekiah.

It is plain that Isaiah would not presage an event to happen hundreds of years later, since his utterance was called forth by the crisis in his day, and his statement, necessarily, would apply to his own time or soon thereafter. To confirm his view that Hezekiah is meant, Rashi cites the rabbinic story that God desired to appoint Hezekiah as the Messiah, and Sennacherib as Gog and Magog. But the ministering angels protested: "Shall he who hewed down the doors of the Temple and sent them to the Assyrian king be the Messiah?"[15]

However, Is. 11 is Messianic. The first half of the chapter describes the exalted character and high mission of the Messiah and the second half tells of the final liberation of Israel. The expression "a second time", in verse 11, means second to the departure from Egypt, which was a complete deliverance. The re-establishment in Palestine after the captivity, cannot be reckoned with because then Israel was subservient to Cyrus.

Rashi holds that Ch. 53 refers to Israel. "This prophet (Isaiah) speaks constantly of the whole people as one man." The chapter depicts Israel's humble origin. As he (Israel) grew older he became hated and oppressed. He was like a lamb goaded on and bruised, yet dumb and unresisting. Both his domicile and his relations were with lowly creatures in abject surroundings. But Israel will ultimately rise triumphant over his vicious foes and seek no retaliation for these many injuries.

The commentator applies the term Messiah, as used in Daniel and in the Psalms, to known historical personages. Thus, "unto one anointed a prince", in Dan. 9:25, refers to Cyrus, and "an anointed one shall be cut off", in 9:26,

---

[15]San. 94a.

refers to Agrippa.[16] "Behold, O God our shield, and look upon the face of Thine Anointed", in Ps. 84:10, refers to David. "For Thy servant David's sake, turn not away the face of Thine Anointed", in Ps. 132:10, is construed as referring to Solomon. Ps. 2 and Zech. 6, are not understood as Messianic by Rashi.

6—The Millennium.

Rashi believed in a future and ideal world, but it is not certain whether he made a distinction between the Messianic state and the future world. One may assume, however, that he merges the events of the two and allows for a short transition period between this world and the next.

The optimistic prophecies in Is. 48-66 depict the resplendent situation of Israel and of the world in the millennium.[17] Joel 3 also pictures brilliantly the future state. Many of the psalms portray the pageantry of the Messianic drama. These psalms are 22, which treats of "the future"; 48, which describes the glory of the new Zion and God's sovereignty; 92, in which the sanctified and Sabbatic character of the "world to come" is portrayed; 93 to 96, which, by the caption "a new song", are undeniably stamped as prophetic; 97, 99 and 118, which tell of the wars against Gog and Magog; and 98, which also deals with "the future".

Regarding Ps. 149:9, the expositor makes an interesting comment concerning the expression "To execute upon them the judgment written". The judgment, he says, alludes to the divine vengeance upon Edom invoked by Ezekiel.[18]

---

[16]The Syriac and Vulgate Bibles equate the "anointed one" with the founder of Christianity.

[17]On Is. 52:1, Rashi remarks: "For all these latter consolations apply only to the ultimate deliverance." Rashi's prophetic method is obvious from the following comments: "Scripture is written for the sake of the future," Gen. 2:3; "Scripture speaks in the language of metaphor," Deut. 1:28. On Ps. 134:2, he writes: "But there are in the words of Torah and tradition, proverb, metaphor, words of sages and riddles."

[18]Ezek. 25:14.

"And if you aver that Ezekiel was not yet born when David made his statement, then one must perforce say that David presaged the end of the redemption, and when that does occur the judgment (of Ezekiel) will have been long written."

The final liberation of Israel from exile of many centuries will be unprecedented in grandeur and in effects. Miracles will be enacted as in olden days. Concerning Ps. 46:3: "Therefore will we not fear, though the earth do change", Rashi comments that the passage points to a similar miracle in the time to come, to the day of which Isaiah spoke when he said: "And the earth shall wax old like a garment." The sons of Korah saw the miracle wrought for them when their surroundings were swallowed up and they stood in mid-air. At that time they declared to Israel, by the power of the Holy Spirit, that the duplication of the miracle would be wrought for them in "the future".

The wonder of the new renaissance and redemption will be equal to all the miracles of Hebrew history.[19] Israel will be set free and gathered into the Holy Land. Deliverance will be as thorough as was the Exodus from Egypt; not a soul will remain under oppression. A Day of Judgment will visit the nations and the wicked. The world will pass through a crucible of fire and many will encounter death. Gog and Magog, while feasting outside the walls of Jerusalem, preparatory to their attack upon the Holy City, will be consumed in the conflagration. The terrific heat of the sun will destroy people, but Israel will go forth unscathed.[20] The inauguration of the blissful age will be celebrated by a great banquet.[21] In this new world, Jerusalem will be the home of the righteous.[22]

---

[19]Ps. 9:2.
[20]Is. 43:2.
[21]Ps. 50:10.
[22]Is. 4:3.

The tokens enumerated in Jer. 31 were not realized in the second commonwealth and must therefore be anticipated with the coming restoration. These tokens included, first, the new dispensation that will seal the spiritual law on our hearts and render the legal covenant superfluous; second, the perpetual independence of Israel; and last, the enlargement of the city of Jerusalem. In the millennium, Israel will receive a new instruction—the secret lore of the Torah, for which she was not fit during the harrowing years of her dispersion. God had shown Ezekiel the pattern of the new temple for the "future to come".[23] Hosea also gives a hint of the third temple.[24] God Himself will rebuild it, so that it cannot be destroyed like the previous man-made sanctuaries.

The present world will be thoroughly transfigured in the millennium. Thus Rashi explains the promise of new heavens and a new earth in Is. 65:17. To prove that the promise is not poetic but that it speaks of an actual and material sphere, he cites Is. 66:22, where the "new heavens and new earth" are posited as a guaranty of the perpetuity of Israel.

Resurrection is alluded to in Ps. 17:15 and 104:30. Considering Ps. 22:30, Rashi follows the Targum when he states that the wicked will not be resurrected.

Unlike certain rationalists, Rashi probably held to a physical conception of Paradise, and considered it as a place affording material delights. It is in this way that he interprets Ps. 45:9: "Better than ivory palaces are the mansions prepared for thee in Paradise to delight thee." "There is a river, the streams whereof make glad the city of God",—Ps. 46:5—is the river of Paradise.

---

[23]Ezek. 40:1.
[24]Hos. 6:2.

Chapter IV

SOLOMON IBN GABIROL

1—*The Philosopher.*

Not only in theological writings and in Bible commentaries, as in the case of Saadia, was the Messianic belief expounded but it was sustained also by the muse of poetry. A vast and rich poetic literature on this theme had developed to console and inspire the people. The first outstanding poet of redemption was Solomon ibn Gabirol (Spain, died 1070) whose personality glitters through history with the double effulgence of philosopher and poet. His philosophy has evoked the highest praise from foremost Jewish historians. Graetz has pronounced him "The Jewish Plato", and Steinschneider says that he is "the most original philosophical writer among the Jews and the Arabs".[1] Yet his philosophic system betrays no preeminently Jewish characteristics. His principal and highly metaphysical works, "The Fountain of Life", and "The Royal Crown", are singularly free from Jewish content and method. He proceeded independently of Bible, Talmud, Israel and the God of the patriarchs. He kept his Jewish interests and recollections in check. His foundation is neither Jewish thought and history, nor our national genius and experience, but the theories of neo-Platonism. On these, with the aid of his own lucid and penetrating mind, he constructed his system. This non-national character of his philosophy attracted early attention. A theologian of the next century, Abraham ibn Daud, rightly describes his speculation as a kind which is not distinctly

---

[1]Graetz, Geschichte der Juden, Vol. VI, p. 25; M. Steinschneider, "Die Hebraische Ubersetzungen", p. 379.

national, but which "pertains to all mankind".[2] Because of its non-Hebraic, but withal deeply spiritual quality, "The Fountain of Life" was welcomed and exploited by the Christian Church while the Jews uniformly ignored it. Indeed, the Christians did not know until half a century ago that the author, whose name had been distorted to Avicebron, was a Jew, the same indeed who wrote "The Royal Crown" and other devotional poems which have become part of the holiday ritual.[3]

2—His Messianic Poetry.

The Jewish basis and sympathies of Gabirol, so conspicuously wanting in his speculative discourses, appear very markedly in his poetry. He was one of the far-famed liturgical poets of the period, and as such, Harizi showers unstinted praise upon him. "Rabbi Solomon, the Small, spread such a fragrance of song as was never produced by any poet either before or after him. The poets who succeeded him strove to learn from' his poems, but were unable to reach even the dust of his feet, as regards the power of his figures and the force of his words."[4]

His poetry commands our interest, not only for its literary excellence, but also as a contemporary source which throws considerable light on the pitiful plight of medieval Jewry. The tenor of his lyrics, like that of other Spanish Hebrew poets, is predominantly nationalistic. It presents the reaction of a Jewish metaphysician of the eleventh century to the harrowing existence of his people in Christian and Mohammedan states. It echoes the cry of a hounded race that prays and pines for freedom and justice. Gabirol protests, implores, pleads, and prostrates himself before the Almighty. He sings of Israel's ancient

---

[2]Quoted from S. Bernfeld, Daat Elohim, p. 62.
[3]I. Davidson's edition indicates poems used on the Day of Atonement, New Year, the three festivals, and on certain Sabbaths.
[4]R. Judah Alharizi in Tahkemoni ed. Warsaw, 1889, pp. 40-41.

glory. He laments the destruction of the Temple, and dwells on the traditional expectation of a happy future. He comforts himself with the hope that God will surely deliver His chosen people from thraldom. He invokes God to remember the pledge which he made to the ancient patriarchs and prophets, and calls upon Him to redeem that pledge. In fine, one concludes that Gabirol used poetry as a vehicle for the transmission of the Messianic ideal.

How variously, through the aptitudes of the scholars, did this faith assert itself? In Saadia, through the labyrinthine paths of theology; in Rashi, through pietism; in Maimonides, through rational conviction and ethical insight; in Gabirol, through the art and genius of poetry. In anguished supplication and lilting lyric he sounded the familiar melodies in the symphony of the Messianic drama. The depth of the philosopher's Messianic yearning is evident from the 150 poems classified by Chaim Nachman Bialik in his edition of the *Religious Poems of Gabirol*,[5] under the heading of "Dispersion and Redemption".

3—*Traditional Character of His Messianic Conception.*

In the highly imaginative poems of Gabirol we find almost all of the typical elements of the Messianic doctrine. The mysticism in his metaphysics appears also in his Messianism. As a poet, he does not dogmatize; with him it is merely a theme for intuitive belief, for meditation, and for exuberant faith to which he gives fanciful and brilliant expression. At the outset, we observe with surprise that the philosopher does not deviate from the line of the agadic conception of the advent. His portrayal of the belief contains many of the particulars and allusions that are current in rabbinical writings, and that

---

[5]For various collections and editions of Gabirol's poetry, see the excellent introduction by Prof. I. Davidson in his edition of Gabirol, Philadelphia, 1923.

were held by the exponents of traditional Judaism in his day. Other important features, however, such as Messiah ben Joseph, Armilus, and the final wars of Gog and Magog are missing.

The specific notions which show the poet's familiarity with rabbinic fantastic conceptions and which manifest his sympathy for the doctrine, both in its derivative and developed forms, are the following:

1. In conformity with Daniel and the Agadah, he characterizes as beasts the four empires that have dominated Israel. When describing the sorrows and agonies of the people in dispersion, he repeatedly alludes to their foes as the lion (Babylon), the leopard (Greece), the wild ass (Arabia), and the boar (Rome).[6]

2. The poet's consolation that ultimate deliverance is inevitable is based on promises made by God to the saints and seers. He refers quite often to the angel (messenger, Elijah), whom he will send to prepare the way for the wondrous event.

> "O break the yoke, the slave release,
>   Rebuke the arrogant again,
> And send thy messenger of peace,
>   Whose feet are welcome as the rain."[7]

3. The story of the Exodus is often mentioned in the Bible and in later literature as the pattern of the final redemption. So, too, the author occasionally harks back to the Exodus as the deliverance par excellence of the past, and as the parallel of the last and permanent redemption.[8]

4. The poet alludes to the Messiah as Yinon, in accordance with Sanhedrin, 98b.[9]

---

[6]Davidson, Nos. 39, 48, 7, 18; Bialik, Vol. II, Nos. 4, 16.
[7]Davidson, No. 21, p. 33.
[8]*Ibid.*, No. 40.
[9]*Ibid.*, Nos. 48, 17.

5. The zealous Phineas is identified as Elijah, wonder worker, at the Messianic advent.[10]

6. He places the redemption in Nisan, after a Talmudic opinion.[11]

7. The poet addresses the Messiah as the shoot of Ammiel.[12]

8. A poem entitled "The Trumpet of the Messenger" deals with the legend of Elijah, who by trumpet call will beckon Israel to Jerusalem.[13]

4—The Dispersion Under Christendom and Islam.

In Gabirol's treatment of Christianity and Islam, the latter is more severely condemned and is more often the target for the poet's wrath and scorn. Israel had suffered more perhaps from the Mohammedan persecution than from the attacks by the Christians.

Gabirol lived under the sway of the crescent and suffered severely from the belligerent invading armies of the Arabs. Again, probably it seemed to him that Rome (Christendom) had already done its worst in the destruction of the Temple, and in the persecutions of the first centuries. Perchance the time was ripe for deliverance, but then the new and furious power of Islam arose to frustrate the Jewish hope, to prolong the night, and add to the general agony. Hence, the torments devised by the "handmaiden" were more deeply registered in the poet's consciousness than the troubles brought on by Edom. The "brood of Hagar", the servant of the matriarch Sarah,

---

[10]Senior Sachs "Shire Ha-Shirim" of Gabirol, p. 100; Yalk. Shim. Numb. 25:11.

[11]Bialik, Vol. II, No. 22; Rosh Hash. 11a and various Midrashic references.

[12]Bialik, No. 25; Book of Zerubabel in Bet ha Midrash, Jellinek, Vol. I, p. 56; Ammiel acc. to I Chron. 3:5 was the father of Bathsheba, mother of Solomon; The Messiah will descend through the line of Solomon.

[13]Bialik, Vol. II, No. 109.

mocks at Israel. They have proven more ruthless than all previous foes. The race of Ishmael came upon the children of Abraham in the dead of night.[14] The poet uses the expression *hazot layil,* midnight. Actually it is the black night of the dispersion, which up to the time of the poet had lasted 1000 years. Half of the night would mean the year 500—about the time when Islam sprang up and became a menace to Israel.

Hence the poet implored:

> "To dust the Arab kingdom sweep,
>   The ravenous beasts who tear and bite,
> Who rend our scattered sons as sheep,
>   Whose motto is to seize by might."[15]

And again:

> "Turn away from the wild ass brood,
> And incline to the dainty roe."

In another selection the writer says:

> "Hardly these creatures had passed,
>   Sated with Judah's spoil,
> Than the wild ass we feared
> Out of the midnight appeared
>   To trample and dwell on our soil."

> "Ishmael's offspring command
> Back to his Arab land
>   As his mother of old
>   To her mistress was told
> To return and submit to her hand."[16]

A thousand years of blight and desolation have passed over Israel since the disaster of the year 70. Four hundred and sixty-one years have already sped by under Mohammedan rule and there is no surcease.[17] The scepter-ed family of David has long ceased to rule. Its pomp

---

[14]*Ibid.,* Nos. 1 and 2.
[15]Davidson, No. 21; p. 32.
[16]*Ibid.,* No. 39; p. 67.
[17]Bialik, Vol. II, No. 5.

and its power have become a mere memory. Perchance the extinct family will be revived, and send forth a renowned son.

> "Root of our savior,
> The scion of Jesse,
> Till when wilt thou linger
> Invisible, buried?
> Bring forth a flower.
>
> For winter is over!
> Why should a slave rule
> The lineage of princes,
> A hairy barbarian
> Replace our young sovereign?
>
> No man in white linen
> Reveals at our asking
> The end of our exile.
> God sealed up the matter.
> And closed up the knowledge."[18]

Israel has served so many "masters", that it has lost its self-respect. It has become an enslaved and abased people. Yet it does not enjoy even the small amount of rest and peace considered necessary for a slave. Its masters are slaves,—what can they expect?

> "Beneath the feet of slaves we bend:
> In pit and prison we are pressed;
> The hunters at our necks impend:
> We labor still and have no rest."[19]

This race of captive bondmen has counted and awaited certain "periods" of release. These have come and gone. There is a Bible statute that Hebrew slaves must be manumitted at the expiration of six years. Israel has been held in servitude for many more years, but still its masters

---

[18]Davidson, No. 43.
[19]*Ibid.*, No. 21; p. 32.

do not heed the Biblical injunction, and there seems to be
no pre-determined end to this enslavement. Israel would
rather be a slave of God forever, than be the slave of
slaves as now.

> "Behold, take me, if thou wilt not deliver;
> I will be thy slave forever, and will not go free."[20]

The figure of Israel as a dove, innocent, helpless, driven
forth, is common in poetry of this kind and in the Midrash.
But Gabirol heightens his effect when he speaks of the
"wounded dove", hunted by the enemy, gripped within a
net. More pathetically he speaks of Israel in the clutch
of the foe, as a dove in the hand of an urchin. The child
lacking comprehension, mercilessly and wantonly maims
the bird, and leaves it to expire. So the nations act toward Israel. The following vivid couplet depicts Israel's
painful life-and-death struggle.

> "I was as a lamb led to the slaughter,
> One man drawing me from the fold and another
> performing the sacrifice."[21]

Again, Israel is like a water-fowl lost in the wastes of
the desert. The world is unfriendly—aye, fatal to it. It
can expect neither relief nor hospitality. Its forlorn position is made clear by comparing the people to a boat that
is fast in a swamp; there is no one to seize an oar and
pull the ship from its moorings.[22]

The Messianic motif is sounded in several long poems
known as Geula or poems of redemption. These were
recited on Passover and on succeeding Sabbaths. Often
they take the form of a dialogue between God and
Kenesset Israel. Israel complains that it has waited so
long in vain. In the past it had been sunk into the lowest

[20]*Ibid.*, No. 9.
[21]*Ibid.*, No. 14.
[22]Bialik, Vol. II, No. 4.

pit of misery, yet through divine goodness it was uplifted. But this time, every avenue of escape appears closed. The nations, like birds of prey, surround Israel and feed on it, and yet are not sated.

Cantor to cong.:

"How long till the turn of my fate shall draw near,
How long ere the sealed and the closed be made clear?
My years have gone in sorrow and in sighing,
I hoped for respite, but instead comes wailing:
Before the balm arrives, behold me dying.
Ah, wait, faint heart, that sighest sick and failing:
Thyself against God's mercy do not harden;
Thou, eased of foes, shalt flower like a garden."

Cong. to God:

"Mine eyes are sick and faint from hope's depression,
Dumb like a sheep I bear thy storm of fury."

God:

"Harken, afflicted one, for hope yet lingers,
And look to Me, whose angel is preparing
My path, for though at night be tears and sadness,
Yet in the morning come delight and gladness."[23]

One of the most affecting Geulas is the dialogue between God and Israel.[24] Israel appeals fretfully to the Almighty to send the promised one; and God in turn sustains Israel's confidence by reiterating His ancient promise to uplift her.

God:

"Where'er thy origin, whosoe'er thy master,
A man shall come—nay, I—thy cause to plead,
Whoever holds the bill of thy divorcement.
Like wall or tower of fire I guard thy seed,
Then wherefore weep or heart affrighted heed?"

---

[23]Davidson, No. 19; p. 26.
[24]*Ibid.*, pp. 28-29.

THE DOCTRINE OF THE MESSIAH

Israel:

"Why do I weep? Because Thou keepest silence,
Though violence rages and, all uncontrolled,
The mob destroys, and we as slaves to strangers,
Master and man together, have been sold,
And no Redeemer do our eyes behold."

God:

"Who art thou thus to shrink from man in terror
And be dismayed because of mankind's scorn?
My angel I will send, as wrote the prophet,
And gather Israel winnowed and new-born:
This miracle shall be tomorrow morn."

Israel:

"To gather me my chieftains Thou didst promise,
The day comes not and miracle is none,
Nor see I Temple built nor any herald
Of peace arrive to be my Holy One—
Ah, wherefore lingers Jesse's promised son?"

God:

"Behold, I keep the oath I swore to gather
My captives—kings shall bring their gifts to thee;
Created for a witness to the nations,
My holy ones shall testify to Me—
Yea, Jesse's son Mine eyes already see."

The writer gives expression to a thought which theologians had stressed, that although the exact duration of previous exiles had been prophetically announced the present one remains a mystery.

"The calculation of the first end to Abraham had been
    vouchsafed.
The time of the second end to Jeremiah had been disclosed.
The third end from every eye is concealed.
Every seeker flounders, every seer is disillusioned.
The vision is hid, the appearance is withheld.
How long, O Lord, till the wondrous end!"[25]

---

[25]Bialik, Vol. II, No. 5.

SOLOMON IBN GABIROL

5—The Restoration.

The poet asks directly: "Why does the son of Jesse not come?" God had promised to do wonders for Israel, but thus far no miracles had occurred; no messenger had appeared to reestablish the Temple. There had been no answer to the insistent and plaintive cry of the people. To all of which God is represented as saying: "Let not Israel fear the abuses of man. There will be rescue from those who belabor her. The extraordinary event will come to pass—tomorrow, in the near and certain future. Israel, the distressed, is holy. That distress is not incompatible with the mission to testify of God in the world."

The poet awaits the dispersion and the resumption of new ties in Palestine with the same anxiety that a widow waits for her brother-in-law to fulfill the levirate vow. The law is clear, the promise is explicit. When the poet is derided by people who do not understand, and who mockingly say: "Why do you wait?"—he relies upon the comforts and the predictions in Holy Script, that at the opportune time God will make known His desire and mercy, and reclaim Israel for His own.[26] The quest for the Messiah, and the royal welcome in readiness for him, is depicted in the following ecstatic lines:

> "Come up to me at early dawn,
> Come up to me, for I am drawn
> Beloved, by my spirit's spell,
> To see the sons of Israel.
> For thee, my darling, I will spread
> Within my court a golden bed,
> And I will set a table there,
> And bread for thee I will prepare;
> For thee my goblet I will fill,
> With juices that my vines distil,
> And thou shalt drink to heart's delight
> Of all my flavors day and night.

[26] *Ibid.*, No. 144.

The joy in thee I will evince
With which a people greets its prince.
O, son of Jesse, holy stem,
God's servant, born of Bethlehem."[27]

Hence, all is not melancholy and despair in the poet's mood and in his reaction to the future probabilities of Israel. There is a cheerful and optimistic note in many of his poems. In the face of the world's ruthlessness, what should Israel do? It has no alternative but hope and trust. Gabirol philosophizes that it would be foolhardiness to expect the rapacious and envious nations to manifest any favor or love toward Israel. Nor could Israel be a traitor to her historic past and national mission by merging with the other nations. She must therefore endure her unspeakable adversities with equanimity, until the Almighty points the way and releases her.

"Though He delays, shall I not start
To seek His face; now of a sooth,
I yet shall find his words of truth
Bring comfort to my bitter heart.
The promise that Zechariah gave,
How sweet it tastes in this our woe;
My soul shall bid my heart to know
I trust the living God to save."[28]

Let not Israel abandon hope because of her affliction. As God has saved her in the past, so will he save her in the future.

"Forget thy affliction and cease supplication,
Recall thy release from Egyptian rod;
The hand is not short that hath laid earth's foundation;
Who stretched out the heavens remaineth thy God.
And at thy *due season* the glory that dwelleth
In Zion shall rest on thy head that great day,
When moonlight as sunlight in radiance welleth,
And sunlight shall glow with a sevenfold ray."

---

[27]Davidson, No. 4.
[28]*Ibid.*, No. 6.

In a Passover psalm he alludes to the Exodus, and ends with this stanza:

"Thus, Lord, do Thou Zion support and uphold,
Be unto Zion a supporter and upholder,
Arise, for the hour of grace is at hand;
The appointed time to sing has come as of old.
God reigneth, His kingdom forever shall stand."[29]

The Messiah is addressed as "Admoni" the ruddy-faced one in accordance with the use of this term as descriptive of King David. The poet exuberantly anticipates his arrival.

"Thrice welcome he
Who comes to me
Of David's line;
My palace treasure
Is at his pleasure
With all that's mine.
My pomegranate, cinnamon, spice
And the jars of my old sweet wine."[30]

The ingathering of the dispersed, an integral part of the structure of the Messianic doctrine, recurs in a number of poems.

"The scattered shalt thou assemble and the sighing redeem:
To the holy house thou shalt lead them with rejoicing,
And from earth's four corners gather the exiles."[31]

A ballad for Simhat Torah ends thus:

"O mighty One, glorious among celestial creatures,
Thou wilt gather in the scattered ones from the four corners,
Proclaim a year of redemption to those who stray like sheep,
However ill favored and lean,
O mighty God."[32]

---

[29]Davidson, No. 47.
[30]Ibid., No. 3.
[31]Ibid., No. 28.
[32]Ibid., No. 38.

There is also an Habdalah, each line of which ends with *"Phineas"*, a designation which applies to Elijah. The Almighty is implored to send his prince to lead the sheep, to proclaim the "end of ends", to bring vengeance upon presumptuous servants, to overthrow Rome as formerly wicked Sodom was overthrown, and to restore the divorced one to her patrimony.[33] He pleads for the restoration of Palestine as the motherland. Let the Almighty preserve and prosper the children, but let him also retain for them their mother, Palestine.[34] He prays for the renewal of the Temple and the altar, and the reinstatement of the priests, the Levites, and the Sanhedrin. The poet cites the statutes of the seventh year for the liberation of slaves, and of the fiftieth year, the Jubilee, when land that had been sold reverted to its original owner. In this way the Holy Land may enjoy a Jubilee of freedom from heathen posession, and become again the hallowed estate of Israel.[35]

A reference to Gabirol's astrological calculations of the "end" is made by Abraham ibn Ezra in his commentary on Dan. 11:30: "Also the words of R. Solomon ibn Gabirol (of blessed memory) who essayed to make the end contingent upon the conjunction of the two highest planets, Saturn and Jupiter. All who compute from words or letters after the manner of the gematria are ridiculous and perverted. For Daniel did not know the end, how much less did those who came after."

Our philosopher believed in two worlds. The second is the ideal one, the world of rewards.

"Thine are the two worlds between which Thou hast set a boundary,
The first for deeds and the second for rewards;
Thine is the reward, which Thou for the righteous hast stored up and hidden,
Yea, Thou sawest it was goodly and didst hide it."

---

[33]Sachs' Shire Ha-Shirim, of Gabirol, p. 100.
[34]Davidson, No. 48.
[35]Bialik, Vol. II, No. 6.

This other world is the world after death to which the
departed souls go, to abide by the throne of God. There
the wicked receive punishment and the righteous are rewarded. The punishment of the wicked will consist in
their being doomed to wander about through the upper
spheres forever.[36] This was the view of Joseph ibn Zaddik
but it is not found among the leading theologians. The
poet, more than the scholastic was the mouthpiece of the
desires and needs of the people. That is why the emotional
and sentimental strain in Gabirol's poetry may be taken
as the true mirror of the intense popular yearning for a
redeemer.

---

[36]"Royal Crown", Ch. XXX.

Chapter V

JUDAH HALEVI

1—Poet and Philosopher.

The fame of Judah Halevi (Spain 1080-1141), a physician by vocation, rests upon his brilliant enrichment of Jewish literature and his stimulating effect upon the Jewish spirit in every age. He devoted a good part of each day, as well as his Sabbaths and holidays, to the study of the Torah and to the composition of poetry. His two outstanding literary achievements were first, the Kuzari, a defense of traditional Judaism and Jewish nationalism against the criticism of philosophers and Karaites; second, several hundred poems; secular, liturgical, and Palestinian. As poet, the distinction of genius belongs to him. He ranks second to none since Bible days. His poetry has vision, fire, determination, ingenuity, and stylistic perfection. It voices his unquenchable love for God and the Holy Land. Again and again he reiterates his hope in Israel's national deliverance. Much of his poetry is Messianic, in the sense that it echoes the people's plaintive cry for redemption. His poetry and philosophy mark him as the greatest exponent of Jewish nationalism in the Middle Ages. He was devoted to his race, his God, his religion, and his ancestral land. He seems to have spent his genius and labor to revivify Israel with national ardor and honor, to guard Judaism from attack, and to bring forth his nation's adequacy and completeness.

He wished his Judaism to be pure and unadulterated. The historic faith was all sufficient for him. He founded all beliefs and axioms on the Torah and on tradition. Hence he was more of a religionist than a philosopher. Yet, he felt that the natural sciences such as medicine, astronomy, and mathematics, should be studied because they are necessary for a full knowledge and proper observance of our religious codes. Metaphysics, however, he disliked. And so he preferred the certainties and postulates of Judaism to the vagaries and frigid intellectualism of Aristotle. He cautioned against the Stagyrite's influence:

> "Let not Greek wisdom entice thee,
>   Which has no fruit, but only blossoms.
> Its upshot is that never earth was stretched
>   And the tents of the firmaments never expanded.
> No beginning there was for the work of creation
>   Nor is there an end for the renewal of the moon.
> Listen not to the misleading words of its adepts,
>   Built upon frail foundations.
> But then thou will turn away
> With a heart empty and faint
> And a mouth full of dross and thorns.
> Why should I seek crooked ways
> And forsake the mother of paths?"[1]

Hence, Judah Halevi, is not one of those who sought to bring harmony between revelation and reason. Undoubtedly he knew well the current speculative tendencies, Greek, Islamic, and Karaite, but he did not accept them either as equal to religion or as its handmaiden. In his opinion Judaism is superior to philosophy, both in method and in conclusions. The disadvantage of philosophy is that it is uncertain; its views change according to the era and the thinker. At best, it is a supposition and speculative, where Judaism offers positive, proven and unvarying teachings.

---

[1]Harkavy's ed. of Judah Halevi's poetry, Warsaw, 1893, I, p. 19.

Furthermore, the best criterion of value and veracity is experience and this has been the criterion of Judaism. Certain leaders of thought argue the existence of God and the fact of creation from abstract principles, but Judaism does so from actual testimony. The revelations of God to the patriarchs, to Moses, and to the prophets were actual manifestations witnessed by the people. The report of these revelations furnishes for us, as it furnished for those who saw them, unshakable evidence that God exists. The truth of Judaism is seen also in the faithful transmission of the Written Law intact from Moses to the present day. The very survival of the Jewish people is an ever-living witness and proof of God's presence and vigilance for them throughout history.

2—*The Messianic Idea in the Kuzari.*

a. Acceptability of the Doctrine.

The Kuzari is a defense of Jewish thought and life as a whole, rather than an examination of its several dogmas. It is a lengthy dialogue between the king of the Khazari and a rabbi. Halevi expatiates on certain metaphysical principles such as causation, divine attributes, the soul, emanation, and the Hebrew alphabet. His idealization of Palestine as the geographic center of the earth, as a most holy land, and as the principal need of the Hebrew people shows the nationalistic quality of this work. As for specific dogmas, he does not analyze them microscopically as do Saadia and Maimonides. He does not feel urged to justify any Jewish doctrine. It is enough that it had been revealed, faithfully maintained and transmitted. Thus it becomes part of the Jewish doctrinal household.

For that reason belief in the Messiah is a matter of course to Halevi, and receives no special treatment. We must bear in mind that Maimonides also omits the Messianic theme in the "Guide of the Perplexed". Said the rabbi to the doubting king: "Why art thou reluctant to accept the firmament and the water above the heavens, and the evil spirits mentioned by the sages, the description of events to be expected during the days of the Messiah, the resurrection of the dead, the world to come?"[2] This is one of a few casual allusions to the Messiah in the Kuzari. To Halevi, the Messiah apparently must be quite human. He places him on the same level with the prophet, the nazarite, or the high priest, at the moment when they are enwrapped by the Holy Spirit. The legend of the Messiah's pre-existence—as found in the Talmudic statement that seven things were created prior to the world: Paradise, the Torah, the just, Israel, the throne of glory, Jerusalem, and the Messiah, son of David means that before God created the world he planned wisely for its future, and for a high destiny for Israel in Jerusalem through the rulership of the Messiah.[3]

b. The Rationale of the Dispersion.

Judah Halevi has more to say on the "rationale" of Israel's disperson than on the fascinating elements of the Messianic drama. He speaks of the humiliating and unhealthy status of the Jews from which they yearn to be delivered. As Israel is the heart of the world, so the Jerusalem Temple was the heart of Israel. Since the loss of the Temple (the heart) and the priests and prophets (the head) Israel has become ossified. The skeleton only remains, and its parts, scattered everywhere, represent a body that once thrived. Still these parts retain vital potentialities, "having once been active with heart, brain, and breath." To this hapless condition the disputed section in Isaiah refers (52:13-*et seq.*). Israel

---

[2]Kuzari, V. 14.
[3]*Ibid.* III, 73.

in the diaspora is like a sick and attenuated person who has been given up by the physicians and yet hopes for a miracle or an extraordinary recovery.[4] On account of its sickly repulsiveness the nations turned aside from Israel in contempt. However, through the divine interposition Israel will recover and be reinstated in his own land. His deliverance is sure to come. Indeed, God had intended to effect a permanent redemption of Israel during the second commonwealth, but the people themselves preferred to remain exiled in Babylon.

Halevi quotes Canticles 5:2-4 as an allusion to the unsuccessful effort toward the restoration from Babylon.[5] The "sleep" is the sleep of the Babylonian exile. "The wakeful heart" is the vigilance exercised by the prophets. "The voice of my beloved" is God's call to return. "The head full of dew" designates the Shekina. "I have put off my coat" refers to the people's recalcitrance in returning. It was only through the urgent appeals of Ezra and Nehemiah that the people responded.

But present weakness means strength in the future. "Israel among the nations is like the heart amidst the organs of the body. It is at the same time the most ailing and the most healthy of them."[6] The delicate functioning of the heart makes it easily susceptible to disease, and yet gives it a certain immunity. Likewise Israel stands exposed to the brutal treatment and to the obnoxious influence of other races, but its unique mission in the world has rendered it forever indispensable and indestructible. The immunity enjoyed by Israel consists in God's protection over it and His forgiveness of its sin.

Hence, the diabolical sufferings of the Jews should not lead anyone to hold them in reproach, nor to conclude that God has cast them off and that they are fated to

---

[4]*Ibid.* II, 34.
[5]*Ibid.* II, 24.
[6]*Ibid.* II, 36.

perdition. In a sense, Israel is only paying the price of its constancy and its glory. That price must be paid in martyrdom.

The founders and followers of Christianity and Mohammedanism also had to pass through a stage of contumely, torture, and death, before those religions became ascendant. Likewise, Israel is now passing through a crucible of fire to prepare itself for a lasting and glorious future. When the King of the Khazari objected, saying that the humility and affliction of the Jews are involuntary and hence not efficacious or deserving of admiration, the rabbi replied—"Thou hast touched our weak spot. If the majority of us, as thou sayest, would learn humility towards God and His law from our station, Providence would not have forced us to bear it for so long a period. Only the smallest portion thinks thus. Yet the majority may expect a reward, because they bear their degradation partly from necessity, partly from their own free-will. For whoever wishes to do so can become the friend and equal of his oppressor by uttering one word and without any difficulty; if we bear our exile and degradation for God's sake as is meet, we shall be the pride of the generation which will come with the Messiah, and accelerate the day of deliverance we hope for."[7]

A theory of unusual interest, found in Halevi and others, which evokes our admiration because it was voiced in the midst of outrageous persecutions, is that the Gentile nations fill a necessary purpose in the divine economy of the world by hastening its moral advancement. Through Christianity and Islam the way is prepared for the expected Messiah. The law of Moses is like a seed which is cast into the ground and changes outwardly into sod. However, the seed remains true to the vegetative function of its species. It refines the soil-elements in

---

[7] *Ibid.* I, 115.

which it is bedded and in time thrusts itself upward and produces fruit. So is mankind the soil, and the Mosaic law the seed by whose wisdom mankind will ultimately be transformed and Judaized. The fruition of this spiritual planting will be the Messiah.[8]

c. Palestine and Israel.

The hub of Halevi's thought is Palestine. Where other theologians made the Messianic advent a dogma of Judaism, Halevi may be said to have made the belief in the Jewish re-possession of Palestine central in the scheme of future things. This is obvious in the Kuzari, and even more so in his poetry. The author, fully aware of the sovereign and spiritual interest of the major religions of his day in Palestine, takes great pains to show that Israel has a prior claim to the Holy Land. Their residence in it antedated the conquests of any living people. From the primitive days of Hebrew history the land has been beloved and sanctified. The Patriarchs dwelt in it. Jacob and Joseph ordered their remains interred there. Moses yearned and prayed unto the Lord to enter it. The Bible speaks of it constantly in relation to God. It is called the gate of heaven—Gen. 28:17; His footstool—Ps. 99-5; His holy mountain—Ps. 99-9. The prophet Micah declares that from Zion shall go forth the Law, (4:2). Halevi also quotes numerous passages from the Talmud to show its sacrosanct character.[9]

As individuals vary in character and ability, and as the races of mankind possess distinctive qualities and aptitudes, so do the many sections of the earth present differences. Some countries are by nature endowed with properties that are conducive to religion; among them is Palestine. It possesses a *genius loci*. Even if it could lay

---

[8]*Ibid.* IV, 23.
[9]*Ibid.* II, 22.

no claim to uniqueness on account of inherent natural qualities, the fact that the Shekina, God's glory, dwelt there for 900 years is sufficient to make it hallowed, and the object of our yearning. The Jew will not attain full development except in Palestine. Many precepts and ordinances depend upon the Holy Land for their observance. Israel needs the visible Shekina or glory of God, and this dwells only in Palestine. Hence the pious Jew prays daily: "Let our eyes behold when Thou returnest to Zion."

In the conclusion of the book, Halevi states his own ardent desire to dwell in the promised land. This is his greatest passion. He utilizes Psalm 102:14-15 to show with what intense emotion the people at large must respond to the call of the mother-land. "Thou shalt arise and have mercy upon Zion, for the time to favor her, yea the set time is come. For Thy servants take pleasure in her stones and embrace the dust thereof." "This means", says Halevi, "that Jerusalem can only be rebuilt when Israel yearns for it to such an extent that they embrace her stones and dust."[10]

There is scarcely any mention in the Kuzari about the Messianic state. The future and last sanctuary will be constructed in accordance with the details of the prophet Ezekiel, as surely as Moses built the Tabernacle and its equipment from the specifications of the book of Exodus, and as Solomon built his magnificent temple according to the model revealed to David.[11]

d. Eschatology.

After the rabbi had set forth, to the delight of the king, the exalted religious life of a virtuous Jew, and explained the daily recitation of the Eighteen Benedictions with

---

[10]*Ibid.* V, 27.
[11]*Ibid.* I, 99.

particular mention of the Messianic prayers, the king replied: "There is nothing to criticize, as I see how settled
and circumspect all these arrangements are. There is
however, still one point to be mentioned, namely, that your
prayers say so little of the world to come. But you have
already proved to me that he who prays for attachment
to the Divine Light and the faculty of seeing it with his
own eyes in this world, and who, nearly approaching the
rank of prophets, is thus engaged in prayer (and nothing
can bring man nearer to God than this) has without doubt
prayed for more than the world to come. If he gains such
communion with God on this earth, he has already won
the other world. For if one's soul is in contact with the
Divine Influence, though still exposed to the accidents and
sufferings of the body, it stands to reason that it will gain
a more intimate connection with the former, when it has
become free and detached from this unclean vessel."[12]

Such theological notions as Paradise, Gehinnom, and
resurrection, all of which are quite important in the dominant religions, are defended by Halevi as originally Jewish. "Our sages long ago gave descriptions of Paradise
and Hell, their length and width, and depicted the enjoy-
ments and punishments in greater detail than is given in
any later religions", he wrote. "From the very beginning,
I only spoke to thee of what is contained in the books of
the prophets. They, however, do not discuss the promises
of after-life with so much diffuseness as is done in the
sayings of the rabbis."[13] Nevertheless, the Bible furnishes
us with our idea of Paradise. It was the exalted place in
which Adam lived in innocence and splendor, and from
which he was expelled for disobedience. Gehinnom too is
an actual place, located near the Temple site. It was a
valley in which the refuse of the Temple and discarded
parts of the sacrifices were burnt.

---

[12]*Ibid.* III, 20.
[13]*Ibid.* I, 115.

The Bible clearly teaches the resurrection of the dead at some future time, and the return of Elijah to earth. Belief in the resurrection is popular in Jewish tradition. The educated as well as the illiterate Jew prays every morning in his daily devotions: "O, Lord, the spirit which Thou hast breathed into me is hallowed. Thou hast created it, Thou guardest it, and Thou wilt after a time take it from me, but wilt restore it to me in the after world. As long as it is within me, I praise Thee and am grateful to Thee, O, Lord of the universe. Praise be to Thee, who restoreth the spirit unto the dead."

3—Messianic Poetry.

The failure of Judah Halevi to expatiate on the Messianic theme in the Kuzari is compensated for by the profuse treatment of the subject in his national poetry. Naturally, we cannot hope for a dogmatic consideration of it in his poems. These are what we would expect them to be—didactic and sentimental. The poet, more than any other writer, is the medium of expressing the best traditional and current sentiment. Although the style and spirit may be new and individualistic, the thoughts are certain to be old and inherited. So the recurrent motif of Halevi's poems is the irrepressible desire of Israel for deliverance from the diaspora. We hear the familiar note of forthcoming divine vengeance upon the merciless adversaries of Israel, and the people's renewed fidelity to God. Palestine is envisaged as the land of popular adoration, and the cynosure of a new spiritual imperium. A great pioneer in the study of the religious poetry of the Spanish Jews characterizes Judah Halevi in the following words: "The longing for the hour of redemption is the dominant note in the Jewish poetry of the Spanish period. With many, it was the oppressive conditions of existence that called forth that irrepressible longing. But with

Halevi this longing is a fine, loving desire, which possesses, on the one hand, the simplicity and naïvete of childhood, and on the other, the glow of a mighty passion. The energy and vividness with which he expresses his confidence in the redemption of his people is only the more gripping because of the fact that in his poetry there is no trace of the gloomy present, and his hope of the future does not appear to be the result of a daring escape from the dark environment which surrounds him, into the shining regions of phantasy. He is confident of his cause and the joy of his belief intoxicates and inspires him."

In the following pages are summarized the emotions and reflections bearing upon redempion, which abound in the collected songs of Zion and songs of Israel published in Harkavy's edition of Halevi's poetry. This material is grouped under the following captions:

> A—Israel in Dispersion.
>
> B—The Poet's Steadfastness.
>
> C—Yearning for Zion.
>
> D—The Deliverance.
>
> E—Glorification of Zion.

a. Israel in Dispersion.

The poet echoes the traditional view that the dispersion is a punishment inflicted upon the people for their misdeeds.

"Behold, my sins have driven me forth from my parental chamber;
The doom decreed by the Father impends upon me;
My brother and the handmaid's son have seized my birthright;
Hence doth my soul pour forth its entreaties before the Rock."[14]

---

[14]Harkavy I, p. 15.

Hence, Israel implores God to let His graciousness descend upon her as formerly His fury distressed her. Will the nation's guilt forever be a wall of separation between her and the Almighty?[15] The life of Israel in dispersion is characterized by the poet as Sheol (hell). He frequently calls Israel a "prisoner of hope" in the dungeon of exile. She is helpless as an orphan, as a disowned child. She is a congregation and a nation of weepers, yet she treads on the mountains of hope. Her calamitous condition is presented by the poet in this "Song of Israel to God."[16]

"My love! hast Thou forgotten Thy nest upon my breast
And wherefore hast Thou sold me
To be enslaved for aye?
And how hast Thou apportioned
My glory away from me?
Thrust unto Seir, pursued, sent forth to flee
Unto Kedar, nor suffered to abide;
Within the Grecian fiery furnace tried;
Afflicted, weighed with care,
With Media's yoke to bear:—
And is there any to redeem but Thee?
Or other captive with such hope above?
Thy strength, O Lord, grant of Thy strength to me!
For I give Thee my love."

Other metaphors applied to Israel denote her timidity and harmlessness, such as the dove, the lost sheep, the lamb and the gazelle. The dispersed elements of Israel are described as "yonot". But Israel also bears the proud name of Messiah. She is destined to be the anointed and ruling nation. The races of the earth are vile, venomous, reptilian creatures, whose embrace or touch means death. Unlike Gabirol, who repeatedly refers to the nations as

---

[15]*Ibid.* I, p. 57.
[16]*Ibid.* I, p. 55. The trans. is from Friedlander's "Standard Book of Jewish Verse", p. 405.

wild beasts of the forests, our poet describes them by such
epithets as adder, scorpion, dragon, and venomous serpent.
He bitterly suggests that Israel should turn the other
cheek to her smiters and perchance such resignation and
self-effacement, in the face of torment, might appease the
enemy and make him relent.

Israel appeals reminiscently to God. How could He
have forgotten the mutual friendship sustained through
all the early vicissitudes of their history? The consequence of His severance from His chosen people has been
their affliction under Media (Persia), Yavan (Greece),
Keder (the Arabs), and Seir (Christendom).

The singer envisages Israel as a bride who seeks
passionately to greet her beloved, but sudden disenchant-
ment keeps her from him and renders her sick unto death.
Likewise Israel is pained at the sight of multitudes of
strangers who visit the Holy Land, particularly at the
ancient seasons of pilgrimage, while she must perforce
stand by and watch. She must remain in distant lands
and be content to prostrate herself beseechingly in the
direction of the sanctuary. In lieu of temple gifts and
offerings she brings her tearful entreaties.[17]

In one of his best-known effusions "An Ode to Zion",
used in the liturgy for the fast of Ab, the poet addresses
Zion and asks whether she is concerned with the welfare
of her people, now prisoners in other lands.[18] Whatever
her response, abashed and broken though she be, her old
patriots remember her, and greet her from every quarter.
The souls of the people are tied fast unto her. They long
for her from the pit of captivity. They do her reverence.
They bow down toward her gate. Although far removed
from the land they love, they have not forgotten its walls,
the Torah, the customs and ideals that governed their life

[17]Harkavy I, p. 62.
[18]*Ibid.* I, pp. 10-14.

there. All the states which flourish now will come to naught, but Zion will regain her faded strength. Her crown will be replaced, for she is indestructible.

b. The Poet's Steadfastness.

The revelation at Mt. Sinai and the Exodus from Egypt are the two incontrovertible evidences of God's greatness which fill the poet with courage and the conviction that He will deliver the chosen people from their present distress. The intense nationalistic faith of Halevi is seen in his belief that Israel will endure forever.

"The sun and moon unchanging do obey
The laws that never cease on night or day
Appointed signs are they to Jacob's seed
That life eternal hath been decreed.
And though, O Lord, thy left hand dealeth pain,
Thy right hand shall lead them back to joy again.
Let not despair oppress their quailing heart,
Though radiant Fortune from their midst depart,
But let this constant faith their soul uphold,
That in the Book of Life their name's enrolled
For all eternity: nor shall they cease
While night and day do alternate in peace."[19]

The poet declares that he is immune from the enemy's enticements and their attempts to convert him, because his Jewish belief is instinctive; he cannot change. It is embedded in his inward parts, in his very bones.

"And his name is within me
Like a fire in my inmost veins
Locked in my heart
Bound up in my bones."[20]

He cannot recede from his God. Even if He should slay him, he will still trust in Him. Despite his suffer-

---

[19]*Ibid.* I, p. 72. The thought of Israel's immortality is borrowed from Jer. 31:35.
[20]*Ibid.* II, p. 16.

ings, he is quite willing to submit to the divine wrath because he is confident that he will be shown compassion
later. God Himself is his pledge, that the yoke of the
Arab will be broken. Should the "end" which appears
near be deferred, he will not be disappointed, for the star
of hope is breaking through.

The poet bears uncomplainingly the ridicule of his
enemies for his uncompromising observance of Judaism.
Their inhospitality has really become his joy and a reason
for glory.

> "They who belittle me do not know
> That my shame for Thy name's sake
> Is my glory."[21]

Even when his suffering grows acute, he will love the
Lord. The nations round about mock us and say that
salvation will never come. They deny that the vision and
prognostications of our holy men will be fulfilled. Apparently we have been given unto them to do with as they
please. We have no redeemer. There will be no offshoot
from the stem of Jesse. But opposed to such boastings is
the reassurance of God Himself that He will deliver us.

God and Israel are unique in that they are necessary
to each other. There is no one requiring deliverance so
badly as Israel and there is no one who can redeem as
well as God. The poet ruminates on Israel's dim past,
the dawn of their history; how God loved and chose them;
how He brought sweet salvation unto them in the land
of the Pharaohs and sealed His union with them by the
giving of the Torah. Subsequently they were humbled
by the four monarchies, Seir, Kedar, Yavan, and Modai.
But his affection will return; He will again free them
from the abusive powers and enter into a new covenant
with Israel.

---

[21] *Ibid.* I, p. 56.

As of yore, He will send a messenger to recall them.

"Through my guilt does now my soul wither,
From my mountain habitation divorced.
Until the Lord will enact a new covenant;
He will yet send forth a messenger to recall me
And render the darkness light unto me."[22]

God exhorts Israel to be firm, loyal, observant in the faith, and unvexed about the "end".

"Strengthen thy heart, and wait for thy time
Why art thou affrighted at the end of thy captivity?
Thy beloved who afflicted thee will make answer,
He who wounded thee, will send for his healing balm;
Thou didst well to wait for thy redeemer.
Haste not, Thou wilt behold his wondrous work."[23]

c. Yearning for Zion.

Halevi's affection for Palestine is not alienated by seductive influences in the diaspora. All the wealth and beauty of his native Spain do not mean as much to him as the dust of the devastated sanctuary. He cherishes a burning desire to dwell in the Holy Land. His heart is in the east, although he lives in the west. He calls himself a prisoner of passion for Palestine. He freely uses hyperbolic language to give vent to his overpowering emotions. His tears pour forth like the dew on Mt. Hermon. He asks for the wings of an eagle to carry him Zionward. There, from pure joy would he water the earth with tears. He would kiss the sod and caress the stones, and they would taste sweeter than honey.

His knowledge of sacred history and his reverence for the past have endeared the land to him. His heart beats with rapturous joy at the prospect of visiting Bethel, Peniel, and other sacred sites. He craves to wander

---

[22]*Ibid.* II, p. 22.
[23]*Ibid.* I, p. 57.

through the places where God's seers and ambassadors received their oracles and visions. He would. meander through Carmel, Gilead, and Mt. Abarim. He would be content to walk barefoot over the desolated places, where the sanctuary stood enshrining the ark and the cherubim. He would stand at the graves of the patriarchs near Hebron. He would scatter his grief, aye the very parts of his rent heart *bisre levovi* over Palestine's spicy mountains,[24] *ben besorayich.*

Aside from the national memories that feed his ardor for the homeland, he longs for it also as a pious Jew. It is essential to him, for without it he cannot fulfill his vows. He cannot live a complete religious life in Islamic lands while Palestine is under Christian control.

Judah Halevi relates a dream in which he found himself within the precincts of the Temple during the Aboda, witnessing the sacrifice of incense.[25] He heard the praise-songs of the Levites and was enchanted by their music. Emotions of self-sacrifice welled up within him, and he too would offer up his heart as a sacrifice of devotion to God. He would gladly die in Palestine that his sepulture might be a witness of his unbounded love.[26]

The following effusion sums up the poet's immeasurable admiration and yearning for the Holy City:

"Beautiful height; O joy! the whole world's gladness;
O great King's city, mountain blest!
My soul is yearning unto thee,—is yearning,
From limits of the west.
The torrents heave from depths of mine heart's passion
At memory of thine olden state;
The glory of thee which was born to exile,
Thy dwelling desolate.
And who shall grant me but to rise and reach thee,
Flying on eagle's pinions fleet,

[24]*Ibid.* I, p. 12. See J. P. S. trans. The Song of Songs 2:17.
[25]*Ibid.* I, p. 8.
[26]*Ibid.* I, p. 33.

That I may shed upon thy dust, beloved,
Tears, till thy dust grow sweet?
I seek thee, though thy King be no more in thee;
Though where the balm hath been of old,—
Thy Gilead's balm—be poisonous adders lurking,
Winged scorpions manifold.
Is it not to thy stones I shall be tender?
Shall I not kiss them verily?
Shall not the earth-taste on my lips be sweeter
Than honey—the earth of thee?"[27]

d. The Deliverance.

Although hope and cheer fill his poetry, here and there are heard the minor keys of protest and vengeance. However, these are not as frequent in his poesy as in that of other bards, Gabirol for instance. His staunch faith and personal integrity embolden him to ask God to hasten the blissful "end". He protests that his position has become unendurable. He wishes to be spared the humiliation of calling his servant, master. It is becoming increasingly difficult to combine a life of godliness with one of affliction and wandering. God has been merciful with non-Jews but severe with Israel.

"And why are thy beloved as forlorn as berries at the top
    of the tree?
Pour forth thy ire upon the stranger and thresh them.
Not upon them is thy dread, only against me art thou
    grieved.
With a pointed metal is the sin of Judah inscribed."[28]

The dove Israel has flown into the wilderness of nations and can not retrace her flight homeward. Why, has God forsaken His tender ward, which He once bore on eagle's wings, and gave a nest, where stood the people's shrine? Why does God act like an enemy, when Israel

---

[27]*Ibid.* I, p. 7; Friedlander, p. 464.
[28]Harkavy II, pp. 31 and 32.

seeks His friendship through prayer and constancy? The lips of the people have become heavy and sore from asking for the day of redemption.

They have prayed for the "end", for the time when God will find the lost sheep, when He will redeem the lost ones in Spain and lead them unto light and liberty through Elijah and the Messiah. Elijah is mentioned as the herald of deliverance, as promised us by Malachi. The Tishbite had performed numerous wonders in former days, and had even restored the dead to life. Surely, in his second coming, he will perform wonders equally great. But thus far 1000 years have elapsed since the destruction and he has not come. The people have considered this a sufficient time for the accomplishment of the "end", but their expectations have been frustrated. Still, God reassures Israel that He will perform wonders on the day of recompense and retribution, when His blessing will rest upon Israel like the gentle dew, and His wrath will come upon the Gentiles. God's word is firm. He is not impotent to redeem. Neither is he subject to time and accident. He will rebuild what others have destroyed. The poet is certain that He will rescue the lamb from the den of lions, and prays for the day of freedom when the sanctuary and Sanhedrin will be restored, when the slave will remove the tattered garb of the exile and be clothed with dignity.

> "Put forth Thy hand again, O Lord,
> To renew the pristine kingdom,
> That ever waileth,
> Dispersed to right and left;
> Confound the Arab and the Greek
> And restore the priesthood anew.
> Sanctified by the hand of Levites
> Be Thy name-exalted everywhere."[29]

---

[29]Harkavy II, p. 12.

JUDAH HALEVI

In a Passover hymn he calls for a second liberation of the people, and after the manner of certain prophets speaks of it in connection with the Exodus:

> "When as a wall the sea
> In heaps uplifted lay
> A new song unto Thee
> Sang the redeemed that day.
> O, let thy banner soar
> The scattered remnants o'er
> And gather them once more,
> Like ours on harvest-day.
> O let them, sanctified,
> Once more with Thee abide,
> Their sunshine far and wide,
> And chase the clouds away".[30]

The motif of revenge is not absent from Judah Halevi's poetry. He warns us specifically that Israel may perish altogether unless the Mohammedan nation is shorn of its power. He recounts a dream he had in which the downfall of Mohammedan rule was foretold to occur in 1130, when the Messianic upheaval would commence.[31] In another poem[32] Halevi cites the belief of a preceding generation that the advent would occur in 1068, a thousand years after the second destruction. "She deemed a thousand years would be the limit of the set Time. But she is ashamed of all whereon she counted." Neither does Christendom, with its gnashing teeth, afford any respite to the people. It is merciless, and from its yoke also, Israel must be freed.

> "Spread forth a redeeming hand unto the broken in spirit
> Who weep over the pain inflicted by enemies.
> Bring near, we pray, the time of our redemption
> From the power of Edom, that gnashes her teeth."[33]

---

[30]Friedlander, p. 376.
[31]Harkavy II, p. 61.
[32]Ibid. I, p. 60.
[33]Ibid. I, p. 59

e. Glorification of Zion.

The poet extols Zion as the acme of spiritual perfection. It epitomizes the grandest ideals of the human race. He is fully imbued with its pre-eminence as a city of God. It is a crown of beauty upon the face of the earth. It is the throne of the Almighty. The Shekina dwells there. Its gates are set opposite the gates of heaven. God, Himself, has chosen Jerusalem as his own. He separated it from the rest of the earth as holy; as the priestly portion, *halla,* sanctifies the dough, so Jerusalem sanctifies the earth. It was the seat of the revelation and of the most righteous dynasty upon earth. It harbored the sacred treasures.

"There the cherubim and engraved tablets
Are hid in clods of earth and secret places;
It is the place of marvels, the fountain of prophecies
Made luminous by the Divine Glory.
Its dust will I beseech, near it will I nestle,
And lament over it, as over a grave.
The intent of my striving is to dwell
At the tomb of my fathers, in the possession of the pure."[34]

The mighty miracle of resurrection will be enacted upon its holy soil.

"There will I await the resurrection.
There doth man await the reward of his deeds."[35]

Egypt is accorded a place next to Palestine and is lauded as the birthplace of Moses and Aaron as well as the scene of many miracles. It has a well-deserved niche in the temple of Jewish memory, for much was wrought in that land for the creation of our nationality. The glory of the Lord had manifested itself there, but not in full-orbed brilliance. It appeared there as a guest, in

[34]*Ibid.* I, p. 27.
[35]*Ibid.*

a temporary and external way. But Jerusalem possessed intrinsic qualities which made her suitable as the permanent abode of God.

f. The Personal Equation.

Someone had dispatched a letter to Judah Halevi in which he essayed to dissuade the poet from making his romantic pilgrimage to Palestine.[36] The writer did not share the poet's ecstatic attachment for the Holy Land. In reply, Halevi re-affirmed that Palestine had not lost its sacredness and potency through its desolation and alien occupancy. No alteration of its political status could divest the land of its holiness and charm for us. It is our inalienable possession, having been promised us in perpetuity. Granted that we have been dispossessed, but only temporarily. The fact that it is now ruled by non-Israelitish governments does not dim the luster of its former glory, since it has been the birthplace of the world's greatest masters and sages, and the creative center for law, morality, and joyous living. Nor does alien control render it unfit to become our homeland once again.

As a matter of fact, when the patriarchs for the first time visited and settled in Canaan, it was a heathen land. Yet they deemed it wise and proper to buy sepulchres there. The poet holds that there is much more reason for Israel to hold it precious at this time, since it is now the home of a large Jewish settlement and still popular. For many centuries Palestine has been the scene of a free and intensive Jewish life. Even after the catastrophe of 70 C. E. it exerted a penetrating mental and moral influence upon the diaspora and fashioned our character and mode of life. In recognition of the debt we owe to Palestine, all Israel follows the custom of turning to the east during prayer.

---

[36]*Ibid.* I, p. 16.

THE DOCTRINE OF THE MESSIAH

Halevi invokes the tenderest and purest emotions to justify his desire to visit Palestine. Nay, it is a duty. He alludes to the popular custom of visiting the graves of kin. Is it right to visit the last resting-places of our dear-departed ones and thereby gain comfort, blessing, incentive, and hope, and yet to forsake the sepulchres where rest the ashes of our nation's immortal rulers and prophets? These tombs are our national shrines. How can we ignore our foremost heritage, the sanctuaries of God, located in the ancestral land? There is no place in the East or West that carries so many associations, sentimental and political, as Palestine. Only upon the Holy Land can we center our hope for the future.

Once Halevi speaks in a very personal vein. He discloses the fact that there were domestic difficulties to surmount before setting out upon his journey.[37] Home ties, as well as kind and loving friendships had to be broken. He left behind him his only daughter, and the recollection of her young son pierced his heart. The pang of separating from his dear family and his esteemed pupils, his regret at missing the pleasurable study-hours in the synagogue, were mingled with his joyous anticipations of being in the Holy Land. The voyage itself brought material loss to him: the loss of his possessions and means of livelihood. It entailed severe hardships in the lack of food, the loss of health and ordinary comforts, and the hazards of the sea. Yet he did not grieve. For in the want of physical necessities he was animated and strengthened by a vital reliance upon God. He could bear every privation and peril because of the glorious goal on which he was bent. Even when his ship was storm-tossed and enveloped by the raging billows he rejoiced, for he was resisting the elements and being carried ever nearer to his beloved Palestine.

---

[37]*Ibid.* I, p. 20.

JUDAH HALEVI

In Judah Halevi, Hebrew poetry reached its highest level, and by the verdict of time he has been crowned the matchless singer of Zion's glories. Perhaps his soul-stirring poems did more to preserve the hope of redemption than the discourses of the scholars.

Chapter VI

ABRAHAM IBN EZRA

1—*His Character.*

Although Abraham ibn Ezra (Spain, 1092-1167), an older contemporary of Judah Halevi, has left us no systematic treatment of the Messianic doctrine, his distinction as a scholar makes it necessary to set down the thoughts on the subject which are found in his commentaries and poetry. His position as a man of learning was unique. He headed no school and wielded no communal authority. He hewed no original paths in theology. Yet his literary remains have been cherished and guarded jealously, and have enshrined him forever in the Jewish hall of fame. His clever poetry, his acute commentaries, his scientific studies and apologetics, considered as a whole, stamp him as one of the greatest intellectual virtuosos of his race, and account for the magnetic hold he continues to have upon every new and inquisitive generation of his people.

No consideration of any aspect of Ibn Ezra's scholarship is complete without reference to his personal characteristics. A trait which distinguishes him from many other celebrities in this series is his wanderlust, his restless and adventurous nature. This manifested itself mentally as well as physically. Upon reaching middle age, he left Spain, his birthplace, and began a nomadic existence, living in North Africa, Babylon, Persia, India, France, and England. Intellectually, too, he was attracted by diverse cultural interests. Like the butterfly that flits from garden to garden and tastes the sweetness of every fragrant flower, so was he stimulated by a curious impulse to enrich his experience and knowledge through poetry, philology, theology, philosophy, medicine, mathematics, and astrology.

Another personal point of interest was his poverty. He very candidly admitted his luckless state due, he believed, to a conspiracy of ill-omened planets at the moment of his birth.[1] Many of his poems echo the plaintive cry of the beggar. He was dependent largely on the gratuities of patrons and friends. His only earned income was from the astrological services he rendered to princes, whose fortunes in war and other matters he foretold.

The weighty influence exerted by Ibn Ezra in his own day is seen from the exalted estimate placed upon him by an unknown writer in a famous "Letter to his Son", which has been attributed to Maimonides.

"And thou, my most faithful son, I command thee not to peruse any commentaries and dissertations, nor to apply thy mind to any but his (Ibn Ezra's) commentaries, dissertations, and books. For they are very good and helpful to anyone who will read them through with proper attention, with clear intelligence, and subtle comprehension. They are not like other dissertations. For he was like our Father Abraham (peace be to him) in spirit. This sage did not fear any person, and did not flatter any creature. He traveled through many lands,—to-day, in one place, to-morrow in another place. Notwithstanding, he served also as minister to various rulers. And know, my son, that a poor man in this mundane despised world has no rest, and, happy is he, whose years are sealed quickly without vexation. And were it not for the sage, R. Abraham ibn Ezra, (of blessed memory) who illumined me on many matters, of which I did not know until after

---

[1]Raphael Levy, The Astrological Works of Abr. ibn. Ezra, Baltimore, 1927, p. 8.

I composed the Commentary on the Mishna, the Mishna Torah, and the Moreh Nebukim, I would enlighten thee on the mysteries to which he alludes in his dissertations and book. Beware, that thou apply not thy pure comprehension and thy precious spirit save to our dissertations and to his. Aside from these, they are valueless and unimportant, time-wasting although they will never end."[2]

2—Messianic Poetry.

Ibn Ezra is more famous for his Bible commentary which outshines the others of his age for its rationalism, than for his poetry. Both of these sources furnish us with enough material to see clearly how he viewed the doctrine. The subject matter of this chapter is divided into two parts—first, Messianic poems, second, Messiology of the Bible. Although he produced a considerable amount of poetry, much of it is secular and occasional.

The Messianic poems lack the intensely nationalistic strain of Judah Halevi or Gabirol, and they are not so numerous as the poems of these authors. The tone of national grief and complaint and the hope of blissful deliverance, sounded so loudly and repeatedly in the latter two poets, are much fainter in Ibn Ezra. He is less emotional. He does not heap fierce denunciation on the Gentile despotism, nor is his poetry pervaded with the mood of exasperation and contempt. The tragedy of his people does not saturate his poetry. It does not overflow with ecstatic rejoicing, nor abound in glowing pictures of the Messiah and the restoration. Perhaps his wit and humor, his volatile nature and cynical mood, helped him to view and carry lightly the burden of his people. It is interesting to notice that he rarely calls Babylon, Rome, or the Arabs by the names of beasts, while among other poets

---

[2]Kobez Teshubot Rambam II, pp. 39d-40.

such allusions are the rule. Not that Ibn Ezra ignores the hapless situation of his people. He bewails their portion bitterly and in several Geulas and Kinot, as well as many other poems, the Messianic motif is distinctly heard. In a dirge on the destruction of the Hebrew communities in Spain and northern Africa by the invading armies of the Almohades in 1140, the poet mourns the excesses perpetrated upon the Jews. In Lucena, where Israel had prospered uninterruptedly for many centuries, the tide of oppression now overwhelmed it. The study of Talmud was prohibited. Synagogues were turned into mosques. In Seville, princes and leaders of the people, together with their families, were forced to accept the alien faith. Cordova the beautiful, the center of scholars and learning, was laid waste. In northern Africa Jewish communities were entirely wiped out. These trying experiences of his people furnished a fertile ground for the poet's vital Messianic hope. Yet to him these afflictions were but an incident in the dispersion. They were the inevitable consequence of the destruction of Jerusalem.

Israel will never fare better in "unclean lands". With aching heart the poet trusts that God will heal the ancient breach between Himself and His people. An unknown writer gave this dirge a more definite Messianic trend when he added a stanza, reading, in part:

"We hope for the time of enlargement
And for the quietude which has not come,
For the advent of the son of Jesse and of the Ephraimite."[3]

In one of his longest and most satiric poems, Ibn Ezra casually, yet ironically alluded to the strained internal life of Israel. He bewails the stupidity and baseness of certain Jewish communities, which aggravate the low estate of Israel by creating:

---

[3]D. Kahana's ed. of Ibn Ezra's Poetic Works, I, p. 143.

THE DOCTRINE OF THE MESSIAH

"Galut within the Galut;
Would that we had died by the hand of God,
Whilst we dwelt in spacious ease,
For we have become bigoted and oppressive."

A common simile for Israel is the dove, peaceful, innocent, and helpless. Afflicted Israel resembles that bird
when it has no resting-place, when its only haven is at the
very mouth of a deep pit and it is in imminent peril of
having its life snuffed out by beast or bird. The frail creature, terrified by every movement and sound of lurking
animals, has actually been plucked of her wings. Israel,
too, is beset by violent adversaries. Hovering on the
precipice between life and death, the people recall the
time they dwelt in a mansion, adorned with purple and
silver, amid great opulence. Who can now infuse into
them new strength and stamina to fly back to their
primeval and secure nest, Palestine? Later the poet
varies the figure of speech, describing Israel as a betrothed
maiden, overpowered when there was no one to shield
her. So had Israel, the betrothed of God, been humbled
by savage suitors, who compelled her to submit to their
designs.[4]

In a Geula, Israel is personified as a woman of beauty,
charm and lovely adornment, who has become an object
of degradation. The decline in her estate, however, is
but temporary.

"Why dost thou mourn, my daughter?
Arise, come forth with me:
I will bring thee, to my beautiful house.
I am thy master, thou art my spouse:
Lay on thy adornments, and be comforted."[5]

---

[4]*Ibid.*, p. 173.
[5]Brody-Albrecht, "The New-Hebrew School of Poets of the Spanish-
Arabian Epoch", p. 155.

— 108 —

ABRAHAM IBN EZRA

The popular hymn included in the Sabbath Eve
Zemiroth, pleads for a speedy advent.

"Remember the love of the fathers
And awake the slumberers;
Bring near the promised days, O Lord,
When Jesse's son once more will flourish.
Regard the mother's truth when tested:
How shrill the handmaid hath protested!
The dead religion—it is thine,
The living one is mine, is mine."[6]

The conduct of Gentile nations toward Israel has been
treacherous in the extreme. According to the traditional
notion Christendom and Islam are brother and servant
of Israel, respectively. The members of the household,
brother and servant alike, who should be confidantes and
supporters, have conspired to supplant Israel. The poet
further pleads that Israel—but a woman, frail as all flesh,
whose heart is not of iron, and whose flesh is not of brass,
—be spared. She cannot endure torment. No doubt, her
lot is deserved, for she had deceived her Lord. Wherefore
she was divorced. Then did her patrimony, her vineyard
Zion, become the plunder of her foes. They razed the
tower in the vineyard, the Temple, to the ground. She
had become homeless. Her erstwhile servant smites her;
her brother is murderous. Will the end of this estrangement be forever delayed? God replies, Nay. He will restore her to His affections and will see that the servant's
progeny shall not share the inheritance bequeathed to
Isaac.[7]

A touching poem, in the form of a dialogue between
Israel and the foe, dwells on several controversial aspects
of the redemption.[8] Zion, representing Israel, complains
of being deserted and desolate, yet is hopeful of the out-

[6]Friedlander, "Standard Book of Jewish Verse", p. 423.
[7]Kahana I, p. 179.
[8]Brody-Albrecht, pp. 156-158.

come. She deplores the absence of her children, who long ago came to her from the desert of Sinai, inflamed with divine zeal. To this the enemy ironically replies that another fire, the fire of destruction, had been decreed and sent to devour them.

"Ye men of Zion, where now is your God?" the enemy asks. Zion answers that her children have been driven forth from the beauteous land and are held like ensnared birds in other countries. The dispersion was caused by the guilt of Israel, who in time of calm and security exchanged faith in God for trust in her own material strength. The enemy contends that Israel's light is extinguished forever and that he has prevailed over her God. He has won from Him the spoils of war, as witnessed by the fact that he has devastated the chosen people before His very eyes. But Zion stands unshaken and interprets her oppression differently. Her troubles, she says, are welcome, aye, they are joys and delights endured for the sake of the most Holy One. The end which shall bring the salvation of Israel is fast approaching.

The foe argues that the religion of Sinai had become corrupt and that the new dispensation was more suitable. The ancient prophets, intended their millennial predictions for the second commonwealth, at which time they were realized. Granted, as everybody does, that these prophets had divine sanction, why, they ask, should the Jews persist in hoping for that which had already come to pass a thousand years ago? In concluding this rhetorical debate, Zion points to the circumstance that nations still resort to war in the attempt to extirpate each other, whereas the prophets prognosticated an age of amity and disarmament. The contradiction should convince one that the ancient vision had not come true, and that we must still await its fulfillment.

ABRAHAM IBN EZRA

The disquieting problem of finding an anchorage for faith in Israel's salvation[9] forces the poet to scan the predictions of Israel's seers.

He communes with Isaiah, who had said that salvation was near. Many ages have since passed and still the mighty shepherd has not come. He addressed himself to Ezekiel, who had spoken in parables, and had seen visions and miracles. Had he, perchance, inquired for the blissful year, and could he disclose it? But no answer is forthcoming. He would fain seek the companionship of the beloved Daniel, to ask whether the time had already passed or was still to come. He is informed that it is a mystery, and that the part of intelligence is to desist from interrogating. Fruitless in his search, his greatest consolation and encouragement come from the divine word spoken to Moses, in which God vowed to gather in the chosen people from every corner of the earth.

The drama of deliverance is presented in a nut-shell in the following allegory. There are four in the *dramatis personae:* God, the captain, the sheep and the enemy. The enemy oppressed the sheep, (Israel); the sheep cried unto the captain (the Messiah), who sought the grace of God. God commanded the captain to deliver his sheep from the molester.[10]

Ibn Ezra frankly and pitifully beseeches God to grant his pious wish:

> "I entreat Thee, to reveal the secret,
> Unhidden from Thee;
> Reveal the mysteries deep set,
> That Thy servant be undismayed.
> Perform the marvel to the imprisoned one;
> Show him the innermost altar,
> Oh, that I might enter thy sanctuary,
> To which I mightily aspire."[11]

---

[9]*Ibid.*, p. 155.
[10]Kahana I, p. 167.
[11]*Ibid.* I, p. 20.

THE DOCTRINE OF THE MESSIAH

The return of the Tishbite is thus invoked:

"Father, Father, when wilt Thou bring
Elijah the prophet?
With a broken heart I greet Thee
That I may find grace before Thee.
See the decimated remnant of Israel.
Not mighty but youthful."[12]

The lighter mood of Ibn Ezra is seen in the question and answer concerning the Messianic advent, which can be read backward as well as forward.

Avi, El Hai Shemeko, Lomo hamelek Meshiah lo yovo.
"Father, Eternal God is Thy name, why does not the Messianic King come?"
Deou m'avikem, ki lo bosh, oshuv alekem, ki vo moed.
"Know of your Father, that I will not tarry; I will return unto you when the time appointed comes."[13]

Among the hundred miscellaneous questions attributed to Ibn Ezra are several that pertain to the advent, here discussed:

> 58. Why has the redemption been delayed so long?
> 65. Why is "my anointed" found in the plural? (Ps. 105:15, "Touch not mine anointed ones".)
> 93. Why is the time of redemption concealed from every person?
> 142. Why did not Daniel specify the time indicated in "a time and times"?[14]

3—*Messiology of the Bible.*

Before setting forth Ibn Ezra's comments on Messiological passages in Scripture, it may prove of interest to know the principles and method of his exegesis. As an exponent of rationalism we would expect him to relegate

---

[12]*Ibid.* I, p. 167.
[13]*Ibid.* I, p. 166.
[14]*Ibid.* II, p. 21.

Midrash and mysticism to the limbo of discarded things. He sought to give the accurate meaning of the Bible. Hence, his commentaries are full of valuable observations and digressions on grammar, chronology, and historic probabilities. Such critical elucidation of Holy Writ led to the novel theories, that certain psalms were not Davidic and that the last chapters of Isaiah dated from the Babylonian period. With all this he did not discard the Midrash, because, after all, it represented the wisdom and authority of the earlier sages. Rashly to condemn their expositions, would be tantamount to severing his attachment to the spirit and substance of traditional Jewish lore.

Ibn Ezra makes clear his attitude towards the rabbinic homily. It is an embellishment of the literal meaning of the text, and serves in the same way that vestment covers the body. In choosing Midrashim he advises us to discriminate between them on the basis of quality and suitability. The Midrash may be precious and fine as silk, or heavy and coarse as burlap. No doubt there are passages which can be understood only by applying to them the homilies of the rabbis, but as a rule Ibn Ezra prefers to give historical and common sense explanations. Many predictions, which other scholars interpret Messianically, are explained by him as referring to events in the days of David, Hezekiah, and others.

Nevertheless, a good many eschatological interpretations are found within his commentaries. In these commentaries he follows the Talmud and Targum, as in his exposition of Isaiah, 40-*et seq.*, of Canticles, and of certain psalms. It is sometimes difficult to understand on what basis Ibn Ezra drew a line of demarcation in Scripture, between Messianic and historical passages. Thus he expounds Gen. 49:10, Messianically, but not Num.

24:17. He refers Zech. 13 to the Messianic epoch, and Zech. 9:9 to the Maccabean events.

The following gives, in Biblical sequence, the Messianic comments of Ibn Ezra.

a. Pentateuch.

Gen. 49:10—
> "The scepter shall not depart from Judah,
> Nor the ruler's staff from between his feet.
> As long as men come to Shiloh;
> And unto him shall the obedience of the peoples be."

Like most expositors, Ibn Ezra also takes the third clause to mean: until Shiloh come. After giving various possible meanings for Shiloh, he excludes the inference that the scepter will depart from Judah when (*ad*) the event indicated by Shiloh's coming occurs. In his larger commentary Ibn Ezra identifies Shiloh with the sanctuary at Shiloh and takes the verb *come* to predict its destruction. The complete thought of the verse is that the tribe of Judah will wax powerful and reach its climax in the overthrow of Shiloh and in the ascendancy of David in Jerusalem, where he will rule many nations. In this connection he also uses Ps. 78:60 and 70. Shiloh cannot logically be construed to forebode the submergence of Israel and the rise of Jesus, because the obvious purpose of the dying patriarch was to bless his progeny, and not to curse them.[15]

Numb. 24:17 is not a Messianic prediction, but points to the historical David. Ibn Ezra fears that his dissent from the Midrashic explanation might be construed as a denial of the advent. He therefore avers that there are other more reliable sources for the belief, notably Daniel. It is also clearly inculcated by Moses in Deut. 30:4: "If any of thine that are dispersed be in the uttermost parts

---

[15]Comm. on Gen. ed. by Friedlander, 1877, p. 67.

of heaven, from thence will the Lord thy God gather thee, and from thence will He fetch thee." He feels perfectly at ease, therefore, in his own interpretation of the text.

Deut. 32:39: "Not one in a thousand understood the matter of a world to come, which is very mysterious. Reward in the world to come depends upon the conduct of the soul, which is in recompense for devout worship, and its endeavor to understand God's work. For they are the ladder whereby one may ascend to the topmost rung of divine knowledge, which is the principal thing."

b. Isaiah.

Is. 7:14: "Therefore the Lord Himself shall give you a sign: behold, the young woman shall conceive, and bear a son, and shall call his name Immanuel."

Ibn Ezra attaches no Messianic significance to this verse. "Immanuel is the name of the prophet's own son, called forth as a symbol that the Almighty will aid Israel in trouble. As proof, note 8:18; where the prophet declares that his children were given him to be used as signs and wonders."

11:1: "And there shall come forth a shoot out of the stock of Jesse. And a twig shall grow forth out of his roots." The commentator does not know whether to attribute this passage to the Messianic king or Hezekiah.

38:18: "For the nether-world cannot praise Thee. Death cannot celebrate Thee; they that go down into the pit cannot hope for Thy truth."

This verse is not a denial of resurrection; it only means that the body has neither power nor knowledge, when the soul has departed from it. Why the wonder? Even while the soul still resides in the body, the latter is void of understanding; how much more so, upon death: Hence, only the soul can be said to live and partake of divine glory. The body is powerless and useless without the soul. This thought is conveyed by the prophet. Maimonides explains similarly the seeming negations of an after-life in this and other verses.

Is. 40: This and the prophecies to the end of Isaiah deal with the present dispersion. Occasionally the prophet speaks of the Babylonian captivity. The very last chapters, however, are all directed to the glorious restoration of the future.

"This parashah is an extremely difficult one. Our opponents say that it refers to their God, supposing the 'servant' to signify his body. This, however, is not possible for the body cannot 'understand' even during a man's lifetime. Moreover, if their view be correct, what will be the meaning of 'seeing seed,' for he (their God) saw no son; or of 'prolonging days,' which is equally untrue of him; or of 'dividing spoil with the strong'? The proof of its proper meaning lies in the passage immediately before (52:1), where 'the barren one' represents the congregation of Israel; similarly, my servant means each individual belonging to Israel, and consequently God's servant who is in exile."[16]

Is. 55:4: "behold, I have given him for a witness to the peoples," refers to the Messiah.

Is. 56:1: "Keep ye justice, and do righteousness, for my salvation is near to come" implies that Israel's sinfulness delays the advent.

Is. 59:20: "And a redeemer will come to Zion," refers to the Messiah.

Is. 65:17: "For, behold, I create new heavens," Ibn Ezra explains that God will form a more healthful air, which will be conducive to longer life and stronger physi-

---

[16]The fifty-third chapter of Isaiah acc. to Jewish interpreters, p. 42.

cal existence in the golden age. Of such a transformation the "newness of the heavens" will consist. The prediction does not refer to the establishment of a new universe in the world to come.

Concerning Is. 66:24 Ibn Ezra approves the views of the Talmudists who say that a judgment day will be held in Jerusalem. He thinks that "neither shall their fire be quenched" refers to the condemned soul which leaves the body at death. If it does merit ascent to the upper regions it is doomed to remain within the sphere of fires. This fate will overtake it after resurrection, as is clear from the passage in which Daniel states that the wicked will arise for perpetual disgrace.

c. Minor Prophets.

Hosea 3:5 is Messianic: "In the end of days" is the Messianic future. "David their king" means the Messiah. In this, Ibn Ezra follows Targum Jonathan.

Joel 3 and 4 are not construed as Messianic.

Obadiah 17-21: Ibn Ezra inclines to assign these verses to the ideal future. Concerning verse 13, he cites three divergent opinions—that of Japhet, which holds that it refers to the future; that of R. Moses which refers it to the age of Hezekiah; and that of R. Jeshuah, which refers it to the second commonwealth.[17]

Mic. 4:1 is Messianic. 4:3: "And he shall judge," means the Messiah.

Hab. 2:3: "And it declareth of the end." Ibn Ezra remarks that "end" here means the overthrow of the Chaldean state.

Zech. 9:9: "Behold, thy king cometh unto thee" alludes to Judah Maccabee.

---

[17]Japhet B. Ali, 10th century, a Karaite teacher, commentator of the Bible; R. Moses ibn Gikatilla, 11th century, a rabbinist opposed to the Messianic interpretation of Scripture; and R. Jeshuah B. Judah, 11th century Karaite.

Ibn Ezra refers the entire section to the Hasmonean conflict, but Zech. 12:10 is explained, in agreement with the Midrash, as relating to the return of Israel under the Messiah ben Joseph.

Zech. 13:1: The unfulfilled prediction, "In that day there shall be a fountain opened," shows that the prophecy is of the future. 13:7 refers to the world war during the days of the Messiah ben Joseph. 14 describes the situation in the Holy Land after the death of the ben Joseph. 14:12 tells of the distress and ruin of Israel's foes, as the punishment by God. 14:21: Ibn Ezra remarks that the final chapters of the book treat of the remote future. "He who maintains that all is past, let him show us the living waters flowing forth from Jersalem in summer and winter."

Mal. 3:1: "Behold, I send my messenger" may appropriately mean the Messiah ben Joseph. 3:23: Ibn Ezra suggests the ingenious theory that the prophet Elijah, mentioned here, is not the one who flourished in the day of Ahab. The appellation, Elijah, is applied possibly to several persons, who in their moral and religious practices, followed the example of the ancient seer. This view is now generally adopted by critical scholars.

d. Daniel.

He approaches the Book of Daniel fully conscious of its difficulties and of the remarkable expositions thereof made by his predecessors. In the introduction to his commentary he says: "This book of a beloved person contains weighty matters and prophecies, some of which have been fulfilled, and some still awaiting their fulfillment. Everything is spoken briefly and enigmatically. It also contains allusions to the nature of the angels. But the commentators did not comprehend its meaning; they erred in their interpretation of the end; they were also confused about the vision of the beasts. I propose to explain it in accordance with the rules of grammar."

Dan. 2: Nebuchadnezzar's dream of the metal-image points to the succession of the following four powers: Babylon, the head of gold; Persia, the breast and arms of silver; Greece and Rome, the belly and thighs; the Mohammedans and surviving Roman races, the legs of iron and the feet part iron and clay. The eternal kingdom that will supplant these is the Jewish Messianic empire.

Dan. 7: The four beasts in this vision—the lion, the bear, the leopard and the nameless, most frightful one—allude to the four mighty universal powers. The ten horns signify the ten territorial divisions of the Ishmaelite world. 7:9: "Ancient of days" is God. 7:13: "One like unto a son of man" is Israel.

Dan. 8: This prophecy "predicts the victories of Cyrus, the successes of Alexander, the division of his vast dominion, and leads up to the outrages of Antiochus Epiphanes, and his punishment." In consonance with this view, Ibn Ezra offers three plausible explanations of the number in v. 14: "And he (the angel) said unto me: Unto 2300 evenings and mornings; then shall the sanctuary be victorious."

a. 2300 half-days, or three years, denoted the period in the reign of Antiochus during which the sacrifices in the Jerusalem temple were discontinued.[18]

b. 2300 days, or six years, coincided with the duration of the rule of King Antiochus over Israel.

c. 2300 months, or 186 years, marks the duration of the Syrian domination in Palestine.

Dan. 9 recounts the course of Israel's history during the second commonwealth, up to the time of the destruc-

---

[18]Ibn Ezra followed a school of exegesis that interpreted the book of Daniel historically and not as adventist; he took the word "days" literally, and not to mean years.

tion by Titus. The outstanding comments of this chapter are:

a. That "seventy septenates" (490 years) represent the period of the second Temple.

b. That "seven septenates" (49 years) cover the interval between Cyrus' proclamation and Nehemiah's visit to Jerusalem.

c. "One anointed, a prince" is Nehemiah.

d. (9:25) Jerusalem will be restored under immense difficulties, and will have a precarious existence for 434 years (62 weeks of years), when it will be overwhelmed and destroyed by a tyrant.

e. (9:27) In the last of the seven year cycles, a truce of peace will be established between Titus and Judea.

f. (9:27) The daily sacrifices will be abolished three and a half years ("half-week") prior to the destruction of the Temple.

Dan. 10, in general describes the wars that raged between Yavan and Ishmael, and the changing tide of Israel's fortune.

Dan. 11:31: Ibn Ezra enumerates several scholars, among them Ibn Gabirol and Abraham b. Hiyya, whose calculations he disparages, because as he says "not even Daniel knew the end."

Dan. 12:2: Ibn Ezra limits resurrection to the righteous of Israel. They will arise at the advent of the Messiah, partake in the great feast, die, and be resurrected again. 12:7—"a time, times and a half" and 1290 days (v. 11) are equivalent to the 3½ years before the destruction, during which the sacrificial services in the temple ceased 12:12—A period of 1335 days will precede the advent of the deliverer, but the difficulty is that the terminus *a quo* has not been disclosed.

e. Psalms.

Ps. 2:12: "Do homage in purity (nashku bar), lest He be angry, and ye perish in the way, when suddenly His wrath is kindled." Ibn Ezra rejects the simple and acceptable meaning of "bar" as *pure* and inclines to translate it as son, referring it to the "anointed one" in v. 2 and making it the apposite of "Thou art my son" in v. 7. *Bar* would then allude to Israel.

Ps. 20:7: "Now know I that the Lord saveth His *anointed.*" David is meant.

Ps. 28:8: "He is a stronghold of salvation to His *anointed.*" David.

Ps. 36:10: "For with Thee is the *fountain of life*"— the divine source of the soul. "In thy light do we see light" represents the reward in the world to come.

Ps. 43:3: "And to Thy tabernacles." "Thy tabernacles" indicate the assembly halls that are to be built in the third temple.

Ps. 45 may concern David or the Messiah, the ideal ruler to come. Targum Jonathan on Psalms, gives it a Messianic interpretation.

Ps. 46:10: "He maketh wars to cease"—in Jerusalem. "Possibly through the holy spirit the psalmist divined the collapse of Gog and his armies."

Ps. 47 applies definitely to the Messianic age.

Ps. 49:16: "But God will redeem my soul from the power of the netherworld." "This," says Ibn Ezra, "is a very distinguished psalm. For therein is taught the nature and light of the world to come—the soul of wisdom— which is immortal and invisible." 49:20: "They shall never see the light." This light is the reward and delight of the soul.

Ps. 50:2: "Out of Zion the perfection of beauty, God hath shined forth." Ibn Ezra comments that Zion is situated in the exact geographical center of the earth, a thought current among Jews and Arabs.

Ps. 69:29: "Let them be blotted out of the book of the living," "I have already explained in my writings, that the book of life is the heavens, where all the decrees of the future were inscribed at creation." This is but proof of Ibn Ezra's faith in astrology. 69:37: "The seed also of His servants will inherit it" (Zion). This may refer to the Davidic or Messianic ruler.

Ps. 72:1: "Give *the king* Thy judgements, O God, and Thy righteousness unto the *king's son*" may refer to Solomon or to the Messiah. 72:17: "May his name endure forever"—either Solomon or Messiah shall flourish.

Ps. 73:17: "Until I entered into the sanctuary of God, and considered their end." "For man was not brought into this world to have pleasure, or to assume regal power, or to possess wealth, but that his latter end may be good. That is the reward of the souls of the righteous." 73:24: "And afterward receive me with glory." "The expression *lokah*—receive, in this sense, refers to the attachment of the righteous souls with the higher ones which are bodiless and eternal."

Ps. 80:18: "Let Thy hand be upon the man of Thy right hand." Either Israel or Messiah ben Ephraim is intimated. This verse is the apposite of verse 16. "And upon the son of man whom Thou madest strong for Thyself." Ibn Ezra's comment coincides with the paraphrase of Targum—"and upon King Messiah whom Thou madest strong."

Ps. 85:1: The psalm relates to the Babylonian captivity, and also, prophetically, to the present dispersion. 85:5: "Restore us, O God" this time, as formerly, from Babylon. 85:6: "Wilt Thou forever be angry with us?" is asked concerning the present exile which appears interminable.

Ps. 89 is eschatological. 89:37: The oath of God on the indestructibility of Israel. 89:50 is a plea for deliverance: Ibn Ezra paraphrases the verse thus, "Fulfill the oath of the coming of the redeemer." 89:52: The psalmist divined the advent of the "anointed one," the Messiah.

Ps. 104:26: "Leviathan"—Ibn Ezra explains this as a name of a species of large-sized fish (hence no particular reference to the fabulous sea monster of the future world). The Targum, however, takes it Messianically.

Ps. 106:47: He quotes views that assign this prayer to the alleviation of Israel's chaotic state in the time of the judges or of the Babylonian captivity. He seems to believe that the psalmist prefigures the situation in his own day.

Ps. 120:1 contains a reflection of the dispersion. 120:6: "My soul hath full long had her dwelling with him that hateth peace" hints at the great length of the exile.

Ps. 125:1: "But abideth forever," unto the Messianic era.

Ps. 137:7: The commentator remarks that there is evidence to prove that the Romans and Greeks were racially the same. In his enumeration of the four empires he mentions Greece and Rome as the third, and Ishmael as the fourth.

Ps. 139: "This psalm is highly distinguished in matters relating to divinity. And in all these five books there is none to compare to it. According to a person's comprehension of divine ways and the ways of the soul, will he understand its significance."

Ps. 147: As its contents prove, this psalm is a prophetic insight into the time of the ingathering and restoration.

Ps. 148 is explained according to his theory of cosmogony. It tells of two worlds: the upper one, which is inconceivably large and wide, and the mundane world which is like a point in a vast circle. The elements of the upper world enumerated in the psalm are angels, stars (hosts), sun, moon, the heaven of heavens, the sphere of fire near the moon, and the sphere of water above the heavens. The beings and phenomena of the earth are sea monsters, atmospheric forces like fire, hail, snow, and smoke; metals, plants; cattle, creatures, fowl; mankind, princes, and Israel supreme over all.

Ps. 149:7: "To execute vengeance upon the nations"— and thus prevail upon them to turn to the service of God in the Messianic era.

Ps. 150:1: "every soul"—R. Solomon the Spaniard takes this as an allusion to the soul dwelling in heaven.

f. Canticles.

The commentary on Canticles, as that on many other books of the canon, was written in two or more versions. The third exposition on Canticles follows the allegorical method. According to this the songs depict the entire course of Israel's history from its genesis in the time of Abraham to its consummation in the Messianic era.

Can. 7:6: "thine head" is King Messiah. "The hair of thy head" is the Messiah, son of Joseph. "The king is held captive" indicates that the Messiah will be withheld until the appointed time comes, for he was born on the day of the destruction.[19]

8:1: "O that thou wert as my brother."—Thus Kenesseth Israel addresses the Messiah. "O that I would find thee and cleave to thee as a brother."

8:15: "Who is this that cometh up?" Thus the nations will say in amazement when Kenesseth Israel marches forth with the Messiah from the wilderness of nations.

8:12: "Thou, O Solomon, shalt have the thousand." Solomon is taken to signify the Messiah. The vineyard is

---

[19]Ekah Rabbati 1:16.

Israel. The sense of the passage is that the ten tribes (the thousand) will unite with the two tribes (two hundred) at the restoration under the Messiah's leadership. The resurrection will usher in only a transitory state, in which the risen will again be subject to death. The souls of the wicked will then perish, while the souls of the righteous will ascend to the luminous region. The "world to come," in the eschatology of Ibn Ezra, is the world of these pure souls. This is also the view of Maimonides.

Chapter VII

MAIMONIDES

Moses ben Maimon (1135-1204) towers majestically above all the other striking personalities of the Jewish Middle Ages. More than any other Jew, he represented the best combination of philosophy and religion. Thus he wrote to an acquaintance, "Were it not for the Torah, which is my delight, and matters of speculation in which I forget my grief, I would have perished in my affliction."[1] In him, Torah and Hokma seem to have formed a perfect, indistinguishable union. He produced colossal works of high purpose, acute analysis, and comprehensive study. He was master of the sciences and philosophies of his day and aided materially in the cultural advance of civilization. Upon the Jews of his own and subsequent days he has exerted a magnetic power. He is reverenced and admired as the protagonist of his race. He strengthened the faith of those who were then on the shoals of doubt and disbelief by reconciling reason and revelation, and for the instruction of his people, he codified Biblical and Talmudic laws on the basis of their underlying motives and common characteristics. He also rationalized the ceremonial and disciplinary phases of Judaism as well as its theology.

1—His Rational Conception of the Messianic Doctrine.

The sources for an understanding of the redemption, as conceived by Maimonides, are rather few and fragmentary. In his luminous work on Jewish theology, "The

---

[1]Kobez Teshubot Rambam, Leipzig, 1859 II, p. 37d.

Guide of the Perplexed", he touches lightly on the Messianic ideals and postulates, and then only indirectly, when he speculates on the theory of the eternity or the destructibility of the universe.[2] The three principal sources, however, are the "Letter to Yemen",[3] which was called forth to meet an historical exigency, and which yields abundant information on the Messianic theme; his copious and edifying treatment of the subject in the tenth chapter of his commentary on Mishna Sanhedrin and the last two chapters of the Mishneh Torah.

The "Letter to Yemen" was sent by Maimonides in 1172 to Jacob b. Nathanael, chief of the Talmudical Academy in Yemen, who sought advice as to what course he should take regarding the appearance of a Messianic impostor. The disturbance in the Jewish community due to the impostor was much heightened by two other causes which created confusion and fright. One was the religious persecutions by the Mohammedans to compel the Jews to embrace Islam, and the other was the treachery of the renegade, Samuel ibn Abbas, a Hebrew poet and philosopher who turned Mohammedan, becoming an enemy of his mother-faith. Between 1165 and 1175, he wrote a diatribe "To the Confusion of the Jews", in which he declared that the words "be'meod meod" (Gen. 17:2) refer to Mohammed, and offered as evidence the fact that the numerical values of the letters of those two words and of Mahmed, i.e., Mohammed, are identical.[4] He also charged the Jews with expurgating the allusions to Mohammed from the Old Testament.

Maimonides counsels the Yemenite Jews not to ignore the Messianic pretender, lest he use his publicity to their detriment, but to have him incarcerated as a menace. He was seized and executed by the king's order. Graetz truly

---

[2]Guide, II, 29b.
[3]Letter to Yemen is in Kobez II, pp. 1-7.
[4]They amount to 92.

evaluates the "Letter" in these words: "In spite of its small compass it contains valuable material and bears witness to the writer's lofty soul and spiritual refinement. He sought in it to elevate the sufferers to the height of spiritual consciousness, on which suffering for religion's sake loses its sting, and darkness appears as the inevitable antecedent of the break of day. He expressed himself on the relation of Judaism and Christianity and Islam with an acuteness and precision which reflect his profound conviction."

In addition to these sources, there are numerous succint statements in the sections on Repentance, Beliefs, and Kings in his code, Mishneh Torah, which offer valuable information. Further light on the Messianic doctrine is reflected from other essays—those on Resurrection, Sanctification of the Divine Name, and from his letters. His authorship of the essay on Bliss is doubtful.

The Messianic ideal advanced by Maimonides is very indefinite in character. He draws only its general outline, and embellishes it with few incidental features. He does not, as many other scholars before and after him have done, particularize the Messianic drama, because he sincerely disclaimed any detailed knowledge of it. In his characteristically modest way, he broached the subject with a plea of ignorance of the character and sequence of events in the millennium. He discouraged speculation on the whole subject and admonished the people to believe and to wait. There are no certainties in regard to the particulars of redemption—except that it must occur. Even the Talmud, that vast sea of Hebrew wisdom, contains no uniform, authentic tradition about this mooted question.[5]

---

[5]"Altogether the sequence in which these things will transpire and their details are not cardinal articles of the faith, and a person should not occupy himself with Agadic matters nor concern himself with such as these or similar to them."—Mishneh Torah, Melakim, XII, 2.

Maimonides, no doubt, was led to this discriminating attitude by the fact that we find in the Talmud an incoherent and often contradictory mass of opinions. It is a medley of outbursts, alternately of joy and sorrow. Apparently the utmost freedom of faith and thought was exercised by the rabbis in the matter of redemption. Otherwise, the paths of opinion would not diverge so widely between the one extreme, which leads to a Utopia of grandiose and impossible situations, and the other which shuts out all hope of salvation—as for example, when R. Hillel denied that Israel has a Messiah.[6] This beclouded situation cleared itself before the spiritual touch and penetrating intellect of the philosopher, by means of which he also brought order and light into the maze of Talmudic Halakah. Maimonides dropped the Messianic hallucinations which sprang from the fevered imaginations of the mystics, and in their place incorporated into his concept reasonable beliefs which answer the need of the devoted yet thoughtful Jew for national salvation and the hope of mankind for a consummate civilization.

Writing to the Jews of Marseilles,[7] Maimonides, following Saadia, states the case for intellectualism trenchantly. No knowledge is truthful and secure unless it is rational and reaches us through the clear and pure channels of intuition, personal experience, and bona fide testimony and tradition. On these premises, Tradition (Torah), Experience (the stirring and sad historic events of his time) and Intuition (the triumph of good over evil), Maimonides built a magnificent eschatological edifice. The result was an ideal, which was the natural product of a long-felt historic want, reflecting the yearnings, moods, and experiences of Israel. It was logical in reasoning, yet warm with the heart-beat of united Israel.

---

[6]San. 99a—Contrast R. Hillel's opposition with R. Gamaliel's exaggerations.

[7]Kobez II, 24-26.

THE DOCTRINE OF THE MESSIAH

The Messianic picture of Maimonides was conceived on a wide plane. The redemption of the chosen people from its age-old lowly position would herald the salvation of all mankind. The coming of the Messiah would mark the penetration of Israel's divine discipline into all lands and among all peoples. Justice, peace, brotherhood, intellectual pleasure, leisure, and long life would bless the human race. The philosopher practically discarded all the supernatural and fantastic features connected with the Messianic figure and era. He justified his liberal interpretation of Messiological passages in the Bible by the frequent opinions quoted in the Talmud that certain sections of the Bible need not be construed literally.[8] Scripture has been variously understood. Some people accept it literally, even its stories and ideas which common sense rejects. Others, also taking the Bible literally, conclude that it is a worthless and absurd book, because its contents are incredible to them. A third group, to which Maimonides belongs, maintains that the Bible has a figurative and a literal meaning. The former is for the philosopher, the initiate, the latter is for the average unlearned person. As he applied the rationalizing method to his theology and jurisprudence, so he followed it in his Messianic speculation. This style required no defense, yet he found specific support for his liberal Messianic views in the oft-quoted Talmudic opinion that the only distinction between this world and the Messianic state will be Israel's liberation from the yoke of its cruel masters. His rationalism brought out in bold relief the realistic and political character of the Messianic teaching. His ethical principles tinged it with the right spiritual color.

2—Ethical and Spiritual Motives of the Hope.

Maimonides idealized the Messianic motive of the Jews. He warned the people not to look forward to the rich and

[8]Ber. 18b; Baba Kama 60b; Baba Batra 15a; San. 92b.

supernal blessings of redemption as compensation for their love of God and their loyalty to the Torah. There are many whose fidelity is born naturally, but improperly, from the expectation of future rewards. Some are sustained by the anticipated pleasures of Paradise, where all material things of life will be supplied in undreamed-of abundance. Others are sustained by the glories of the Messianic state, the remarkable achievements of the King Messiah and the independent and opulent position of Israel in those days. Still others affirm that the desired good will consist in the joy of resurrection. A fourth class is of the opinion that our reward will not be in a remote eschatological era but will consist in the attainment in this world of physical happiness: as for example, bodily health and security, fertility of lands, and abundant wealth. The last group combines all these expectations and hopes for the coming of the Messiah, the resurrection of the dead, and eternal bliss in Paradise.[9]

Maimonides criticizes the ignorant attitude of the people toward the eschatological problem. "But with regard to this strange point—I mean the world to come—you will find very few who will take the matter to heart, or meditate on it, or adopt this or that principle or ask to what—the world to come—refers. What, however, all people ask, both the common folk and the educated classes, is this: In what condition will the dead rise to life, naked or clothed? Will they stand up in those very garments in which they were buried, in their embroideries and brocades and beautiful needlework, or in a robe that will merely cover the body? And when the Messiah comes, will rich and poor be alike, or will the distinctions between weak and strong still exist?—and many similar questions from time to time." The sharp tone of this reprimand reflects the gap between the vagaries of the people and the philosophic idealism of Maimonides.

---

[9]Comm. on Mishna San. X. This section is translated in J. Q. R. 1906-07, Vol. 19, pp. 24-58.

It is wrong, he argued, to make the relation between the Torah and the future state one of cause and effect, of reward for service done. The Torah has a present value and a direct reward to give day by day. Its discipline satisfies. It spiritualizes. It brings life and light to the soul. It is a mistake to ignore the dignities, the joys, the eternal verities of the Torah, and to consider only the boon that will be awarded in the remote future.

The prophets, psalmists, and Talmudists who in lyric song, impassioned speech, and aphorism, embodied the popular yearning for a redeemer had no material or chauvinistic ambitions. They did not seek prosperity, world dominion, or retaliation upon their enemies. Instead, they prayed to be delivered from the thrall of the enemy, in order that they might study the Torah, observe its discipline without hindrance, and thus become worthy of spiritual communion with God in the future world.[10]

Consistent with this broad spirit the motive of revenge, which asserts itself so forcefully in some passages of the Talmudic, Agadic, and Geonic writers, plays a minor part in the final drama of the great rationalist. Edom, the antagonist of Israel in most of our sacred literature, is not depicted as the object of divine wrath; Armilus, the hideous monster who will lead the opposing forces against Jerusalem in the day of deliverance, is not mentioned. The final and furious wars of the mythical Gog and Magog against the newly-established state, which make up an essential part of the eschatological scheme, receive scant mention.

Palestine, the home-land, is an element which furnishes an incentive and great warmth to the Messianic belief. The author alludes to it as the land to which the Jews are bound by sacred associations, by an heroic past, and by the divine assurance that they are destined to possess

---

[10]Mishneh Torah, Teshuva, IX, 2.

it forever. The glory of the land is Jerusalem, and its crown the Temple. Even in dispersion Israel is in duty bound to manifest reverence for the sanctuary that once adorned the Holy City. It symbolizes the religious ideal which Israel may never forsake.[11]

3—*Belief in Redemption Raised to a Cardinal Dogma.*

Maimonides deviates boldly from his predecessors in the presentation of the Messianic teaching. Engaged largely in Halaka and in philosophy, he expressed his aver· sion for Agadic ideas and stories in writing of the Messiah. We are, therefore, surprised at his inconsistency in making the belief an impregnable doctrine of Judaism. Perhaps the philosopher Crescas, and such men as Albo and Abra· banel, attacked Maimonides' creed because they found it difficult to reconcile his liberal method with the inclusion in the Creed of such beliefs as Messiah and Resurrection on a par with its philosophical articles. Maimonides may be said to have been the first to elevate this belief to such an exalted rank. In earlier writings it was regarded by some as a postulate of Jewish life, somewhat fantastic, but necessary, and within the power of God to effect. The geonim cling tenaciously to the hope that Israel is inde· structible and that she must and will be redeemed. Their trust is firm that God will not abandon Israel to the merci· less foe. Maimonides, however, goes a step further and changes the belief into an indispensable dogma.[12] He takes away its circumstantial character and popular sanc· tion and puts on it a cosmic stamp, making it a universal necessity. He enumerates it among his thirteen articles of the Jewish religion and gives it the same strength and validity as belief in monotheism.[13] One who disbelieves

---

[11]Sefer Hamitsvot—positive commandments, 21 ed. Heller, pp. 15b.
[12]R. Hananel mentions the advent of the redeemer as one of the four principles of Judaism. See Migdal Hananel ed. Hoffman, Berlin, 1876, pp. 35.
[13]Comm. on Mishna San. X.

the Messianic dogma is a *kofer*, a heretic, and has no share in the future life, because he denies the infallibility of Moses and the prophets.[14]

The coming of the redeemer is clearly promised in Numbers 24 and Deuteronomy 30.

4—Scripture and Faith as Sanctions of the Dogma.

If we exercise unquestioning faith in the revealed words of the Torah, we have a solid foundation for our trust in the ultimate deliverance of Israel. Such faith is natural. As a blind person relies upon a guide to conduct him and as a sick person places his confidence in a physician, so must we, in matters spiritual, rely upon the prophets who knew and spoke the truth. Their prophecies are replete with sanctions and supports for our Messianic hope. The picturesque language of the prophets amplifies the simpler utterances of similar import in the Pentateuch. God had plainly promised Moses that He would redeem Israel from her sore straits and give the people everlasting security and peace. To doubt that God will effect His promise is virtually to negate the veracity of the Scripture. Furthermore, belief in the redemption is a corollary of our faith in the indestructibility of Israel. The Almighty had affirmed that Israel will endure forever, yet so intolerable and infirm has her position become that unless salvation be effected she may succumb to noxious forces and crumble to dust. But God will not fail!

After dilating on the rich and unfailing source of redemption, which is the goodness and the pledge of God and despite his assertion that "one need not look for proofs in the prophets because their writings are full of this subject,"[15] the sage resorts to the usual rabbinical methods of exegesis, such as the flimsy inference from

---

[14]Mishneh Torah, Teshuvah 6.
[15]Twelfth Principle, Comm. on Mishna San. X.

Deut. 19:8, in which he follows an old theory. The promise made therein, that the territory of Israel would be
greatly enlarged and that three additional cities of refuge
would be allocated, had not been fulfilled in Biblical days;
hence, the expectation will be realized in the Messianic
state.[16]

The Messiah himself is prefigured according to the
sage in the following verses.[17] Peculiarly he construes
some of the parallel clauses as referring to King David;
these are marked "a"; the Messianic clauses are marked
"b".

  a. "I see him, but not now;

  b. I behold him, but not nigh.

  a. There shall step forth a star out of Jacob,

  b. And a scepter shall rise out of Israel

  a. And shall smite through the corners of Moab

  b. And break down all the sons of Seth.

  a. And Edom shall be a possession,

  b. Seir also, even his enemies, shall be a posses-
     sion,

  a. While Israel doeth valiantly.

  b. And out of Jacob shall one have dominion,

  a. And shall destroy the remnant from the city."
                  —Numbers 24:17-18.

"And when he seeth a troop, horsemen by pairs,
A troop of asses, a troop of camels,
He shall hearken diligently with much heed."
                  —Isaiah 21:7.

Maimonides construes this Messiologically. He assumes
that "a troop of asses" alludes to the Messiah and finds

---

[16]Mishneh Torah, Melakim. XI, 2. Abrabanel also points to this
Deuteronomic passage as an assurance of a future redemption.

[17]Letter to Yemen, 6a; Mishneh Torah, Melakim XI, 1.

support for his view in Zechariah's allusion in 9 :9; "Lowly, and riding upon an ass." "A troop of camels" refers to Mohammed. From the coordinate mention of the Jewish and Mohammedan Messiahs, he adduces the inevitable appearance of the Jewish Messiah because Mohammed has already appeared.[18]

5—Controversial.

a. Attitude Toward the Dominant Religions.

The Messianic belief is the bone of contention between Jews and Christians. A considerable polemical literature, some of it contributed by the authorities in this book, was written about this question. The writings of Maimonides, however, were not of a controversial nature. Yet, his attitude toward the two militant religions of his day certainly comes within our scope.

The contention of Christians that the second person of the trinity is the prophesied Messiah is only one of the several ways by which Israel's foes have planned to overthrow Judaism. Jew-haters have employed varied tactics;[19] some have resorted even to violence and bloodshed, to harass the children of Abraham, and to force them to submit to tyrannical rulers. Among these were Amalek, Sisera, Sennacherib, Nebuchadnezzar, Titus, and Hadrian; others used intellectual strategy to crush the spirit of the people by heaping calumnies upon them, as did the historians and philosophers of Persia and Greece who attacked the Jews and Judaism in their writings. The third method, used by Christianity and Mohammedanism, combined violence with vilification. They proclaimed a new divine law and dispensation which they alleged superseded the older one. The last group, says Maimonides, will go the way of the two former. It will fail. Christ-

---

[18]Letter to Yemen, 6b.
[19]*Ibid.*

ianity and Islam are merely imitations of Judaism. They are no more like the veritable faith than a statute is like the living person whom it represents. The extinction of the three types of Israel's foes is hinted at in Dan. 7:8: "I considered the horns, and behold, there came up among them another horn, a little one, before which three of the first horns were plucked up by the roots; and behold, in this horn were eyes like the eyes of a man, and a mouth speaking great things." The last phrase describes the presumption of Jesus.

Maimonides delicately discriminated between the attitudes of the two dominant religions towards Judaism. In reply to the question as to whether the Talmudic statement that a non-Jew who studies Torah deserves death, is or is not law, Maimonides subtly observes that the statement holds true for Mohammedans but not for Christians, since the Mohammedan denies the divine inspiration of our Scriptures which to him is a fraud, replete with untruths and expurgations. The Christian, however, accepts the God-given and revered character of the Torah, but deviates from its Jewish interpretation in believing that it prefigures the founder of his own religion.[20]

As for Jesus and Mohammed, they were both false prophets, mere pretenders to the Messiahship, since they promulgated the new faiths and discipline. They dispensed with the Torah and ordained laws after their own hearts. Above everything else, the criterion of the true savior must be rigid adherence to the revealed law of Moses. It is true that non-Israelitish prophets have been recognized as mouth-pieces of the one God, but the content of their prophecy and their ministrations were not in accordance with the spirit and the letter of Judaism.

Maimonides refutes the erroneous and futile attempts to discover allusions to Mohammed or Jesus in the Bible

---

[20]Responsum—No. 58, in Kobez.

and prefers to follow the adopted and usual meaning of the text.[21]

b. Mohammed not Prefigured in the Bible.

As for Mohammed, the verse, "He shined forth from mount Paran"—Deut. 33:2—cannot signify his future appearance, for the obvious reason that the verb, "he shined" indicates a past event. The notion that *b'meod meod* Gen. 17:2, alludes to the prophet of Allah because the numerical value of the Hebrew letters of the two words and of the name Mahmad is, for each, 92, is unsubstantiated. The Hebrew phrase simply means "very much" and describes the greatness of numbers. It could not logically refer to an honored successor to Abraham, because Isaac had already been designated the heir of the patriarch and the recipient of God's promise and blessings. The same explanation is given to Gen. 17:20, where *great* denotes size of numbers, and not eminence in prophecy or spirituality.

Maimonides refutes the charges made against his people by Islamic polemicists that the Jews expunged many references to Mohammed in Holy Writ. The sage points to the numerous ancient translations which never mention the prophet of Mecca. Furthermore, he declares the text of the Bible has been jealously guarded and has come down to us without the change of even a vowel or letter. Any deletion, such as is charged against the Jews, would surely have been noticeable.

As for Christianity, Maimonides asserts that it did not fulfil the hope of prophetic Messianism. He particularly levels the shaft of vigorous criticism at an alleged view that the founders of Islam and Christianity are presaged in Deut. 18:15. When studied in connection with the

---

[21]Letter to Yemen, pp. 3-4. Mishneh Torah, Yesode ha-Torah, VIII, 9, 10, for discussion of the true prophecy. See H. Hirschfeld, Mohammedan Criticism of the Bible, J. Q. R. 1901, p. 222 *seq.*

entire chapter, the verse does not foretell the coming of
a particular prophet, but states the lofty character of the
Hebrew prophetic type. He shall be of a higher order
than prophets who resort to primitive heathen practices.
The passage is not concerned with a new dispensation that
may be promulgated by a new teacher, but warns Jews
that the man of God they seek must be an Israelite. The
qualifying phrases, "from the midst of thee", and "of thy
brethren", preclude him from being a descendant or fol-
lower of Edom or Ishmael. The true prophet must adhere
to the Torah—this was not so with Mohammed and Jesus.
Jesus did the very reverse of what the Messiah must do.
He and his followers abrogated the Law. Yet no evil is
unmixed with good; the spread of Christendom is helping
to bring on a purer civilization. Through the prevalence
of error truth becomes more urgent and evident.[22]

6—*The End.*

a. Trend of the Times Suitable for Redemption, as Evidenced by Oppression and Enforced Apostasy.

To the community of Yemen, Maimonides wrote
sorrowfully, though not in despair, about the wretched-
ness and dismay of the Jews in the Orient and in European
countries, averring that the calamitous events of the day
betokened the "birth-travails of the Messiah". The Messiah might soon be expected. Scripture had veiled the
exact year of the advent, but it had indicated the general
character of the period immediately preceding it. The
prophets had such dire situations in mind when they
exclaimed: "O Lord God, cease, I beseech Thee; How shall
Jacob stand for he is small"—(Amos 7:5); "My heart is
bewildered, terror hath overwhelmed me; the twilight that
I longed for hath been turned for me into trembling"—

[22]Letter to Yemen, p. 32, *et seq.*

(Isaiah 21:4). Thus the times were ripe for the blessed intervention. Israel is governed and prostrated by Edom (Rome) and Ishmael (Mohammedanism). Maimonides is especially bitter against the latter's tyranny and finds his sentiments suitably expressed in the words of the Psalmist

"Woe is me, that I sojourn with Meshech;
That I dwell beside the tents of Kedar!" (Ps. 120:5).

Pleas for salvation are heard everywhere. Their souls long for release. But they must not lose hope, nor despair. Many attempts had already been made to annihilate the sacred seed, but all have failed. Israel can only submit and forbear. The fact that many Messianic pretenders have appeared in their generation, in Fez, in Cordova, and in Spain at large, indicates a groping toward the light which will be satisfied in the speedy advent.

The doubt and the apostasy which had spread in Israel, owing to the people's abasement, had been foreseen by Dan. 12:10; hence, let not the people take their weakened position and decimated ranks as a token of certain downfall and swift obliteration at the hand of the Gentile nations. Maimonides called upon his persecuted brethren to martyr themselves for the holy cause. Every material sacrifice, be it removal from birthplace and dear kin, or loss of position and wealth, is insignificant compared with the duty of remaining faithful to the God of Israel. Interpreting Canticles as an allegory, Maimonides followed the Midrash in explaining the four-fold mention of the word "return" in 7:1 as indicative of Israel's (Shulamith's) restoration from Egypt, Babylon, Greece, and Rome. All but the last have already occurred. The present Roman sovereignty, too, is destined to end very soon.

In his day, as in all the Middle Ages, the question of enforced apostasy was pressing. His generation turned to Maimonides for light in its perplexity and we have from his pen an unusual disquisition which is interesting from more than one angle—the "Epistle on Apostasy". To begin with, he says, those who of their own volition lapse from the faith and embrace another, show that they are not of the blood of the race which pledged unqualified obedience to the Torah at Sinai. Such a one is a "Mumar", an unpardonable apostate, who is knowingly induced by Israel's abject position to prefer the religion of the majority and the powerful.[23]

He excused, however, those who had violated under duress even the major ordinances of Judaism, including foreign worship. They cannot be penalized, for the Jewish law, the very Bible itself, recognizes the principle that compulsion exonerates a person who has committed a wrong. In judging enforced apostasy, one must also consider that the prevailing apostasy is quite different from what it was in the past, when the Jew was required to abandon essential Jewish institutions such as the Sabbath and circumcision. In his time a mere lip-service, the recital of a theological formula, sufficed to satisfy the cross or the crescent. "It has become common truth among them that we do not believe the affirmation we make, and that it is only uttered as a subterfuge to save ourselves from the ruler, to placate him. . . . One who asks whether he should be slain or affirm, we say to him, 'Make the affirmation and be not slain.'" But Maimonides cautions these pretending apostates not to conclude that because they have taken the fateful step, they may with impunity discard or transgress the Torah. Nay, it is incumbent upon every person in time of stress to observe the laws secretly to the best of his power. Moreover, such converts must not be reviled nor ostracised by the congregation, but cordially welcomed and considered a part thereof.

---

[23]Mishneh Torah, Teshuvah III, 9.

An account of an enforcèd conversion in the boyhood of Maimonides shows how the sword of Damocles hung over their heads: "In the year 1142, the armies of Ibn Tamurt appeared. A proclamation was issued that anyone who refused to adopt Islam would be put to death, and his property would be confiscated. Thereupon the Jews assembled at the gate of the royal palace and implored the king for mercy. He answered—'It is because I have compassion on you, that I command you to become Moslems; for I desire to save you from eternal punishment.' The Jews replied, 'Our salvation depends on our observance of the divine Law; you are master of our bodies and of our property, but our souls will be judged by the King who gave them to us, and to whom they will return.' 'I do not desire to argue with you,' said the king; 'for I know you will argue according to your own religion. It is my absolute wish that either you adopt my religion or be put to death.' The Jews then proposed to emigrate, but the king would not allow his subjects to serve another king. Thus many congregations forsook their religion; but within a month the king suffered sudden death; the son, believing that his father had met with an untimely end as a punishment for his cruelty to the Jews, assured the involuntary converts that it would be indifferent to him which religion they professed. Hence many Jews returned at once to the religion of their fathers, while others hesitated for some time, fearing that the king meant to entrap the apparent converts."[24]

b. Advent Will Occur Upon Termination of Rome's Allotted Period of Prosperity.

Although Maimonides did not doubt that the end must arrive, and believed that the low ebb of Israel's fortune made the redemption imminent, he was reluctant

---

[24]Ibn Verga's Shebet Jehuda, ed. M. Wiener, Hannover, 1855-56, p. 3.

to commit himself to a definite date. In his open-mindedness he agreed with an oft-repeated view that utter ignorance prevails as to the exact year of redemption, and that our attitude, meanwhile, should be one of resignation. The fact is, he did not believe it possible to compute the Messianic year, and condemned attempts made in that direction, in accord with the well-known Talmudic malediction hurled upon those who calculate the "end". A curse was heaped upon foolish calculators, because the repeated failure of the Messiah to appear at the predicted time caused the mass of Israel to despair and to abandon all hope of a final redemption. Maimonides severely rebuked the people for attempting to prognosticate the advent from the planetary movements. He held astrology in contempt and dissuaded his Yemenite correspondent from placing faith in it.[25] He was further convinced of the ridiculousness of astrology from the fact that in the alleged year of redemption new and merciless persecutions were raging against the Jews of Spain.

In general, he maintained that the rule of Edom (Rome) must first reach its allotted end. Its prolonged and world-wide supremacy is not without valid reason. It is God's way of rewarding the progenitor of the race, Esau, for the honor he showed his aged father, when he, albeit deceitfully, asked him the law on tithing salt. This characteristic spark of filial fidelity and love in Esau deserved to be requited here on earth. When the measure of Esau's reward has been filled in the form of a flourishing temporal existence, the Messiah will follow.[26] If the compensation of Esau be so great, how immeasurably

---

[25]"Letter to Yemen"; Kobez II, p. 5b; In the Guide III, ch. 37, Maim. condemns astrology as witchcraft.

[26]Maamar Kiddush Ha shem in Kobez, II, p. 12. "The son of David will not come until Esau receives reward for respecting father and mother." Comp. Yerush, Kiddushin I, 7; 61b, "The Holy One, blessed be He, does not delay the reward of Gentiles, for performance of Mitzvot."

greater will be the bliss of the descendants of Jacob for the martyrdom they have exhibited all through history. Maimonides reveals by such rationalization his desire to justify the success of forces hostile to Judaism.

c. Reluctantly Calculates Year of the End.

As to a definite year for the climacteric event, there are two possibilities: first, it depends solely on repentance; second, it has been predetermined by a wise Providence. Maimonides chose to believe in the first possibility which was favored by numerous rigid rabbinical authorities. He insists on the conversion of all Israel to the divine way as a *sine qua non* of the redemption,[27] the deliverance of the people from sin, and their acknowledgment of God the Lord of all. Since it is impossible to tell when all Israel will be repentant, no one can tell when the "end" will arrive.

The difficulty of determining the precise year was further realized by Maimonides in the instance of the Exodus. Four hundred years of oppression in Egypt had been clearly foretold, and yet it was not known exactly when the four hundred years would terminate and the Exodus occur. Nor was it known whether to count from the time of God's covenant with Abraham, or from Jacob's descent into Egypt, or from 70 years later, when the actual servitude commenced. Actually, the birth of Isaac was the *terminus a quo*. Still more uncertain is the exact end of Israel's present insufferable exile, since no time-limit for it has been set. Quite differently, Saadia arrived at a terminal year from the conflicting figures in Daniel, using as an analogy the several time-limits mentioned for the Egyptian Exodus.

It is interesting to note, that the law of contraries holds true in the case of Maimonides, as it does of most

---

[27]Mishneh Torah, Teshuvah VIII, 5.

people, great and small, genius and dullard. His aversion
for adventist dates did not prevent him from defending
Saadia Gaon, who offered abundant evidence for the
Messiah's arrival in 965, on the ground that Saadia sustained the courage of the people in an age of extreme distress and despair.[28] He himself, in an ingenious family
tradition, derived from Num. 23:23 that the Messiah
would appear in 1216.

"For there is no enchantment with Jacob,
Neither is there any divination with Israel;
Now is it said of Jacob and of Israel;
'What hath God wrought.'"

The return of pristine prophecy would unmistakably
hail the incoming Messianic age. By a forced interpretation the calculator reads the return of prophecy into the
words: "Now is it said of Jacob and of Israel: what hath
God wrought;" and he believes it would take place as
many years after Balaam uttered his prayer as had already elapsed since creation. In other words, Balaam's
prediction was spoken at a time equi-distant between creation and redemption. Balaam lived forty years after the
Exodus, which would set the date of his utterance at 2488.
Doubling this, we have 4976 (1216).[29]

Maimonides rationalized his disclosure of the end with
the usual argument that it was close at hand, and would
serve to sustain the people and tide them over the years of
frightful oppression. His death came twelve years before
the computed "end".

[28]Azariah dei Rossi similarly defended Maimonides, in *Imre Binah*
Ch. 43, p. 104, ed. ben Jacob, Wilna, 1863.
[29]Letter to Yemen, 6bc. This calculation is traceable to statement of
R. Hanina, Yerush, Sabbath, VI:9. "It appears that Balaam, the wicked,
lived at the middle of the world's duration, when he said, 'Now it is said of
Jacob and of Israel, what hath God wrought.'" M. Friedlander in his
intro. to the Guide, p. xxi, thinks that this date-passage is spurious and had
perhaps been added by the translator of the "Letter to Yemen."

d. Warns People Against Religious Laxity.

He counsels the Jews, the world over, not to grow lax in the observance of Jewish law because of their anticipation of the advent. One should not voluntarily remain in a country where the Torah has fallen into neglect, or where it is proscribed, in the hope that a Torah-less world will hasten the Messianic order. In such cases, it is mandatory upon Jews to migrate from lands of oppression and go to places where they may freely observe the faith. "The observance of religious ordinances does not depend upon the Messiah's advent, but we are required to engage in the Torah and in the ordinances at all times. After we have done what is expected of us, and if God will deem us or our grandchildren worthy to behold the Messiah, well enough; but if not, we will have incurred no loss."[30] The Torah has been in our possession from time immemorial and cannot be suspended under any circumstances. The binding power of the Torah will continue in the Messianic world. The redemption, however, is now only a promise awaiting fulfillment in some distant time, and should not be the cause of any laxity in the people's observance of Judaism.

7—*The Messiah.*

a. Not Superhuman, No Wonder Worker.

As a philosopher who tried to naturalize the miracles of the Bible and who took liberties in defining Jewish theological truths, Maimonides, quite consistently, divests the Messiah of all supernatural powers. The Messiah will be born in a Davidic family through Solomon, and will trace his lineage back to Ruth, daughter of Eglon, King of Moab.[31] King David is the prototype of the future redeemer, and both are placed on a par in char-

---

[30]Maamar Kiddush Ha shem, p. 15b.
[31]Ozar Nehmad, II; pp. 44-45; Nazir 23b.

acter, achievement, and authority. A descendant of the great David who will emulate his sire in his zeal for the Torah, who will espouse the Written Law, fight the battle of the Lord, and prevail upon all Israel to obey the Law, may be assumed to be the Messiah. If he has, furthermore, rebuilt the sanctuary and gathered in the dispersed tribes of Israel to the Holy Land, he is certain to be the long-awaited Messiah. The *locus classicus* for a description of the Messianic personality is Is. 11:2. The Messiah will not be an ignoramus who will rise to world-mastery through adventitious circumstances, wealth, or cunning. He must excel in learning and wisdom. He will be wiser and mightier than Solomon and well-nigh the equal of Moses in prophetic power.[32] The doctrine of the supremacy of Moses (even above the Messiah) was posited to oppose the contention of the dominant religions that their alleged Messiahs were greater than Moses and could abrogate the Torah.

Like his illustrious forebear, King David, he will be Israel's savior. He will free the nation from foreign domination, enlarge its boundaries, and implant the love of God in every home and heart. His sway will extend as far as India. Maimonides placed a premium on the wisdom, or as we would say in modern terms, the common sense of the Messiah. In his "Letter to Yemen", he showed the imprudence of the Messianic impostor who appeared amongst the Jews of Arabia, in ordering equal distribution of private wealth among the poor. This communistic principle seemed absurd to the great sage, because it would merely impoverish the rich.[33]

Among all the earth's rulers he will stand incomparable for personal rectitude and eminence. The attempts to offer Jesus or Mohammed as the Jewish Messiah, as well

---

[32]Mishneh Torah, Teshuvah IX, 2; Letter to Yemen, p. 6.
[33]Letter to Yemen, p. 6d; Mishneh Torah, Deot. V, 12.

as the appearance of Messiahs who rescinded the Jewish law in his own day, undoubtedly moved Maimonides to stress the religious side of the Messiah to make him an observant Jew, absorbed in the study of Torah and scrupulous in the enforcement of the rabbinic law. The Messiah will not be a thaumaturgist, and will not, as imbeciles believe, perform the miracle of resurrection. This common-sense position is strengthened in the mind of Maimonides by the historical fact that Akiba, leading tannaitic authority, acknowledged Bar Kochba who neither promised nor performed miracles, as the Messiah. In this characterization, Maimonides deviates essentially from the usual course of mystic Messianism, according to which the Messiah was pre-existent, or inhabited Paradise. The philosopher humanized him, and ascribed to him natural excellences in a superlative degree.

The difference between the common-sense conception of Maimonides and the mystic conception of the Cabalists may be made very clear by the illustration of two kinds of mirrors. One reflects the body as it is; the second distorts it—the body appears ill-shaped, the limbs elongated or shortened. The philosopher, with his well-balanced mind and lucid language, gives us a Messiology which truly reflects the opinion and the need of the average religious person. The Cabala stretches the essential features so far that the result is an awkward and grotesque picture of the redemption which fits in neither with our experience nor reasonable expectation. We have instances of this exaggeration when it speaks of his angelic nature and his exploits in Paradise.

The manner of the Messiah's advent and its immediate effect upon the world is set forth by the sage of Cordova who is fully aware that he is treading on thin ice. He will make his first appearance unexpectedly in the land of Israel. The Messiah himself will not be aware of his royal origin nor of his princely mission, and until he has disclosed himself, his family and immediate parentage will not be known.[34] However, his high destiny will manifest itself in due time. His achievements on behalf of Israel and mankind will testify to his exalted rank and will set the seal of Messiahship upon him. Upon his coming the rulers of the earth will be seized with fear for the security of their thrones and will conspire to overthrow him.[35]

b. Maimonides' Conception of the Revived State.

Unperturbed, he will set about the task of reviving the dynasty of the ancient legitimate throne. The temple will be rebuilt, and the dispersed tribes of Israel gathered unto the Holy Land. The sacrifices, the Shemitah, and the Jubilee will be reintroduced. He will reinstate the Levites and the priests in their sacred brotherhoods and apportion to the tribes their old territorial divisions. In this difficult task he will be guided by the Holy Spirit.[36] The Messiah will die and his rule will become hereditary.[37]

It is singular at first to see that the Messiah ben Joseph, that lesser light of the redemption, the herald of the Davidite, does not appear in Maimonides. The omission is easily explained. The dramatic role traditionally assigned to the Josephite, is that of an avenger of Israel's enemies. He towers high in the preliminary events of the Messianic regime and in the severe warfare between Israel and other nations. Maimonides minimizes the retaliatory and military aspects of the redemption, believing that it must issue peacefully and naturally out of the bosom of time. He can therefore find no need for the meteoric appearance of this military figure.

---

[34]Zech. 6 :12 and Is. 53 :2 are the basis for this thought.
[35]Letter to Yemen. pp. 6d, ff.
[36]Mishneh Torah, Melakim, XII, 3 and XI, I.
[37]Comm. on Mishna San. Bahya b. Asher believes that ben David would live forever. See Bahya on Gen. 11 :11.

Altogether, the Messianic account of Maimonides is not as dramatic and fascinating as that of the Talmud, the geonic writers, or the later Abrabanel. The principal personages who move to and fro on his Messianic stage are kept in the background. Crucial and central events are not treated stirringly and imaginatively. He writes of the redemption in a calm, reverent and resigned manner. What interests him more than the paraphernalia and the exterior side of redemption is its motive and purpose. He views redemption *sub specie aeternitatis*, as the consummation of the ages, as the fruition of the divine promise, rather than as a relief from distress and oppression. And it was no doubt due to his philosophic attitude and rationalizing method that he could look upon the Messiah's coming from the angle of God and not from the angle of man. Not that Maimonides was oblivious of the people's desire for one who would deliver them from oppression, but the material aspect was overshadowed by his wider and more idealistic outlook.

8—*The Messianic Era.*

a. The New Israel.

Sometime after the Messiah's revelation, will occur the fierce and decisive warfare with Gog. During the early turbulent years of the Messianic regime, the Jews will be sifted at the hands of their oppressors, all the faithless ones will be weeded out of the body politic of Israel. Only the purest of the pure will survive to share in the glory of the blessed state. The Torah will then come into its own. Though oft fallen into neglect, it has never been changed nor eclipsed, and in the new state it will be re-established as the great code. The early civil and ritualistic system, such as the Sabbatical and Jubilee years, will be reintroduced. These pristine institutions will show to the world the excelling wisdom of Israel.

MAIMONIDES

In addition to the eternal improvements of the social and economic order, the new state will enjoy political independence. This freedom will be thrice-blessed for its own sake, because it will enable Israel to give its undivided self to religion and to solidify its sublime ideas and teachings. Israel will be the lode-star, the exemplar of nations. Then will Israel be prepared for the supernal bliss awaiting it in the future world.

Maimonides maintains that the Messianic state will endure for 2000 years and will be an unbroken continuation of the existing order. There will be no miracles, and natural laws will not be suspended. Is. 11:6 is an hyperbolic picturization of the rule of peace, brotherhood, and felicity in that period. However, in the Guide of the Perplexed, the philosopher wisely says:[38] "All the great evils which men cause to each other because of certain intentions, desires, opinions, or religious principles, are likewise due to non-existence because they originate in ignorance, which is absence of wisdom. . . . If men possessed wisdom, which stands in the same relation to the form of man as the sight to the eye, they would not cause any injury to themselves or to others; for the knowledge of truth removes hatred and quarrels, and prevents mutual injuries."

Although the philosopher insists that the new era will not need miracles to make it the wonder age, he does not deny the possibility of miracles occurring then, but explains them in his own way. Miracles are possible because they are foreordained changes in nature. They do not violate natural law, but are rather in consonance with the original plan of God to cause certain changes at definite times. But no contra-natural changes have been designed for the Messianic state. There will be no difference in existing things, except that Israel will be a sovereign nation.

[38]Guide, III, Ch. 11.

THE DOCTRINE OF THE MESSIAH

The divine promise of a new heaven and a new earth, found in Is. 65:17, is construed in two ways.[39] First, as impassioned, metaphoric language which indicates merely the exalted and happy condition of future Israel; second, that the new heaven and the new earth have existed since creation, and are merely waiting to be transplanted in Messianic days. Is. 11:6-9, which states that beasts will lose their ferocity, that the wolf shall dwell with the lamb is figurative. It signifies that Israel, the lamb, will dwell peaceably with its erstwhile foes, the beasts that once preyed upon it. In the same way, the awful celestial phenomena narrated in Joel 3:3-4, is a poetic representation of the defeat of Gog in the time of the Messiah.

b. Amelioration of Human Society.

The political and moral stability of the revived Hebrew state will be paralleled by the betterment of human nature, and of human inter-relations universally. Man will have reached the profoundest knowledge of God, of the exterior world, as well as the complex secrets of his own being. The greatest quest of man will be for God. Peace and union will be established everywhere. Discord will cease. Knowledge will be universal. This perfect condition will not result from the innate equality of people, because all people cannot be like-minded, nor can they all attain to the same rank. The familiar divisions of rich and poor, strong and weak, will remain in the new society. But a change to brotherhood and peace will come in the course of thousands of years through the eradication of the primitive instincts to fight, to envy, and to ridicule. Man will put forth no painful energy nor experience any hardships in gaining a livelihood. This simple and unworried existence will prolong life. Such is the meaning that the sage places on the Talmudic statement—

---

[39]Guide, II, 29; Mishneh Torah, Melakim, XI, 12.

Sabb. 30b—that "the land of Israel will one day produce cakes ready baked, and garments of fine silk." It is a popular way of expressing the "good times" of the Messianic future.[40]

9—Resurrection.

a. Dogmatic Statement.

Maimonides reckons the belief in the quickening of the dead among his thirteen basic principles of Judaism.[41] This principle—together with the twelve other doctrines —has been liturgized by the synagogue. "I believe with perfect faith that there will be resurrection of the dead at the time, when it shall please the Creator, blessed be His name, and exalted be the remembrance of Him, for-ever and ever."[42] One who denies a Scriptural origin for this belief will himself not be resurrected. It is the key to all miracles, and must be accepted as a matter of faith. No philosophic or empirical evidence can be relied upon to convince us that it must happen.

The doctrine of resurrection was the subject of acri-monious discussion between Maimonides and other theologians, notably Samuel b. Ali of Bagdad. His admirers besought him to clarify his position, his opponents charged him with denying it altogether. To satisfy friend and foe alike, he wrote the important treatise, "Essay on Resurrection,"[43] in which he treats the subject from many angles. Here Maimonides says that he "firmly believes in the

[40]Comm. on Mishna, San. X.
[41]Ibid.
[42]Singer's Prayer Book.
[43]Essay on Res. Kobez 11, pp. 7-11—The material here is based on this essay, unless otherwise indicated. For the large controversial correspondence between Meir b. Todros Halevi of Toledo, anti-Maimonist and the Lunel scholars on Maimonides' conception of Resurrection and the Hereafter see Kassav Alrasail, ed. by J. Brill, Paris. See also M. Wolff, Eschatologische Gedanken Musa ben Maimuns, 1890. Wolff contends that Maimonides did not believe in re-existence of the body, but only in the soul's survival, p. 14.

resurrection as a miracle whose possibility is granted with the assumption of a temporal Creation." The belief has plowed itself deep into the religious consciousness of the Jew, and its wide acceptance is attested by frequent mention in his prayers, in the Bible, and in the Talmud.

b. Difficulties in the Way of Belief.

One may deny resurrection for either of two reasons. First, on the ground that it is unnatural; but this attitude is irreligious because it virtually gainsays the possibility of miracles. To the believing mind that begins with faith in the divine creation of the world, everything is possible.[44] Second, on the ground that Scripture does not clearly teach re-existence after death; this says Maimonides, is untrue.

Although there are not many affirmations of this exalted miracle in the Bible, there are several which indubitably point toward it. Dan. 12:2 distinctly predicts it. "And many of them that sleep in the dust of the earth shall awake, some to everlasting life, and some to reproaches and everlasting abhorrence." 12:13 reads: "But go thou thy way till the end be; and thou shalt rest, and shalt stand up to thy lot, at the end of the days." It should be remembered, moreover, that the mere reiteration of a proposition does not establish its truth. So primary and requisite a teaching as the "Unity of God" is mentioned only once in the Canon, and yet no one will for that reason question its importance.

It appears from his correspondence and essays that the philosopher was suspected of having denied the doctrine. The following causes probably gave rise to the suspicion: (a) his inclination to expound certain Scriptural verses metaphorically, as *meshalim*, and the possible

---

[44]Letter to R. Hasdai Halevi, Kobez 11, p. 24a bottom. Most of the theologians here considered employ the same logic.

use of this method to explain resurrection passages; (b) his divesting the Messiah of thaumaturgical powers, while the miracle of resurrection had been traditionally ascribed to the Messiah; (c) his regarding the world to come as the goal of achievement and as the highest reward, with the consequent subordination of the resurrected life; (d) his belief that since spirit is the true reality, and retribution is spiritual only, the resurrected body will be unnecessary; (e) his interpretation of Ezekiel's vision of the re-animation of the dead as a dream and not an actuality.

c. Not Clearly Taught in Scripture.

The question why the Pentateuch does not clearly predict resurrection is answered by the sage in the following manner. It was feared in those primitive days that Israel, steeped in heathenism, would not comprehend the purpose and far-reaching effects of resurrection, and therefore would reject it. As the miracle was to be enacted in the distant future, it was necessary to inculcate in them a firm and general belief in divine creation and in the possibility of miracles, before they could be promised the resurrection.[45] This the Pentateuch does by spreading the idea of God's omnipotence and of the creation, in opposition to the prevailing unenlightened view that the universe was uncreated and without beginning. The Jewish conception was instilled by way of miracles which occurred even in the early history of Israel. These miracles proved the power and control of God over nature, and pointed to a divine creation of the world. The people's rooted belief in miracles prepared the way for faith in resurrection as expounded by the prophets at a later time.

---

[45]Kobez, II, p. 11a-b. A similar thought is expressed by Bahya ibn Pakuda (11th Cent.) in his "Hobot ha-Lebabot", IV, on Faith.

Again, this teaching is intertwined with the idea of retribution for good and evil. If resurrection had been taught in the Mosaic law, it is doubtful if fear of punishment or anticipation of reward at a distant time would have influenced the people. Hence, formal promulgation of the belief was delayed until a much later period.

d. His Defense of the Doctrine.

Maimonides also considers the objection that a number of Bible verses like Job 7:9, 14:14; Is. 38:18; 2 Sam. 14:14 and Ps. 72:29 obviously deny corporeal life after death. The superficial sentiment in these verses is one of despair at the hopelessness of life beyond the grave. Intrinsically, they state the common law of nature, that physical substances must decay and dissolve into minute elements. But we need not conclude from these verses that resurrection, God's greatest miracle, will not happen. The verses referred to belong to the same class as does the question: "Shall we bring forth water out of this stone?" It was natural to suppose that a stone could not melt into water. Yet this happened by the command of God. Of the same character is the rhetorical question: "If a man die, will he live?" Death naturally is the end of life, but God can restore life.

Maimonides makes a distinction between the Messianic state and the future world. Resurrection will occur in the former period. Following Saadia and others, he held that the miracle would take place soon after the Messiah's appearance, and would constitute the first great act of redemption. He sees a veiled reference to resurrection in the last verse of Malachi, which speaks of God sending forth Elijah before the great and terrible day. Elijah was not translated alive to other regions, celestial or mundane. He actually died in the flesh. The promise therefore, of Elijah's reappearance, means that he will be revived at the deliverance. His return is complete proof that the resurrection depends upon the Messiah, for Elijah will precede and prepare the way for the redeemer. This assumption does not conflict with an opinion, elsewhere stated, that the Messiah will not perform miracles. In reality, the opinion implies that the Messiah will not need to perform resurrection or any supernatural deeds to prove his genuineness. His identity will be quickly established by the course of historic events, and by his self-revelatory nature. The supreme miracle will be performed by God himself. It is a reward only for the righteous.[46]

10—The Future World.

a. General Characteristics of the New Existence.

In Jewish eschatology the conception of a future world is at times confused with that of the Messianic future. It was Maimonides who separated these two periods. Maimonides derides the materialistic theology of his day which aims not to clarify and idealize the future world, but concerns itself with silly questions such as: "will the dead arise naked or clothed? in their embroideries or in the shroud? and will the Messiah equalize rich and poor?"

All who are resurrected will die after a long and consecrated life. The souls of the righteous will then pass into a future world, where, upon reaching the stage of spiritual completeness, they will abide forever.[47] Thereafter, the body, which is but the tenement and the instrument of the soul, will be shed. There will be no further need of it because the new world will be of a spiritual instead of a mechanical order. It will be pop-

---

[46]Mishneh Torah, Teshuva. VIII, 2.
[47]*Ibid.* See Kassav Alrasail for arguments pro and con. This must be the explanation of the Talmudic statement that the righteous sit with crowns on their heads and enjoy the radiance of the Shekina, which Maimonides uses to portray eternal bliss.

ulated with soul-beings whose exclusive delight will be intellectual and eternal association with God. The master explicitly states that the soul which is immortal is not the physical but the rational or psychical soul.[48] This will constitute the reward for which the pious have waited. The banquet of which legend speaks must be understood figuratively as the feast of the soul, or the intellect. God, the secret, will be known. God, the perfect one, will be imitated. God, the brilliant, will illuminate all space. The soul-being will find itself in harmony with God and will enjoy endless bliss.

The reverse of this glorious spiritual state is the perdition of the wicked soul at death. Unlike other theologians, Maimonides does not allow for intermediate stages in the purging of the soul toward perfection. Nonetheless his admirer, Nahmanides, defended the sage against the view that the unworthy soul met an absolute and speedy end when the person died.[49]

The great master laughs out of court the common-sense contention that it is difficult to conceive of a being that has no corporeal substantiality. Man, says the sage, cannot be taken as a measure of divine possibilities. Our minds are bounded by finite spheres. He is a fool who insists that individual personality in the future world must be corporeal. The practical purpose of the human anatomy, of its internal and external organs, is to preserve the human species. In the future world, however, life will be endless and will render unnecessary the presence of any physical frame. The opposing view, that denizens of the future world will be physical, is a concession to the popular prejudice. In reality, intellect separated from body is more real than body. Thus it is not impossible to believe that the world to come will be peopled with the highest

---

[48]*Ibid.*
[49]"Chapters on Bliss."

realities—souls or intelligences, that will mark man's perfection to the nth degree.

Maimonides condemns as puerile the arguments of those who point to Moses and Elijah to prove that the highest spiritual status can be enjoyed in a corporeal frame. The instances are not adequate because Moses and Elijah lapsed into the higher state for intervals only. Before and after such lapses they participated in the physical life about them. They were part and parcel of this world. But there is a wide gap between an occasional spiritual exaltation in this world and the continuous and purely glorious existence in the world to come.

Yet Maimonides has no quarrel with those who persistently maintain that corporeality is essential for existence. They are safe theologically so long as they do not trespass on heretical ground and extend their theory to propound a corporeal God. He admits, too, that his view of a disembodied soul-existence has given rise to abuse and misunderstanding. It has misled people into believing that if there is no corporeal existence in the world to come, there need be no resurrection. But this does not deter him from espousing his view. He would rather be right alone than wrong with a thousand.

Paradise, according to Maimonides, is on this side of the grave. It is part of this mundane existence. The supreme, substantial characteristic of that enchanting region will be the superfertility of the soil. It will be rich in streams and delectable fruits, and may possibly yield hitherto unknown plants of extraordinary value. In view of this opinion, it is strange that he considers Gehinnom not a locality, but a mere figurative term, to describe the affliction of doomed souls.[50]

The essentially philosophic Maimonides here and there shows the mystic strain, as when he says that the world

---

[50]Comm. on Mishna, San. X.

to come has already been created and is now in existence
—but is invisible. It is not future in the sense that it
will succeed a temporal or destructible earth; it is
future for those individuals who are destined to enter it.[51]

b. Disclaims Knowledge of Details.

Maimonides does not pry into the more detailed character of the new world. He cites the Talmudic view,
with which he evidently agrees, that the prophets presaged
only the marvels and glories of the Messianic state, and
that they said nothing about the new world. Here they
found themselves blocked. Their subtle insight could not
penetrate the world beyond. Neither shall we succeed.
Language and reason are adequate to describe the infinite
possibilities of earthly felicity, but the infinite possibilities
and phenomena of a world remade transcend the widest
stretches of human imagination. We cannot comprehend
the future world because it is of an order entirely different from the present. The fish do not share the instincts
of land creatures. The animal does not possess the cogita-
tive powers of humans; the blind man has no sensation
of color. In a higher sense, our bodily senses cannot know
the elements and delights that make up the ideal spiritual
world.[52]

The world will never come to an end, nor will its
existence be interrupted by a period or periods of destruction. The Cabalistic notion of a cycle of worlds each
lasting 7,000 years, and created and destroyed successively,
finds no lodgement in his eschatological scheme. The view
of the Talmudic scholar that the present world will be
demolished in the seventh millennium is a personal opinion
and not the teaching of Judaism. But what shall we
make of the Scripture passages which tell of the oblitera-

---

[51]Mishneh Torah, Tesh. VIII, 8.
[52]Ibid., VII, 6.

tion of the world? They are merely exaggerated pictures, describing the dire misfortunes and utter ruin that will follow the adversaries of Israel.[53]

Maimonides' liberal definition of certain traditional ideas connected with the Advent and the Hereafter shows in general the new tone of his theology. For his new ideas he was charged with unorthodoxy; the "Guide of the Perplexed," and the "Book of Knowledge," were inter-dicted and even burnt. Perhaps if he were living today his views would be regarded as untraditional and even heretical.

---

[53]Guide II, Ch. 29.

Chapter VIII

NAHMANIDES

1—Cabalist.

The theologian Moses ben Nahman (Spain, 1194-1270) is a fine contrast to Maimonides. Although he did not share many of the theological ideas of the philosopher, Nahmanides held him in the highest esteem, and in the desperate struggle of the conservatives to proscribe the "Guide" and "Book of Knowledge," Nahmanides pleaded eloquently with them not to besmirch the just fame of the master. Nahmanides was hailed as the most enlightened champion of the school of Jewish mysticism, or as it is known in Hebrew, the Cabala. This grotesque religious movement did not spring, Minerva-like, from the minds of medieval rabbis. Its origin is to be discovered in the remote past although it reached its zenith in the centuries of which we write. Representing one of the many streams of Jewish cultural activity that rose out of faith in one God, its influence was so pervasive that it affected alike the rabbinist, Karaite, philosopher, scientist, and statesman.

An essential difference between scholasticism and Cabala was that the former considered philosophy and revealed religion as disparate, and tried to combine and harmonize them, while the latter regarded philosophy and religion as being identical, and merged them into a system without being aware of any incompatibility between them. It is generally assumed, and rightly so, that the Cabala protested against the systems of the ancient Greek thinkers which had been accepted by the foremost rabbis. It placed faith above logic, and stressed the feelings, intentions and duties of the heart more than the postulates of the intellect. The cabalists refused to circumscribe their concepts and desires by conventional forms. Nothing that the mind could conceive or the heart yearn for was impossible in fact and in reality. By its symbolism, its picturization of God and the angels, its imaginative conception of the operation of the universe, and its moral treatment of the parts of man, of the sanctuary, and of natural objects, it brought a new romantic freedom and activity into Jewish thought, and although it was repugnant to most sober minds, it offset, in a measure, the rigid Talmudism and rationalism of the day.

Yet it would be incorrect to say that the Cabala was anti-intellectual. In Germany and France, where Jews did not engage in the study of philosophy and the sciences, Jewish mysticism grew up completely divorced from systematic philosophy. In Spain, however, where the contact with Mohammedan philosophic forces had created a center of general culture, the mysticism had a philosophic background, and consequently was not as free and bizarre as in Germany and France. Of this enlightened mystic school, Nahmanides was the venerated leader.[1]

It should not surprise us therefore if his presentation of the Messianic doctrine is warped by mystic vagaries. On the whole, he follows the orthodox lines of the Midrash and the geonim. Hence he sees no difficulty in believing that the Messiah might be in actual earthly existence one thousand years before he appears to perform his mission. The following writings[2] deal with the Messianic ideas:

1. "The Book of Redemption."

2. "The Gate of Recompense," being the last chapter of a book entitled "Torat Ha-adam."

---

[1] See Graetz, Geschichte, Vol. VII, p. 38ff., for a splendid characterization of him.
[2] Sefer ha-Geula; Shaar ha-Gemul; Wikkuah ha Ramban.

THE DOCTRINE OF THE MESSIAH

3. The Debate of Nahmanides with Pablo Christiani.

4. His Commentary on the Bible.

2—The Rationale of the Messianic Doctrine.

Each of the scholars studied in these pages approached the treatment of the Messianic belief from a slightly differ-ent angle. Nahmanides believed that it is closely inter-woven with the idea of future reward and punishment for the individual and the entire human race. Hence the sages rightly call a person who rejects that belief a heretic, on the ground that such rejection undermines the principle of compensation, the basis of Biblical teaching. Such a person also reveals a disloyal and untrustworthy nature because he repudiates the patent promises of Moses and the prophets.[3]

Israel's long cherished hope for a golden future is purely religious and should be a source of pride to the race. Be the present dispersion of Israel ever so long and severe, it should not cause us to lose faith either in the validity of the Torah or in the worthiness of its goal. It is true that the highest goal of the believing Israelite is not the Messianic age but the future world and the felicities of Paradise; nevertheless, the importance of the Messianic era should not be minimized. The latter is the ante-room that opens into the magnificent chambers of the millennial world. The redemption in itself will bring about a com-plete transformation of the present status of Israel and of mankind in general. It will draw man closer to God. The Temple and its services, the Holy Land and the Shekina, the purging of the evil inclination of man in order to bring about an era of peace and purity—all these will characterize the Messianic regime. "Know that should we grant that our transgressions and the sinfulness of

[3]Ha-Geula, p. 21.

our forefathers have effaced all consolations and that the
dispersion will prolong itself interminably; should we even
admit that God is pleased to afflict us in this world by
foreign domination; all this will not impugn the essential
doctrine of the Torah. For the pinnacle of our recompense and aspirations is the world to come, the pleasure
of the soul in Paradise and its escape from punishment in
Gehinnom. With all this we cling to the redemption,
because it is an illustrious truth among the masters of
the Torah, which we willingly acknowledge. We await it
in the hope that we will attain a nearness to God, when
we are in His sanctuary among his priests and prophets.
We will possess some of its purity and holiness and will
abide in the chosen land, with His Shekina dwelling
among us; more than we can ever attain in the diaspora,
among nations who lead us astray, and with the impurity
and abomination that attach to us. In the Messianic days
the evil inclination will be rendered futile, that we may
attain the truth as it is, or in another mystical sense that
I have mentioned. This is the quintessence of our own
desire and yearning that comes from the Torah, wherein
it is clearly taught that so long as we are sinful we will
remain in dispersion to be corrected, and when we serve
Him properly, God will again do good unto us."[4]

An eminent ideal of this sort should be embraced for
its own sake. But in showing how characteristically Jewish this ideal is, the theologian pleads a special motive for
the Jew's devotion and constancy to it. He appeals to our
racial instinct, calling upon us to believe in the idea
because of its distinctly national character. Our motto
should be fidelity to all that is Jewish. We are the trustees
of an ancient, honorable faith. It is not seemly that we
should alter our faith for novel and fugitive creeds. Perchance other religions are better or have merits and virtues

---

[4]*Ibid.* p. 20.

which Judaism does not possess; yet, while not disparaging them, we should cleave to our own and show the world we are neither cowardly nor fickle. By unswerving championship of all that is admittedly Jewish, particularly of the advent, we shall gratify our God and Father.

3—*Scriptural Origin.*

a. Pentateuch.

Nahmanides follows his predecessors in deriving the hope of final salvation from the Bible. In justification of his method he ingeniously avers that the desire of humankind of every race "is to know the future destined for it." It is natural to attempt to foretell the unknown. Primitive and heathen races have devised superstitious means to discover what may betide. They resort to magic, necromancy, and astrology. Scripture condemns all this as unworthy of man, who is created in the God-like image. Israel, too, seeks the future. But its medium is divine revelation—prophecy—the true word of God Himself, that unveils the fate of the individual and of the race in the distant future, and unlocks the secret of human happiness.[5]

Together with other mystics, he discerns in the six-day creation a cryptic archetype of the progress of the human race during six millennia.[6] The coming into existence of fruit trees on the third day alludes to the Torah—the fruit of eternal and spiritual life. The lights placed in the firmament on the fourth day represent the Solomonic and the second Temples erected in the fourth chiliad. The formation of sea monsters on the fifth day represents the tyrannical empires. The rise of man in the sixth day has its counterpart in the Messiah, who will appear in the

---

[5] Torat Adonai Temimah ed. Jellinek, Leipzig, 1853, p. 12.
[6] Comm. Gen. 2:3; and in Torat Adonai, p. 32; see Abraham b. Hiyya, p. 316.

sixth millennium—to be exact, in 5118. The seventh day symbolizes the world to come, the millennial Sabbath, when God will reign supreme. Certain episodes that follow Genesis prefigure the subsequent course of events. Jacob and Esau are the prototypes of Israel and Edom, and their ruptured relationship betokens the conflict between the two races. The battle of Moses and Joshua with the Amalekites is a prophecy of the war which Elijah and the Messiah ben Joseph will wage against Edom (Rome) before the arrival of the Davidite in the year 1358. The blessings bestowed on his sons by the patriarch Jacob, while the hand of death hovered over him, have a Messianic import, as the words "in the end of days" always denote. In this manner should Gen. 49:10 be understood.

"The scepter shall not depart from Judah,
Nor the ruler's staff from between his feet,
As long as men come to Shiloh (until Shiloh come);
And unto him shall the obedience of the people be."

The dying patriarch predicted that the tribe of Judah would enjoy an ascendancy among the tribes, which would culminate in the enthronement of King David. Then after a long lapse of time, a scion of David will arise as the Messiah (Shiloh[7]) and to him all nations will submit.

However, it should be borne in mind that the Pentateuch does not concern itself primarily and exclusively with the future. It does not purport to reveal the unknown. Moses, its author, was a lawgiver. He promulgated a set of laws and precepts for Israel, and did not prognosticate. His interest in the future was ethical rather than eschatological.[8] Only once, when he admon-

---

[7]From "Shelya"—see def. in Talmudic dictionaries.
[8]Ha-Geula, p. 4.

ished Israel concerning the curses or blessings to befall
them for their obedience or disobedience to his revealed
law, did Moses venture to look into the future. Some of
these have come true; for example, the contents of Leviti-
cus 26, which point to the captivity in Babylon and the
release that followed. Others will come true. These, says
Nahmanides, are Messianic. Deut. 28-30 speaks of our
present affliction and the joy of the forthcoming redemption. It is true that the promise of the ingathering in
Deut. 30:1-3 is predicated upon Israel's return to God.
Nevertheless the condition is stated in positive terms only.
The possibility that God may eternally abandon the people
if they fail to respond to his teachings is not stated.

Again the divine promises of goodness can never fail
of fulfillment. Deut. 31:21 is a promise of Israel's perpetuity. "Then it shall come to pass when many evils and
troubles are come upon them, that this song shall testify
before them as a witness; for it shall not be forgotten
out of the mouths of their seed." An unforgettable Torah
(this song) implies that Israel will be imperishable. Deut.
32:36 gives assurance of God's merciful interest in Israel.
"For the Lord will judge His people and repent Himself
for His servants; when He seeth that their stay is gone and
there is none remaining, shut up or left at large." Deut.
32:43:—"Sing aloud, O ye nations, of His people; for He
doth avenge the blood of His servants and doth render
vengeance to His adversaries and doth make expiation for
the land of His people." This command that the nations
celebrate the triumph of Israel does not apply to the second
commonwealth because at that time Israel was abhorred
and assaulted. Therefore it necessarily refers to the final
redemption and the Messianic state.[9]

Other pledges of certain salvation occur in the Pentateuch. Deut. 4:29-30 reads: "But from thence ye will seek

---

[9]Ha-Geula, p. 6.

the Lord thy God and thou shalt find Him if thou wilt
search after Him with all thy heart and all thy soul.
In thy distress when all these things are come upon thee,
in the end of days, thou wilt return to the Lord thy God."
For two reasons, it is impossible that these verses refer
to the return of the people from Babylon. From the
general nature of the promise, it is clear that all Israel
will benefit. However, only a fraction of the people was
restored from the Babylonian captivity. Again, chrono-
logically, "end of days" implies a much more distant time
than that of the Babylonian event. Furthermore, the
Mosaic promise presupposes a moral condition of the
world that would make it ripe for a climacteric redemption.

Balaam's four oracles are taken to be a progressive
unfolding of Israel's history. The first oracle states the
unique position of the people under Providence. Israel is
the select of God and under His control. No star or celestial power can change her destiny, and she is immune from
the curses and contrivings of the guardian angels of nations. The second prophecy of Balaam presages the conquest of the Holy Land. The third foretells the tranquility
and the ascendancy of Israel in Palestine under the first
kings. The last oracle, Num. 24:17-19, is Messianic. "I
see him but not now." It signifies the mystery and the
remoteness of the Messiah's domination over the entire
world. It cannot point to the gallant King David, because
he appeared four hundred years after Balaam, while "in
the end of days" and "not now" seem to imply a much
more distant occurrence.[10] The comparison of the Messiah to a star is apt. As the stars are at extreme distances
from the earth, and yet are a unified system under the
direction of a divine intelligence, so the Messiah will
gather in all Israel, even if they be dispersed to the farthest
corners of the earth.

---

[10]Ha-Geula, p. 7.

b. Prophets.

Nahmanides cites what he deems unmistakable testimonies of the future redeemer in the prophets. He refers to commentators who conveniently divide the book of Isaiah into three parts: chapters 1-39, which tell principally of Israel's plight and the eminence of Hezekiah; 40-51, depicting deliverance from Babylon; 51:12 to the end, the import of which is Messianic. The idealizations (consolations) in the first part of Isaiah are said by many to be directed toward Hezekiah. Some of these have been realized. Others are of a mixed character, that is, historical and eschatological. It is patent that the exaggerated prophecies were not fulfilled at any time in the past. We must therefore wait for their realization in the person and period of King Messiah. Nahmanides attempts to prove his point also by explaining that the Isaianic predictions were conditional upon the merit of Hezekiah and his people. If they proved worthy, the Messianic drama might be staged in their time and all the marvels might come to pass. But as they were found undeserving, the fulfillment of the prophecies must be postponed to a future time. The sage strengthens his contention by arguing that the conditional character of the promises did not lapse upon the return from Babylon. The nation always possesses the privilege and the ability to merit salvation through repentance.

Nahmanides correctly refers Isaiah 53 to the past, present, and future experiences of the nation. "My servant," in 52:13, is equated with the same term in 44:2 and 49:3, where it signifies Israel. However, he sees fit to expound it also in accordance with the tradition which applies it to the future advent.[11] The chapter speaks of the reproach to be heaped upon the Messiah at his coming,

---

[11]Yalk. Shim. on Is. 52 and 53.

and how at last he will be accepted during his life-time. He will be invincible and invulnerable.

"Behold my servant shall be wise" means that the Messiah will sense the ripeness of the time for his manifestation.

"He shall be exalted and lifted up"—to perform great things for Israel.

"He was despised"—like Moses riding upon an ass.

"Man of pains"—grieving over the sins of the people which retarded the advent. The Christological explanation of the chapter is made impossible by the absence of any reference to the crucifixion. Nowhere is it stated that "he would be slain or hung upon a tree"; on the contrary, the very opposite is foretold of the promised one. It is stated that he would have children and a long life.

Is. 63:4 reads: "For the day of vengeance that was in my heart, and my year of redemption are come." As the redemption of Israel did not follow the day of God's vengeance upon Edom, we must wait for it. It is still bound up in the bosom of time. Is. 65:17 describes the altered condition of the world in the Messianic age. There will be a new heaven and a new earth. The youngest person will live a hundred years. This is not sheer exaggeration or fancy, it will be so actually. The fact that the prophet particularizes and states specific numbers, proves that he is not talking figuratively. The world will renew its infancy, and man will again attain a great age, as did Adam and Methusaleh in the antediluvian period.

Jeremiah, too, prophesied the liberation of Israel from its present exile. In 30:24 and 31:1 he says, "In the end of days, ye shall consider it. At that time, saith the Lord, will I be the God of all the families of Israel, and they shall be My people." The return from Babylon was too near Jeremiah's time to be designated as an event of the "end of days." Besides, the verse includes in the reclama-

THE DOCTRINE OF THE MESSIAH

tion all the families of Israel, the twelve tribes. The earlier deliverance, however, included only the southern tribes. It must necessarily follow that Jeremiah had in mind the final redemption by the Messiah.

Ezekiel repeatedly announced the re-establishment of the northern and southern tribes, and their complete fusion into one indissoluble state. This did not occur in the return under Cyrus. Chapter 38, concerning Gog, is unquestionably concerned with the future redemption. The distribution of land to the tribes and families, as detailed in Chapters 47 and 48, had never been made, nor do we know of any waters that issued from under the threshold of the "house." These things, therefore, must come to pass in the future. Likewise, we must still look for the realization of the glorious utterances of Zechariah and Obadiah, for their prophecies were made after the departure from Babylon.

Nahmanides controverts the view that the restoration under Cyrus was the great deliverance that the people and prophets had anticipated. This could not have been, he states, because the return from Babylon was by no means complete. Only the tribes of Judah and Benjamin responded to the proclamation, and consequently the return was on too small a scale to be final. It was like a fugitive's escape to his old haunt. "The words of the prophets," he says, "are loud and firm for the ingathering, and for salvation, but the individuals who are thus saved must not flee like thieves to return to their land."[12] Prophecy is one of the spiritual boons promised in the restored state, but in the second commonwealth it flourished for only a little while, at the beginning. Hence the continued hope for a Messianic state in which prophecy will flourish uninterruptedly.

Nahmanides combats the Christological explanation of Daniel. He holds that the seventy weeks or 490 years

[12]Ha-Geula, p. 16.

— 172 —

(70 weeks of years), forecast in Ch. 9:24, measure the time from the close of the first commonwealth to the end of the second.[13] This period is divided into three parts, consisting of seven weeks of years, sixty-two weeks of years, and one week of years. At the end of seven weeks (v. 25), or 49 years, the anointed prince, namely, Zerubabel, will appear. This could not have been a prediction of the coming of Jesus, because he was born more than 500 years after the rebuilding of the second Temple. Verse 26, "And after 62 weeks, 434 years, shall an anointed one be cut off," points to Agrippa. "And the people of a prince that shall come shall destroy the city and the sanctuary" (v. 26) foretells the devastation of Europe. "To seal vision and prophet" (v. 24) alludes to the advent, at which time prophecy would reach its consummation and fulfillment. In making the words "to anoint the most holy place" (v. 24) refer to the Messianic David, Nahmanides differs from most Jewish commentators. Sarcastically he remarks that the predictions unfulfilled at the advent of Jesus do not vex his followers, who declare that he will come again to fulfill what had been left unrealized.[14]

4—The "End."

We cannot help seeing a double conflict of motives and actions in Nahmanides' treatment of the year of the advent. Fixing the time of the "end," he admits, is of primary concern to him. Yet, his finding is tentative.[15] He is aware that the Talmud disapproves of Messianic calculations, but at the same time, permits himself to indulge in them. True, the sages were right to advise prudence. They knew with what hope the people awaited a

---

[13]This accords with the opinion of R. Jose, who says, "From the destruction of the first Temple to that of the second Temple was seventy weeks of seven years"; Seder Olam Rabba ed. by Ratner, Ch. 28.

[14]Ha-Geula, p. 9.

[15]*Ibid.* p. 30.

projected "end," and the Messiah's failure to appear at the putative date.[16] Then, too, the vitality of Israel was so low that it would no more be sensible to knowledge of the "end" than would a dead body to a keen knife in its flesh. Again, what encouragement could the attempt to ascertain the "end" provide for Israel, in view of the failure of the redeemer to arrive at the "ends" computed by "the mighty ones" of the past? Nahmanides excused his own efforts in this direction on the ground that he was living in the "end of days," and that therefore his computation could not be erroneous, and was allowable. He adds that the providential design to conceal the "end" might have been given up, since the right and suitable year of grace is nigh.

How near, indeed, is it? There are two ways of answering this question, both of which Nahmanides follows. The Great Fulfillment will occur when Israel repents. The weight of our sins, however, has projected this event far into the future. Nevertheless he could not resist the temptation of believing in an end, which is calculable and definitive. It is disclosed a number of times in Daniel. The cryptic phrase, "until a time, times, and half a time," recurring in 7:25 and 12:7, yields a clue to the appointed year, which even Daniel could not unravel. He admitted: "And I heard but understood not." "Time," he calculated, equals 440 years of servitude in Egypt, and "times" equals 880. Hence 440 plus 880 plus half of 440 equal 1540, the number of years that Israel will be subject to Rome. Roman domination began 138 B. C. E.; hence Israel's liberation will take place in 1302. Chapter 12:11 gives the year—"From the time that the continual burnt offering shall be taken away and the detestable thing that causeth appalment set up, there shall be 1290 days." Days

---

[16]*Ibid.*, p. 29.

stand for years. The redemption will be enacted 1290 years after the ruin of the second temple, in 1358 C. E.[17] The Messiah ben Ephraim will appear that year, wipe out idolatry, gather in Israel, and lead them to the Holy Land. These tasks will require forty years. At the end of that period, the Messiah ben David will arrive, wage war with Gog, and subject Israel to a final test of loyalty. His preliminary tasks will consume five years. Hence in 1403 C. E. they will be firmly and peaceably settled on their own soil, under the Messiah ben David. In this way, Nahmanides explains the discrepancy between 1290 in verse 11 and 1335 in verse 12. To the objection that an individual cannot wait 1335 years, Nahmanides answers that the thought is of Israel the nation, hoping for deliverance century after century.

This date is confirmed by Dan. 8:13: "Then I heard a holy one speaking; and another holy one said unto that certain one who spoke, 'How long shall be the vision concerning the continual burnt-offering, and transgression that causeth appalment, to give both the sanctuary and the host to be trampled under foot?' And he said unto me: Unto 2300 evenings and mornings; then shall the sanctuary be victorious." 2300 represented the years from the beginning of King David's rule until the termination of the present exile. This is the calculation:

Reign of David	40 years
First Commonwealth	410 years
Second Commonwealth	490 years
From Destruction to Messiah	1335 years
	2275 years

The 25 years which 2275 lacked of 2300 is explained by the phrase "ad erev" (toward evening) which signified

---

[17]A similar date is given by Levi b. Gerson, in his Comm. on Daniel. Rashi's date was 1352.

that 2300 was not to be the precise year of the advent, but that it would occur several years sooner.

Nahmanides also indulged in gematria, the addition of letter values, to substantiate a given interpretation. Thus, imbedded in' Gen. 15:13, he found that the dura- tion of the exile was to be 1293 years.[18] This equals the 1290 years given in Daniel as the duration of the exile, plus half of the week, approximately three years., Deut. 4:30 equals 1291;[19] from the destruction until the arrival of the Messiah ben Ephraim. The adverse criticism of those who held that this method was an abuse of the Bible, that it was irrational, and that it could be used to prove almost anything caused Nahmanides to reply that the use of gematria had always been sanctioned in Agadic and even legal matters, and that Messianic numerations had been handed down as authentic tradition from Moses at Sinai.[20]

5—*The Disputation with Pablo Christiani.*

a. Questions at Issue.

The public debate between Moses ben Nahman and Pablo Christiani, an apostate Jew, was held in Barcelona, Spain, in the year 1263, before King James of Aragon. It is of primary importance in this study because much of the argument centered on the Messianic question. The three principal points argued were: first, whether the Mes- siah had already appeared as Christians believed; second, whether he was divine or human; and third, whether Jews or Christians possessed the true faith. Of this spectacular four-days disputation, the victorious Nahmanides, himself, left a record.[21] Controversies of this sort were provoked

---

[18]This was obtained by calculating the numerical value of the Hebrew passage, "And they shall afflict them 400 years."

[19]Obtained from the Hebrew passage, "In thy distress, when all these things are come upon thee, in the end of days."

[20]Ha-Geula, p. 4.

[21]Wikkuah ha-Ramban, ed. Steinschneider, Stettin, 1860, see Revue des Etudes Juives Vol. XV, pp. 1-18. The sessions were held on July 20th, 27th, 30th and 31st.

frequently by Christian zealots, and the Jews in self-respect and self-defense, had to meet the challenge.[22] These disputes cast a significant light on the precarious situation of the oppressed race in Catholic Spain. During the period of the dispute the Jews lived in a state of alarm and fear, for regardless of the logic and merit exhibited by their learned and imposing spokesmen, the outcome of each debate was usually a fresh assault upon the holy congregation. To the strenuous and often burdensome duties and sacrifices of the Jewish leaders and rabbis was added the ordeal of being summoned to defend their ancestral faith in the presence of royalty and the highest clergy. As we look back today at those scenes from our point of vantage, we draw courage and satisfaction from the fact that the synagogue, even during that era of rigorous oppression, showed sufficient strength to be deemed worthy of being a rival of the Church. In the debate under consideration, Nahmanides easily won the laurels of victory. Nahmanides remained in the city to await the king's visit to the synagogue on August 8th, as had been arranged, and as a token of good will the king gave him three hundred gold dinars and royal protection on his homeward journey. However, the bigotry of the Dominicans reasserted itself. In the next year, 1264, all Hebrew books in Aragon were confiscated and anti-Christian passages struck out. Nahmanides' published account of the controversy was condemned, and he was ordered to leave the country.

b. The Belief Not Central in Judaism.

Nahmanides gained a point over his opponent, when he declared to the king that the Messianic belief is not the pivot of Judaism, as it is of Christianity. The whole of

---

[22]The principal disputations in the middle ages, besides the one in which Nahmanides participated, were (1) Paris, 1240; (2) Burgos and Avila, 1375; (3) Pampeluna, c. 1373; (4) Tortosa, Feb. 1413, Nov. 1414; (5) Granada, c. 1430. See ibn Verga, "Shebet Yehuda".

the new religion hinges upon Jesus as the central and indispensable divine savior. But Judaism has flourished through the centuries without any Messiah whatsoever. The Hebrew's obligation is to the Torah, and not to a Messiah. The Jewish concept of a future redeemer is not one who will displace God, but rather of a human sovereign who will exercise political dominion and be invested with spiritual leadership. The Messiah will be born of human parents, from the family of David.[23]

Another consideration which makes the Messianic dogma of lesser import to the Jew than to the Christian is that the latter requires Jesus—the Messiah—for his salvation, while the former needs no such pillar to lean upon in order to earn for himself an eternal reward. The vexed Israelite, who in dispersion serves his God, Creator, and Preserver, and martyrs himself for his religion, is deserving of a richer reward than that due to a faithful Jew for obedience to the King Messiah in the future golden age. The former has met the test of courage, and loyalty, while the latter will follow with ease the higher law of the new era, because all his foes will have been vanquished, his nature purged, and the blandishments of enemies will not mislead him into ignoble ways.[24]

c. Sages Rejected the Alleged Christian Redeemer.

At the outset Pablo tries to prove from the Talmud and Midrash that the redeemer had already come in the person of Jesus. Even our sages believed this. To this premise, the rabbi replied that if the doctors of the Talmud had accepted Jesus as a Messiah, they would have abandoned their own faith, apostasized and adopted the new discipline.[25] Instead, we know that they did not alter their Judaism, but abided in their original faith and died pro-

---

[23]Gen. 49:10; Is. 11:1.
[24]Schechter, Studies in Judaism, First Series, p. 106.
[25]Wikkuah, p. 6.

fessing Jews. In fact, the Talmud, which, according to the antagonist, is suspected of exerting a Christian influence on Israel, is today a source and bulwark of traditional Judaism.

Nahmanides fearlessly and unequivocally denied that the Messiah had appeared. As for Jesus, he himself and no one else proclaimed his Messiahship. He appeared as the living, divinely appointed Messiah. As such he had the rare opportunity to present his credentials and to gain the confidence of our forefathers. It is claimed for him that he displayed superhuman power. If so, he should have been able to convince and convert all. Yet his authority was denied by many. In view of his own failure, how weak and blatant are the arguments in favor of his Messiahship, framed by kings and apostates who mouth the traditions and legends fabricated after his death.

For many other reasons it is impossible to accept him. Principally, he fell short of the ideal of the redeemer and the scope of power that was claimed for him. Ps. 72:8 characterizes the Messiah's might as existent everywhere. "May he have dominion also from sea to sea, and from the river unto the ends of the earth." But the alleged Messiah wielded no power; instead he was pursued and persecuted. He was a victim instead of a victor. He could not save himself, much less deliver Israel and mankind. Nor did he possess any latent power which ripened and grew effective after his death. It was not through his influence that the solid Roman Empire was built. Rome was in the ascendancy many years before he appeared. Nor does Christendom even today represent the sole universal imperium. It is challenged by Mohammedanism, and other mighty religions which hold sway over great sections of humanity. Besides, the millennial blessings of the universal knowledge of God, of peace, and of widespread innocence and joy, did not descend upon the earth when the pretended Messiah appeared. Instead violence, immorality, strife, and terror—often incited by Christians themselves—increased. Another undoubted mission of the Messiah was to enhance the prestige of Israel. He was to gather in all the twelve tribes. He was to rebuild the Temple and shield Israel with his rod and sword. But none of these tasks did he perform. The reverse happened, and the followers of the pretended Messiah have become the inveterate foes of the Jewish people.

d. Interpretations of Shiloh, Is. 53, Book of Daniel.

The method of the debate was by affirmation and refutation. Pablo quoted Hebrew texts to establish his claims, which Nahmanides readily refuted. Once in the course of the dispute Nahmanides, wishing to be on the offensive, asked for the privilege of interrogating his op-ponent. The presiding king denied his request. Pablo first confronted the rabbi with Gen. 49:10: "The scepter shall not depart from Judah . . . as long as men come to Shiloh." Shiloh, he argued, meant the Messiah. The verse predicted that when Israel suffered the loss of her national power, the Messiah would appear to safeguard and control her destiny. Pablo contended that the suprem-acy of Judah had ended with the destruction of the Temple, and that the Messiah, indicated by the phrase *ad ki yovo Shiloh*, had appeared. To this Nahmanides retorted that the verse did not foretell the termination of Hebrew nationality, but only its suspension, and that the Messiah's coming still was an event of the future.[26]

The loss of Jewish independence is only temporary, like the intermission of Hebrew kings in the Babylonian exile and in the Hasmonean era. Pablo countered with the assertion that the absence of Hebrew kings for 1000 years, truly an abnormal length for a nation, is decisive proof

---

[26]Wikkuah, pp. 7, 8.

that the scepter of Judah had irrecoverably departed. The fact is that even Jewish ecclesiastical authority had ceased with the loss of temporal power. Rabbinic ordination has fallen into desuetude. The very title Rabbi and Maestro, borne by Nahmanides is a misnomer.[27] Nahmanides facetiously admitted that he may not be a Maestro, not even a scholar of any merit, but he would have his opponent remember that ordination actually was continued until the fifth century of the present era.

The apostate adduced further arguments from Isaiah, chapters 52 and 53, beginning, "Behold My servant shall prosper; he shall be exalted and lifted up, and shall be very high." This section, he contended, related the death of the alleged Messiah. In reply, the rabbi unafraid stated the correct view accepted by most critical scholars today: that the "servant" is collective Israel, personified as the humble servant of God. This is borne out by Isaiah 44:1, and 45:4 where Israel is clearly referred to as the servant. Pablo argued that the sages construe the chapter Messianically.[28] This, admitted the rabbi, is true, but the chapter does *not* mention crucifixion, and nowhere in the great writings do we meet with the conception of a crucified Messiah who would be hung among criminals. The sufferings spoken of in verses 3 and 4 represent the redeemer grieving over the sins of Israel, which retard his coming, but they do not refer to the Passion. Hence the interpretation of this chapter by some rabbis may be Messianic, but it is not Christological.

Nahmanides vigilantly and dextrously met the sallies of his opponent against the Book of Daniel. Pablo tried to read Christological references into Daniel 9:24, 25— "Seventy weeks are decreed upon thy people and upon thy holy city, to finish the transgression, and to make an end

---

[27]On the conferring of the title Rabbi in Talmudic era, see Moore, Judaism III, pp. 15-17.
[28]Yalk. Shim., Is. 52-13 and 53. Wikkuah, p. 9.

of sin, and to forgive iniquity, and to bring in everlasting righteousness, and to seal vision and prophecy, and to anoint the most holy place." The apostate avers that 70 weeks of years or 490 years signify the duration of the second Temple, including 70 years of the captivity. The terms "most holy" and "the anointed prince" both apply to Jesus. To all of which Nahmanides responded by saying that Jesus lived at least 70 years before the nation fell, and so the term "most holy" cannot mean him. Neither is he the "prince" predicted at the end of seven weeks, for he appeared at a later period. In these passages, Scripture speaks of Zerubabel. The title, Messiah, "anointed one," may be correctly conferred upon him, only as it had been upon Cyrus and the patriarchs, in a generic sense.

e. Agadah is not Authoritative.

Pablo resorted to several fanciful legends in his attempt to convince the Jewish sage that the Messiah had already performed his task. In explaining these legends, Nahmanides made it clear that they need not be accepted at their face value and as authoritative. We have three literary sources of Judaism: the Talmud, which amplified the basic laws and which is binding upon us; the Bible, to which we owe unstinted faith; and the Midrash, which our author translates by the Latin word, "sermones," sermons —personal opinions and embellishments which carry no authoritative weight. One need not believe the Midrash. It neither harms nor benefits.[29]

The following legend was first offered by the apostate as proof of the Messiah's birth.[30] "An Arab was traveling through the Holy Land, and came upon a Hebrew farmer plowing his field. He heard the ox bellow and straightway

---

[29]Wikkuah, p. 10.

[30]Yerush. Ber. II, 4; 17b; Ekah Rabbati I, 57; Wikkuah, pp. 8, 9.

exclaimed: 'O Hebrew, leave thy ox and thy plow, for the Temple is destroyed.' The Jew did so. A short while thereafter the ox bellowed again, and the Arab called out: 'Yoke thy ox, for your Messiah is born.' " To the astonishment of Pablo, Nahmanides declared that he did not believe the story. It probably had a mysterious import, but even if it related an actual occurrence, it could not be accepted because it was inaccurate and belied historical facts. If the Messiah was born the day the Temple was ruined, the date of his birth was 70 C. E. Actually, Jesus was born long before then—some 200 years before the destruction.[30a] Furthermore, the tale does not say that he came, but that he was born. It is worthwhile to note the distinction. The mention of his *birth* leads to the view that an interval will elapse between his birth and public appearance, for he must be hailed everywhere and anointed, before he enters upon his redemptive mission.

The familiar story of Joshua ben Levi and Elijah is then cited by the Dominican priest.[31] The saint once asked Elijah: "When will the Messiah come?" The prophet replied: "Ask the Messiah himself." "Where is he?" "At the gates of Rome among the sick." He went and found him there and interrogated him. Nahmanides cleverly replied that the tale showed plainly that the Messiah had not yet entered upon his mission, for why else would Joshua B. Levi inquire about his advent? Here King James interposed the following objection: "If the Messiah was born on the day the Temple was ruined, he is now more than 1000 years old. This is incredible and impossible; it is contrary to human experience and natural law." The sage quickly responded that Adam and Methusaleh had enjoyed similar longevity, and that Elijah and Enoch had even longer lives. They are deathless. Life is

---

[30a]For this legend see Sefer Yuhasin ed Filipowski, 1857, p. 15a.
[31]San. 98a. Wikkuah, p. 9.

a gift of God, and, following the Talmud, he claimed that Ps. 21:5 referred to the Messiah.[32]

> "He asked life of Thee, thou gavest it him;
> Even length of days, for ever and ever."

f. Messiah is not Divine.

When the Dominican broached the second question of the debate, namely the divinity of the redeemer, Nahmanides pleaded that since he had successfully refuted the first premise that the Messiah had come, it was absurd to consider the question of his divinity. At another time, the rabbi refused to proceed because his Jewish constituents had asked him to end the controversy lest it should lead to dire consequences. The nobles, too, had confidently advised him that it was imprudent and dangerous to criticize the religion in power. He had unhorsed his opponent, but still he feared that the rascality and revenge of the bigoted Dominicans might bring harm upon his flock. The king, however, enjoyed the theological wrangle and insisted that the witty rabbi bring it to a finish in public.

Pablo contended that the alleged Messiah, Jesus, was divine, because the Midrash ranks the Messiah above the angels.[33] He cited Is. 52:13: "He shall be exalted and lifted up, and shall be very high,"—on which the Midrash comments that "he shall be superior to Abraham, Moses, and the angels." Nahmanides explained the passage as a simple homily. It is a usual expression to say that the righteous are superior to angels. It does not mean superior in divinity. Thus, when the Talmud declares that Israel is more beloved than angels, we are not to infer that Israel is more divine than angels.[34] The precise sense of the homily is that the Messiah will be bolder in affirm-

---

[32]Sukkah 52a. Wikkuah, p. 10.
[33]Yalk. Shim. on Is. 52:13.
[34]Hullin 19.

ing his trust in God and Israel than were Abraham, Moses and the angels. These three distinguished themselves in glorifying God; Abraham at great risk withdrew from idolatry; Moses fearlessly faced Pharaoh and demanded the release of the Hebrews; the angels bestir themselves for Israel's deliverance. The Messiah, however, will surpass them all in the heroic performance of his gigantic task. He will "enter in and lay his commands upon the pope and all the kings of the nations in the name of God, saying, Let my people go that they may serve me; not fearing them but performing in their midst great and destructive signs and wonders; he also will stand in their city, even in Rome until he lay it waste."

An interesting legend read to Nahmanides related that the Messiah supplicated God in behalf of Israel, and that he took upon himself sufferings in order that Israel's sins might be pardoned.[35] The Messiah declared: "I assume sufferings on condition that the resurrection occur in my days, and not only those who die in my time, but those who died since Adam; those also who died unnatural deaths, as from drowning and wild beasts." The apostate identified the Messiah of the Agadah with Jesus, and contended that his suffering was the crucifixion. This explanation provoked the rabbi to laughter. Jesus' very requests of God, he stated, show unmistakably that he was human, and had no power to revive the departed. We have no record that the alleged redeemer ever resurrected the dead, from Adam's time to our own. This legend merely declares that the true Messiah grieves and suffers because his intervention is delayed while everywhere Israel is in distress.

Another fantastic Agadah offered by the opponent told how the Messiah entered Paradise, and received shelter there as a reward for giving up idolatry.[36] Hence he

---

[35]Pesikta Rabati, ed. Friedman, ch. 38, p. 161b.
[36]Derek Eretz Zuta, end. Wikkuah, p. 11.

shared the divine nature, since he dwelt in Paradise. According to Nahmanides, the full statement clearly indicates that the Messiah was not considered a god. It speaks of fourteen persons, two of them women, who entered Paradise. Can it be supposed then that the divine redeemer has his abode among women? In the opinion of the Jewish spokesman the legend informs us that the Messiah still bides the time of his coming and is waiting in the Paradisaic mansion of Adam.

Pablo expounded Psalm 110 Messianically. He contended that the opening verse: "The Lord saith unto my Lord, 'Sit thou at my right hand,'" obviously speaks of the Messiah as divine, since "my Lord" implies divinity. If, as the Jews believed, the redeemer were human and of the family of David, he would not be graced with the name "Lord." Nahmanides, in his rejoinder, explained that the psalm must be understood in its historical setting. Actually, it speaks of David, and only symbolically of his spiritual successor, the Messiah. The psalm was sung by the Levites, who called David their "Lord." "Sit thou at my right hand" should not be taken corporeally. The "right hand" of God, often mentioned in the Bible, is the emblem of His might. The meaning of the psalm is that God has ever shielded David and gifted him with extraordinary strength. Pablo justified his argument by resorting to the Messianic interpretation given to this psalm by our sages.[37] They say, he pointed out, that in the future world God will seat the Messiah on His right, and Abraham on His left. Nahmanides, quoting the second half of the legend, laid bare the fallacy of Pablo's claim. This part reads: "The face of Abraham will turn crimson, and he will say, 'My grandson will sit on God's right and I on the left?' But God will conciliate him." From this it is self-evident that the Messiah is no god. If he were, the patriarch would

---

[37] Yalk. Shim. on Ps. 110.

feel no embarrassment nor ill-will because a god should receive greater honor than he. Furthermore, he is represented as occupying a seat in the same physical sense as Abraham. Lastly, the legend speaks of the Messiah in the future, while Jesus has already appeared.

Finally, the apostate referred to the Midrashic commentary[38] on Gen. 1:2 in which it is stated that the words "The spirit of God hovered over the face of the waters" means that "the spirit of the Messiah moved over the waters." Hence, the Messiah is not human but divine. To this Nahmanides straightway replied that the same paragraph declares the "spirit of God" to mean the "spirit of Adam." Shall we conclude that Adam was a god?

It might have been expected among the Jews that Nahmanides, the foremost Talmudic sage of his day, and the master of many sciences, would be more than a match for the apostate Pablo. And so he was. If he could be vanquished, thought the Dominicans, the loss to the Jews would be overwhelming. With dignity, brilliance, a tolerant spirit, and a sense of humor, Nahmanides stood his ground against the challengers, and his triumph in this memorable disputation adds to the prestige of his illustrious name.

6—*Eschatology.*

a. Sequence of Eschatological Periods.

Of the utmost importance in studying Nahmanides' theology is his view of the Hereafter. He has expressed his thoughts on it clearly and quite fully unlike Maimonides who hesitated to describe specifically the character of the world to come. In fact, Nahmanides and Maimonides have often been contrasted for their divergent eschato-

---

[38]Ber. Rabba. II, 5.

logical principles. The sequence of the eschatological periods,[39] according to Nahmanides, is as follows:

1. Paradise and Gehinnom. The souls of the righteous and wicked repair to these now existent regions immediately after death. The Olam ha-Neshamoth (world of souls) is Paradise.

2. Messianic Age, which will last during the sixth millennium.

3. Judgment Day, for eternal reward and punishment. There are two other judgment periods, one is the New Year Day, when every person is tried and his fortune and welfare upon earth is determined; the second is the judgment at death, when the soul's fate in the world of souls is decreed.

4. Resurrection, reward for body and soul.

5. Future World, where the bodies will become spiritualized and the souls will attain the highest degree of divine knowledge.

b. Paradise and Hell are Actual Places.

Our author does not, like many of the philosophers in his own day and in ours, explain Paradise and Hell as mere personal states of feeling. He mentions, especially, his disagreement with Maimonides, who suggested that Hell (Gehinnom) is a figurative term to describe the suffering of the wicked. To Nahmanides, it is an actual place existing in space. In Gehinnom the souls of the sinful suffer in a manner which we cannot know or conceive. We can experience corporeal punishment only; but soul-punishment is of a higher order and of greater intensity. Punishment varies according to the nature of the subject upon which it is inflicted. If the subject belongs to a higher

---

[39]This section on Eschatology is based on the Shaar ha-Gemul.

species, its pain will be keener. Thus man is more sensitive to pain than the beasts. And even among men there are different degrees of suffering occasioned by the same amount of torture, the degree varying according to the individual's mental and moral development. The doom of the wicked will not be delayed until the Messianic age or the world to come, but will commence soon after death. The first instinctive movement of the sinful soul, when released from the body, is upward unto its pure source; but the weight of its sins will keep it down. It will be drawn into the fiery sphere, thence to be dragged into the river of fire which flows through Gehinnom.

The author discusses Maimonides' opinion that the wicked soul does not continue to exist after death, but is at once destroyed.[40] This immediate annihilation, which deprives it of participation in the future world, is said by Maimonides to be its greatest punishment. Nahmanides seeks to harmonize this idea with his own, that the sinful soul survives and receives punishment. He asserts that Maimonides' view of the soul's annihilation refers to its final stage, after it has passed through its necessary period of punishment. In another statement, Maimonides distinguishes between moderately sinful persons, who will undoubtedly suffer for their sins and recover their moral balance to receive their share in the world to come, and the heretics, who will be condemned to everlasting extinction.

Paradise is the counterpart of Hell. It is the place which the righteous enter after death. There they receive what they have merited while they were alive, not, however, in its entirety. The complete reward is reserved for them in the future world.

---

[40]Mishneh Torah, Sefer ha Mada.

THE DOCTRINE OF THE MESSIAH

Nahmanides states clearly his conviction that Paradise, too, is an actual place. Gen. 1:10, he says, gives an accurate description of it. Its location is now unknown; the ancients knew where it is, and men of science have located Paradise under the equator. Early Greek medical books and Asaph, the Jew, tell of an expedition made to India by Aesculapius and forty scholars in search of the tree of life and curative plants.[41] They came within the confines of Paradise, saw the flashes of the revolving sword, and were all consumed by the fiery sparks which flew from it.

As Nahmanides stated clearly that the Messianic belief is part of the doctrine of reward and punishment, so he no doubt had greater reason to connect the belief in the existence of Paradise and Gehinnom with the same doctrine. It was Maimonides who in his introduction to Mishna Sanhedrin, Ch. XI, asserted that these were not the highest motives and best guarantee for eternal life. But then it should be remembered that Nahmanides belonged to a different school. His entire theology was materialistic and represented a system of thought which Maimonides tried to combat in his Guide and the theological parts of the Mishneh Torah.

But if Paradise is a terrestrial, substantial, and dimensional abode, how can we conceive of it as suitable for the soul's reward? Such reward must obviously be spiritual and celestial. Nahmanides solves this difficulty by supposing both an earthly and a celestial Paradise.

The disembodied souls share in the pleasures of the lower and upper Paradise. This is explained according to Sabbath 152b, which says: "Until twelve months after death, the body remains, and the soul ascends and

---

[41]To Asaph, the Jew, was attributed a medical book mentioned by a number of Jewish Medievalists, Donolo (925) Hai Gaon, Rashi, and Kimhi. Aesculapius was the Greek and Roman God of medicine. See Bet Ha-Midrash III, pp. 155-156, where these two figures are mentioned and L. Venetianer, Asaf-Judaeus, Strassburg, 1917.

descends." For the first year, then, the soul shares an attachment with the body, and is weighted down by the burden of its past corporeal existence. It must, therefore, find gratification in the lower Paradise, and prepare itself for full entrance into the realm of rarefied souls. The upper Paradise is where the purest souls gather for eternal bliss. The souls will dwell in the celestial Paradise, until God summons all of them, good and bad, to judgment. According to His sentence, they will join their former bodies, and the great miracle of the reawakening will have become a reality. In defense of the resurrection Nahmanides quotes Talmudic proofs derived from forced interpretations of the Bible. He does not doubt the soundness of these proofs, nor does he see any difficulty in accepting the doctrine. It is an axiom of faith, like the mathematical axiom that two plus two are four. The resurrected persons will be denizens of the future world, which will be a new world created by God after resurrection. Qualitatively it will mark the acme of man's progress toward the divine.

Chapter IX

HASDAI CRESCAS

1—*Crescas and Maimonides Compared.*

Hasdai Crescas (Spain, 1340-1410) rabbi, philosopher, and leader, whose fame passed beyond the boundary of his native city and province, and who became the ardent spokesman of Jews and Judaism, was among the last in the galaxy of immortal philosopher-rabbis of the Middle Ages. Vast erudition and a new theological outlook won for him the esteem of his own age, and he exercised a strong and beneficent moral influence over his times. His friendship with the rulers and nobility of Spain enabled him to intervene for the Jews in time of trouble and there was indeed, trouble enough. The following historic reminder will illustrate the unhappy situation which rabbi and congregation faced in those days. For several centuries the beautiful skies of Spain had showered a golden light of spirituality and intellectualism upon Israel, and except for a few clouds which sporadically darkened the horizon, Israel prospered. Toward the end of the fourteenth century, however, it became the avowed policy of the Church to convert or to crush the Jew. In 1391, Spain instituted the fatal policy of persecution with its forced conversions, its *auto-da-fes,* and its expulsions. Hasdai Crescas did not escape the general misfortune. He too drank from the bitter cup of persecution. His only son met death at his own hands rather than embrace the religion of the persecutors. There is extant a letter sent by Crescas to the Jews of Avignon in 1393, in which he describes the extermination during the preceding year of the holy congregations in Seville, Cordova, Toledo,

Valencia, Majorca, Barcelona, Laredo, and Gerona.[1] The communication speaks of the defections from the Jewish fold, and as a contrast, of the thousands who accepted martyrdom rather than abjure their faith. As Maimonides has become the standard by which to gauge other scholars of his stamp, a brief comparison of the two may prove beneficial. Both sought to achieve one supreme purpose; to propagate their holy faith. This they did by declaring its excellence, by rationalizing it, by showing how it accorded with the dictates of reason, and how it could meet the challenge of opposing and alluring faiths. The quest of Crescas was to find a means to harmonize religion or Judaism with common sense. In his "Light of the Lord", one of the choice literary products of Jewish scholasticism, he sought to carry out this aim. Although it is not as comprehensive nor as large as Maimonides' "Guide of the Perplexed", it is quite as profound and subtle.

In the main, his task and endeavors coincided with those of Maimonides, yet they differed in a number of ways. Each saw Judaism and life from a slightly different angle. The ideal of a good life, according to Crescas, is ethical; according to Maimonides, it is philosophic. The former believed that the object of the Torah-discipline was to effect the moral advancement of the human species, to refine human nature, to establish society on the immovable foundation of justice, truth, and peace, and to lead man to a mountain-top where he may be suffused and sustained by faith, hope, light, and tranquility. Maimonides, on the other hand, believed that the most desirable perfection to be attained was intellectual, and that the ideal world will be possible only when every man's mind reaches such maturity and power that it will grasp the philosophic basis

---

[1]The letter is printed in the edition of the Shebet Jehuda, by Dr. M. Wiener, Hanover, 1924—p. 128.

of God, of soul, of the world's beginning, of nature's laws and of the other imponderables which are at present un-known to us. In the introduction to the "Light of the Lord", Crescas rehearsed the familiar contentions of the Anti-Maimonists. He made little of the intellectual gym-nastics of Maimonides and his love of Aristotelianism. He opposed their synthesis into any system of Jewish phil-osophy and condemned Maimonides for using the proposi-tions of the Stagyrite as premises for the Jewish belief in one God. He held that while Maimonides may have acted in good faith and was well fortified in his logic, many scholars who came after him abused his method and thereby were led to heretical conclusions. Crescas also deplored the manner of the great codifier in stating deci-sions and opinions in the Mishneh Torah without giving their sources and divergent views.[2]

2—*Dogmas of Judaism.*

For our purpose, the chief line of cleavage between Maimonides and Crescas is their divergent concepts of Jewish dogmas. Maimonides had proposed thirteen card-inal principles, making no gradations as to their relative importance. His creed, which eventually won favor, was differently received. Some criticized it as being either too inclusive or too exclusive. Following his example it be-came the vogue to make dogmatic formulations of Judaism. Crescas represents one of the more important dissenters from the Maimonidean creed. He was selective, and divided the articles of belief into four groups, to each of which he devoted a section of his book. The first section deals with the existence of God, the root and indispensable belief of all religions. Without God, creation and life are unthinkable. This assumption is not only Jewish but universal. Hence he does not consider the existence of

---

[2]End of introduction to "Light of the Lord" (*Or Adonai*).

God a distinctive Jewish principle. The cardinal tenets of Judaism are six in number; Omniscience, Providence, Omnipotence, Prophecy, Free-will, and Purposefulness. These doctrines comprise the foundation stones of our religious structure, and without them Judaism ceases to be Judaism.

The third group embraces the generally accepted doctrines which are primarily Jewish, and consists of *creatio ex nihilo,* immortality, reward and punishment, resurrection, eternity of the Torah, supremacy of Moses as a prophet, the Urim and Thummim,[3] and the coming of the Messiah. These are binding upon the entire race, but are not basic to the faith. One who abandons any one of these teachings may be guilty of heresy but he cannot be accused of destroying the valid foundations of our faith. He has not denied Judaism, nor has he severed the bond that unites him to the congregation of Israel.

The last group consists of miscellaneous notions, which have not yet crystallized into definite principles, but concerning which we should nevertheless entertain the Jewish point of view. Among these are enumerated the teachings relative to Paradise and Gehinnom, devils, the first cause, transmigration, the multiplicity of worlds, and the indestructibility of the universe.

This selective classification of Jewish concepts indicates a finer discrimination of theological values and a more liberal attitude than is displayed in the thirteen formulations of Maimonides. Crescas manifested greater originality and self-reliance than his renowned predecessor. He dared to swim against the current of high philosophic opinion, to speculate on Jewish dogmas, and to unyoke Judaism from Arabic psychology and Aristotelian philosophy. The courage evinced by Crescas in

---

[3]Objects placed on the breastplate of the high priest, that served as a divine oracle (Ex. 28:30).

rejecting extraneous philosophic influence likewise accounts for his restatement of the essential doctrines of Judaism.

3—*Statement of the Belief.*

It is especially encouraging to note the straightforward manner with which Crescas deals with the subject of our study. Although he assigns a lesser dogmatic position to the Messianic belief he avers that the indisputable elements of the Messianic drama are derived from the Scriptures and are amplified by tradition.[4] He states the essential political Messianic belief that one who will arise from the seed of Jesse and David will be king and prophet. This Messiah will assemble and solder the dispersed tribes of Israel and Judah, and the state will never more be sundered. Neither will the government ever end, nor a Davidic ruler ever cease to occupy the throne chosen by God. The Messiah will be an extraordinarily perfect being, and as expounded in the Midrash, he will excel Moses and the angels. He will surpass the lawgiver in the possession of a composite perfection of the body and soul. This union will render the perfection of the Messiah even more remarkable and more unique than that of the angels, who are hampered by bodies.

In thus making the Messiah superior to Moses, Crescas parts company from Maimonides and others who held the contrary view in order to counteract the force of the Christian argument that their savior surpassed Moses. This question of the superiority of Moses or the Messiah involves also the doctrine of the Torah's immutability. The law of a Messiah superior to Moses, would naturally supersede the Torah. This is what Christians contend.

Concerning the Messiah ben Joseph, Crescas modestly affirms that he has little to say and he maintains that we

---

[4] *Or Adonai*, p. 81a.

have no certain knowledge of him in spite of the many prophecies and the Midrashim and geonic writings which set forth his activities.[5]

4—Controversial.

The bitter clash between the two religions and the alertness of versatile Jewish thinkers to throw down the gauntlet to the foe appears from the polemical essay "A Refutation of Christian Principles",[6] by Crescas, in which he enumerates ten Christian teachings which are controverted by Judaism. He analyzes the Church doctrines quite frankly, and successfully shows their fallacious and unhistorical character. The author argues that if the evidences of both religions were equal in number, credibility, and cogency, and were it difficult to decide to which religion the verdict should go, the benefit of the doubt would be in favor of the more ancient faith, Judaism. We are here concerned with what Crescas has to offer on the eighth debatable point, which deals with the Messiah. Christians believe that he has already appeared; we believe that he is still to come. His argument proceeds in the following manner. The savior did not possess the individuality attributed to the prophetic Messiah. He had neither divine wisdom nor prophecy. He did not spring of the consecrated Davidic family, nor did he ever attain a position of exalted and acknowledged authority. Neither in word or deed did he represent the glory of Jerusalem, of Israel, or of the Temple. What militates very strongly against our acceptance of him as the predicted redeemer, is the fact that his coming did not transform society. He did not inaugurate universal peace and justice, nor did he purge the uncleanliness of man.

---

[5]*Ibid.*

[6]Written in Spanish and translated by Joseph Shem-Tob, a polemist, into Hebrew in 1451.

It is also strange, notes Crescas, that the Christian Messiah, acclaimed as God's own messenger and the fulfillment of prophecy, should have been challenged in his own day. He was not even able to impress upon his own generation the truth that the Church claimed for him, to wit, that he had eradicated all wickedness from the earth. In fact, it is somewhat discreditable to assert that his advent as a Messiah had wiped out all sin, since the circumstances of his death are positive proof that the world was still in bondage to sin, and required purification. His very death placed a burden of guilt upon the shoulders of Israel. He condemned mankind and left the world in as pitiful a condition as he found it.

If the supposed Messiah had appeared for the purpose of wiping out all sin, then mankind today should be pure and faultless. Instead, the world is still immersed in wrongdoing and vanity. Crime, corruption, and misery abound. The tokens of spiritual supremacy—prophecy, priesthood, and the Urim and the Thummim—sacred in ancient Israel, which should have enjoyed an added influence have, instead, fallen into desuetude. Surely the guidance and inspiration of prophecy is needed today to lead mankind from error and hate. Sarcastically, Crescas points to the Christian schism of the rival popes as evidence that the prince of peace and unity has not appeared.[7]

5—Some Questions on the Redemption.

Among the vexing problems inherent in the Messianic belief is the question: "Will the Messianic era witness the supernatural events clearly foretold in the prophecies?" We cannot answer this question with certainty. There is, to be sure, the assertion of Samuel in the Talmud that the Messianic era will differ from the present order only in so far as Israel will then be free from foreign

---

[7]The rival popes were Urban VI and Clement VII, 1378-1417.

domination.[8] Another moot point concerns the resurrection: "Will it occur at the precise time of the Messiah's appearance or at a later stage?" However, the principal difficulty is concerning the commencement of the Messianic era. All endeavors to determine it must of necessity prove fruitless. Both Scripture and Talmud have taken a decidedly negative stand in the matter of Messianic calculation. The former boldly withholds the date: "I heard but did not understand, for the words were shut and sealed until the end of time."[9] As for the sages of the Talmud, they heaped curses upon those who would attempt to compute the "end."[10]

6—Explanation of the Present Prolonged Dispersion.

Concerning the cause of the prolonged exile and the appalling delay in the coming of the Messiah, Crescas had much more to say than upon the previous questions.[11] If we compare the length of the present exile with the previous one in Egypt and Babylon, we find that the present one is unreasonably longer than either of the former. The affliction in Egypt lasted 210 years, while the captivity in Babylon covered 70 years. The present dispersion seems interminable. The disproportion in the various exiles becomes more inexplicable if we seek their causes. Israel suffered expulsion in 586 B. C. because of the weight of its sinfulness. It committed the capital crimes of adultery, idolatry, murder, and public desecration of the Sabbath, all of which warrant severe punishment. But the subsequent exile brought on by Rome, was caused by the sin of unjustified animosity in their own ranks or by the lack of reverence for their sages. It is obvious that these offenses are not so grievous as the crimes which brought

---

[8]San. 99b.
[9]Daniel 12:8.
[10]San. 97b.
[11]Or Adonai, pp. 81a, 82b.

on the Babylonian exile, and therefore it seems that the penalty should not be so severe.

If we assume then, as we logically should, that the severity of the punishment is commensurate with the gravity of the offense, the present dispersion should be shorter than the earlier one. Then why has it lasted so long? The theologian opines that it is a mystery of the same sort as the baffling paradox of the prosperity of the wicked and the suffering of the righteous. It is simple enough for us to reason from cause to effect and to make inferences for we live in a small, bounded, accessible world. We create our own codes, and set our own standards and gradations of happiness. But, truly, our experiences and wisdom are inadequate for a full understanding of our life-course and destiny. We cannot grasp or fathom God's cosmic ways and purposes, nor do we comprehend the operation of the universe or His eternal standards of retribution.

Crescas also offers an historical explanation for Israel's long dispersion, namely, that it is a continuation of the earlier expulsion of the Jews to Babylon.[12] Israel is still paying the penalty for grievous crimes and errors which date back to the time of the Kings. The release of the Jews by Cyrus the Persian, in 536, was not a final and complete redemption of Israel, but merely a respite. This view is supported by the fact that only a fraction of the people returned to Palestine and dwelt there under foreign sway. While on this subject Crescas expounds Psalm 136:23-25 in a Midrashic way. "Who remembered us in our low estate," he states, implies God's visitation, not the redemption of the people in Babylon. "And hath delivered us from our adversaries" refers to the forthcoming complete deliverance of the people. The amelioration of mankind and God's providential rule over the world are in-

---

[12]*Ibid.*, p. 82a.

timated in the words: "Who giveth food to all flesh"; for
in that blessed day all mankind will be sustained by the
grace and glory of God.

Despite its length and burden of sorrow, the dispersion is not an unmitigated evil. In the end it will yield
a harvest of rich and significant benefits to Israel and the
world. As the servitude of Israel in Egypt led up to the
glorious and epochal revelation at Mt. Sinai, so Israel's
present affliction is a preparation for the chief divine
event which will seal the past, inaugurate a new theo-
cratic era, and transfigure the whole of mankind. The
deliverance of Israel from its sore trials and tribulations
will impress upon all the people the power and goodness
of the Almighty. Israel will cling to God with greater
zeal than before. The Gentiles will behold the might of
God, and will be drawn unto His worship. Thus through
the instrumentality of Israel's merit and purification all
humanity will be uplifted. Crescas cites the epigram of the
sages as an example of God's gratuitous benevolence: "All
the world is fed for the sake of Hannina, my son; and Hannina, my son, is sated with a measure of carobs from
Sabbath to Sabbath."[13] Through the merit of one, many
are benefited. The disbeliever, in this instance, the nations
at large, will profit through Israel.

7—Resurrection.

a. Its Importance.

The miracle of resurrection is described by Crescas
with even greater clearness and fulness than the Messianic advent. Tradition, Scripture, and personal judgment are the sources or criteria for ascertaining the truth
about resurrection, and for formulating the doctrine.[14]

---

[13]Taanit 25a. The quotation alludes to Hannina, son of Dosa, a tanna
of the first cent. known for his piety and miracles.

[14]The subject of resurrection is treated in "Or" pp. 75ab, 77ab, 78a.

THE DOCTRINE OF THE MESSIAH

Each of these is of equal importance and contributes its share towards the clarification of the theme. At the outset Crescas asks four pointed questions, which, correctly answered, adequately represent the Jewish teaching.

1. Will the resurrection be universal or partial; if partial, what part of humanity will be included?

2. When will it take place?

3. Will the resurrected live an earthly life as in the first existence, and then die again?

4. Will resurrection synchronize with the day of judgment spoken of in our sacred literature?

At this point, it may be well to fix the position this belief holds as a dogma in the philosopher's creed. He maintains that the denial of resurrection does not exclude one from the Jewish fold. Nevertheless, it is a grave and serious offense, for which the disbeliever will fail to be revived, and so be excluded from the world to come. The gravity of gainsaying the miracle becomes plain when we bear in mind the high principles which are involved in it, such as the perfectibility of the human species in mind and matter, the justice of God, and the dissemination and strengthening of universal faith in Him.

In the sequence of eschatological events Crescas places resurrection immediately after the judgment day. It will merely be the execution of God's sentence upon the dead. This is implied in Dan. 12:2: "And many of them that sleep in the dust of the earth shall awake, some to everlasting life, and some to reproaches and everlasting abhorrence." Hence, for some the new life will be a reward, for others a punishment. Crescas seeks to know precisely whether it will occur in the Messianic interim. There is first the broad statement of Samuel, which implies that the Messianic state will not differ radically from the present

order.[15] Since this state will bring with it no extraordinary phenomena, we may conclude that resurrection will
not occur during that period. On the other hand, another
passage permits us to assign this miraculous occurrence
to the Messianic era. The question is asked: "Mitre and
girdle, which preceded in the attirement of the high
priest?" The sages were astonished at the question and
finally replied: "When the Temple is rebuilt, Moses and
Aaron will wear them."[16] The fact that the reappearance
of Moses and Aaron is connected with the building of the
long awaited sanctuary is ground for assuming that the
resurrection will occur during the Messianic era.

Crescas reconciles the dissenting views in Samuel and
the second quotation by declaring that a considerable
interval must elapse between the appearance of the Messiah and the building of the Temple. The early part of
the Messiah's regime will not witness any preternatural
changes. After Israel has been settled within its domain,
and the Temple has been rebuilt, the miracles will occur.
Among the miracles is resurrection. He adds that
Samuel's opinion that the Messianic era will be devoid of
miracles does not express the prevailing opinion of the
Talmud.

b. Selective.

Dan. 12:2—"And many of them that sleep in the dust
shall awake, some to everlasting life and some to reproaches
and everlasting abhorrence"—shows clearly that the resurrection will not comprise all the dead. The sages took this
view, for they qualified the phrase "and many"—but not
all. The difficulty remains in determining what portion
of humanity will be revived. Our sense of justice would
incline us to limit the number of resurrected to the right-

---

[15]San. 99a.
[16]Yoma 5b.

eous; to those who deserve to re-exist and receive the *summum bonum* in the hereafter. But this assumption is ruled out, because the verse in Daniel clearly predicts the resurrection of the wicked. If we establish the purpose of the miracle, it will be possible to determine what part of mankind will be revived. Its exalted purpose, then, is to demonstrate before the whole world the equity and retributive power of God. Bearing this purpose in mind, and also the fact that Daniel indicates that resurrection will not embrace all humanity, we conclude that it will be restricted to the extreme classes, the very wicked and the most righteous. The intermediate group will not be eligible. The individuals in this last group will each receive in this life, according to his deserts, spiritual reward or physical recompense. Or, God in His wisdom might, in certain deserving cases, combine both rewards.[17]

c. Moral Purpose.

The act of resurrection will realize the moral purpose for which the human species was created. The goal of the Torah-discipline will be attained. The miracles will be patent to the eyes of all, and parents and children will tell each other of the marvelous experience of coming to life. The atheists and the sceptics will exult in the glory of God. Resurrection will mark the evolution of man into a consummate being, a superman. The recombination of body and soul will demonstrate, par excellence, the majestic power of God, and will also enable Him to execute His judgments, since true and final justice demands that the entire person be affected. It would be unfair to inflict judgment upon the soul alone or the body alone. As they have been associated and have sinned or merited together, so must the sentence be meted out to them jointly. Hence,

---

[17]The word *yahdov*, together, in Ps. 19:10, is taken to allude to the double reward.

to prove beyond doubt His wisdom and omnipotence, the perishable body must be assembled, revitalized, and re-united with its tenant-owner, the soul.

d. It is not Impossible: Analogies.

The question as to the possibility of reviving the soul-less body and enabling it to assume its previous form, is weighed very thoroughly. How shall the decomposed body be restored when its substance has been scattered like dust, devoured, or drowned. If the second body is formed out of the dissolved particles of the first, it represents a new creation. The old and the new bodies will not be identical, and hence re-existence of this sort will defeat the purpose of the miracle, which is to do justice to the first individual. It cannot be just and genuine unless the same individuality is affected by the ultimate reward or punishment.

The solution to these difficulties is God. He is infinite. His knowledge compasses all remote possibilities. A deed may be contrary to nature, but it cannot defy God's ways. Nature represents no barriers to the Almighty. He con-trols nature. Hence resurrection, which appears to us well nigh impossible, could be performed by God through the simple process of endowing the substances of the body with the magnetic virtue of coming together at an ap-pointed hour for the purpose of forming the body anew. There is, however, another explanation. It is the soul which gives individuality to a person. And this soul, being an entity, does not alter. At the resurrection God will create a body like the first in substance and form, and set the old soul in it. In this way the former person-ality will be continued. If, in addition, the memory of its former existence is restored, the original individuality of the human being will be completely established.

The body will be merged into the spiritual character of the soul and will lose its own external aspect. It is only the vesture of the soul, and need not be identical corporeally with the body that perished.[18]

The author offers an analogy between resurrection and the growth of man. The newly-born infant is a personality that possesses organs, muscles, instincts, and powers. In order to grow, the babe requires outside food. When nourishment enters his system, it is absorbed and assimilated, and with time his physique develops. In the same way the soul in its fleshly abode represents a living entity. Yet it is only the beginning, the infant stage, which, having received the nourishment of spiritual impulses and activities, will thrive and reach maturity in the resurrected life.

e. The Mediacy of Elijah.

Crescas fondly reiterates the thought that Elijah will perform the miracle of the resurrection basing his assumption on several grounds.[19] The end of Malachi clearly foretells his reappearance and his mission as a restorer of human beings. "Behold, I will send you Elijah, the prophet, before the coming of the great and terrible day of the Lord, and he shall turn the hearts of the fathers to the children, and the hearts of children to the fathers." Common sense also makes him the most likely agent. Every wonder in our sacred history has been wrought through the mediacy of a prophet. Now, among the inspired ambassadors of Scripture none can be found more suitable to revive the dead than Elijah, who was a perfect man. The purities of body and soul were admirably encompassed in his nature. Again, since the purpose of the miracle is to exhibit the complete justice of God toward

---

[18]*Or Adonai,* p. 75b.

[19]Mishna Sota IX, 15 says "Resurrection of the dead will come through Elijah the prophet."

man, and as this cannot be done save where the body and
soul are joined together, it is fitting that Elijah, who was
translated body and soul to his eternal reward, should
perform it. Furthermore, since he approached the status
of an angel, and thus exemplified the union of man with
God, who, other than the Tishbite, could better effect the
transformation of man into a being of the highest order?

f. The Resurrected Life.

One of the problems which divided the theologians
concerned the nature of the resurrected life.[20] One school,
of which Maimonides was the exponent, held that the dead
would be fully revived and would lead a normal existence.
They would eat, drink, reproduce their kind, and die
again. Upon this second death, they would enter the spirit
world. The interesting Talmudic statement which says
that in the next world man will not indulge in the gratification of his senses,[21] is referred by Maimonides to two
periods. The one immediately following the departure
from this normal life, in which the body ceases to function. The other is the world to come that will ensue after
the Messianic era, when the spirit alone abides, awaiting
resurrection. The contrary opinion is put forward by the
Anti-Maimonists, among them the celebrated Nahmanides,
who maintains that the resurrected will have bodily existence, but that they will not exercise their corporeal powers, organs, and senses, and furthermore will abide eternally in this condition. Crescas mentions Meir ben Todros
Halevi, an inveterate foe of Maimonides, especially on the
question of resurrection. This view that the resurrected
life will be eternal finds endorsement in the rabbinic statement: "The dead whom God will revive will not return to
dust."[22] Nahmanides' self-contradictory view of a highly

20*Or Adonai*, p. 75a.
21Ber. 17a.
22San. 92a.

spiritualized body tempts one to ask: "Why have the body?" A second physical existence without the exercise of the bodily functions is absurd, and betrays uselessness in God's world. To this, the theologian offers a two-fold reply. First, God does not desire the obliteration of anything, and since the body once flourished, it is not seemly that it should be completely destroyed. The other reason is mystical. The form and parts of the human organism symbolize certain occult powers and meanings which will not be made manifest nor be utilized until the Hereafter.

Crescas inclines to favor the theory of Nahmanides, and assures us that the consensus of Talmudic opinion bears him out. He stresses the point that the attainment of spiritual perfection is possible through the union of the body and soul, even though the body fail to exercise its functions. Moses and Elijah reached this stage. Although they appeared in bodies of flesh and blood, Scripture tells us that for long periods of time they abstained from sensual acts and stood in perfect communion with God.

In Crescas then we have another instance of a renowned and most original Jewish thinker who did not deviate from the traditional Jewish conception of the redeemer and of the miracle of resurrection.

Chapter X

JOSEPH ALBO

1—Polemical: Disputation in Tortosa, Is. 7:14.

The doctrinal exposition of Judaism was continued in a more popular way by the theologian, Joseph Albo (Spain, 1380-1440), pupil of Crescas. His survey of the Messianic idea omits several outstanding features of the Messianic drama, including the Messianic figure, the ingathering, the "end", the final titanic struggle between the nations, and the glories of the millennium. His chief contribution lies not in the embellishment of the Messianic picture, nor in any special re-affirmation of it, but in giving it a suitable place in the Jewish doctrinal household. He aims to make clear the position of the Messianic idea as an article of faith, and no doubt he accepted the form and content of the dogma in the same manner as the Synagogue had taught it before his time.

At the disputation held before Pope Benedict XIII at Tortosa, between February 1413, and November 1414, Joseph Albo was one of the principal Jewish representatives to refute the arguments of the apostate Geronimo de Santa Fe, who aimed to demonstrate from the Talmud and the Agadah that the Messiah had already come.[1] The seriousness of the event appears from the fact that sixty-nine sessions were held. The charge that the Messiah's previous advent is proven by the Talmudic statement (San. 97a) that the fifth and sixth millennia form the Messianic era is refuted by Albo in two ways. First, the passage can be interpreted in too many ways to be used

---

[1]An account of the debate is found in the *Shebet Jehuda* ed. Wiener pp. 68-78. See Revue des Etudes Juives, 1922, 1923, also Husik, trans. of Ikkarim, 1930, vol. 1, pp. XV-XVII.

as a decisive proof for the Christian contention.[2] Second, as the statement is Talmudic in origin and in tradition, the Talmudists would not have included it unless it harmonized with their belief. The scholars believed there are two "ends"; one predetermined by God, the other contingent upon the people's moral worth. Hence, the passage does not state an exact time but implies that the advent is possible during the next two thousand years. The redeemer may arrive at the beginning, middle, or end of that period. There is nothing to indicate, therefore, that the Messiah (Jesus) has arrived.

At another time the apostate offered the passage (San. 97b) wherein Elijah said to R. Judah: "The world will not endure for less than 85 Jubilees (4250 years), and in the last Jubilee he will come." R. Judah inquired: "At the beginning or the end?" Elijah replied: "I do not know." Albo resolved the difficulty by saying that the phrase "not less" implied that the world would not endure less than 4250 years, but could last much longer, and that he would come in the last Jubilee of the world's duration, whenever that event will occur.

The "Book of Principles" was intended not only to improve upon all earlier expositions of Judaism and the doctrines, but to defend the Torah against alien theological systems. This appears clearly in Part III, Ch. 25, where Albo refutes the malevolent arguments of a Christian theologian against the Hebrew Scriptures intending to show the superiority of the New Testament. The only points in the discussion that belong here relate to the Messiah. Albo argued against the Messiahship of Jesus on the ground of conflicting statements in the New Testament. Whereas the Gospel of Matt. 1:6 traces the ancestry of Joseph, the husband of Miriam, to Solomon and David, in Luke 3:31, Joseph is said to have de-

---

[2] *Cf.* Maimonides, Kobez II, p. 9b.

scended from Nathan, the son of David. Aside from this
contradiction the fact that Joseph is said not to have
lived with Miriam certainly deprives Jesus of any Davidic
origin. He refuted also the claim of Matt. 1:22, that
Is. 7:14, "Behold the young woman shall conceive and
bear a son," pointed to the birth of Jesus. That prediction must be understood in the light of political events
that occurred 700 years before the Christian founder was
born. The prophet Isaiah was speaking to King Ahaz and
offered him a sign that the kingdoms of Syria and Israel
would be destroyed and Judah only would remain.[3]

2—Classifies Dogmas Under Three Principles: Belief in the Advent not an Indispensable Doctrine.

The doctrinal discussion is amply set forth in the first
and fourth sections of "The Book of Principles," the last
of the decisively religio-philosophic works in the Middle
Ages, long treasured for its elegant and didactic treatment
of the tenets of Judaism. We may venture the assertion
that Albo's discourses are the first of their kind in our
literature. No earlier authority ever assumed the task
of setting forth for the layman, with such simplicity, the
varieties and relative importance of Jewish doctrines.
There were, of course, the major theological works of the
renowned sages, Saadia Gaon and Maimonides, who felt
keenly the need of laying bare to the eyes of the Jew and
the non-Jew, the firm and perfect foundation upon which
the edifice of Judaism stood. But while Saadia and
Maimonides formulated articles of faith which they defended as fundamental, it was Albo who weighed the com-
ponent parts of Judaism and stated their rightful value.
Albo strenuously combats the thirteen articles of
Maimonides.[4] He contends that if these articles repre-

---

[3]See E. G. Kraeling, The Immanuel Prophecy, Jour. Bib. Lit., 1931, pp.
277-298.
[4]Sefer Ikkarim, Warsaw, 1877, pp. 21ff., and 26ff.

sented general Jewish concepts, Maimonides should have added the belief in free will and in the authority of tradition. Had he intended not to enumerate either the basic doctrines or general concepts, but only the tenets of our faith which every faithful Jew is expected to accept, he should have augmented the list to include beliefs in creation *ex nihilo,* miracles, and the influence of the Shekina upon Israel. These are theologically on a par with faith in a Messiah. Other beliefs which belong to the same category are the immutability of the Torah, the prophetic superiority of Moses, the perfection of man through the pursuit of the Torah, and resurrection. It is obvious from the order in which these are listed that belief in a Messiah is not a fundamental dogma. Neither is it a particularly distinctive Hebrew teaching. Other religions have postulated similar beliefs, and some have even gone so far as to make it the cornerstone of the theological system. Christianity wields this belief as its deadliest weapon in the attempt to overthrow the Mosaic law.

Following the worthy precedent of his master, Crescas, in liberalizing the formulation of a creed, Albo condenses the whole mass of Jewish belief into three unifying principles:—the existence of God, providence, and revelation.[5] These are the categories from which emanate all our beliefs and dogmas. To use the beautiful symbolism of the author, they are the roots out of which grew our multifarious tenets and teachings. Thus, belief in the existence of God naturally gave rise to the essential articles of His pre-existence, unity, and incorporeality. The idea of divine revelation involves His omniscience, the infallibility of prophecy, and the supremacy of Moses among the messengers of God. The root of the belief in providence branched out into the ideas of reward and punishment in this world and in the Hereafter, the Messianic state and resur-

---

[5] *Ibid.,* pp. 31ff.

rection. Subordinate dogmas are the branches and the twigs on the tree of Judaism. He who cuts off a branch or a twig is not a heretic. It is only when he rejects any of the three major principles, and uproots the tree, that he may be branded with this opprobrious term.

Albo made this classification in opposition to that of Maimonides, which he deemed an illogical grouping. It includes: 1. The Existence of God; 2. Unity; 3. Incorporeality; 4. Eternity; 5. God Alone to be Worshipped; 6. Prophecy; 7. Supremacy of Moses; 8. Revelation; 9. Immutability of Torah; 10. Omniscience; 11. Reward and Punishment; 12. Messiah; 13. Resurrection.

Albo contends that these are not all of equal importance. Belief in God is a major principle and presupposes His unity and incorporeality. One who denies the unity of God and His incorporeality is guilty of violating the commandments which affirm that God has no body and that He is one. Judaism conceives of the Divine Being in a specific manner, which it is incumbent upon all professing Jews to accept. Thus, a corporeal or "multiple" God is not in perfect accord with our theology. Yet, one who rejects this Jewish conception of God's nature cannot be adjudged guilty of undermining Judaism. He is guilty only of holding an erroneous opinion, and will no doubt receive punishment for it. But he has not denied the *existence* of the Almighty and hence has not taken the step which severs him from the Jewish communion.

Another central belief of Judaism is revelation, or reward and punishment, which embraces the eschatological ideas of Paradise, Hell, immortality, resurrection, and the Messianic state, as well as divine retribution in this world and in the Hereafter. The origin of our belief in resurrection, for example, is not traceable to the Hebrew canon, for it developed out of an intense spiritual experience, and became a part of the traditional mental stock of the Jew. It has been treated and transmitted as a Jewish belief, and its acceptance is binding upon us, since tradition, in its way, is as obligatory as the Written Law. We owe obedience to both. Hence, disbelief in resurrection is an act of infidelity, a betrayal of inherited trust, and deserves punishment. However, it is not a denial of the root principle of reward and punishment, which is a general principle and is capable of varied and elastic interpretation. Surely, the disbeliever in resurrection or the advent does not impugn the validity of the divine Law or the Mosaic system.

Albo also makes a dialectical distinction in favor of a liberal formulation of the creed. If resurrection will benefit all the departed, one who denies it merely rejects, as was said before, part of the general scheme of providence. But if resurrection is limited to the righteous, it will rank with the unique miracles of history, and the rejection of it discredits only the omnipotence of God to perform miracles.

3—The Origin and the Fulfillment of the Hope.

Albo indirectly infers the obligation to believe in the advent from Deuteronomy 18:15: "A prophet will the Lord thy God raise up unto thee, from the midst of thee, of thy brethren, like unto me; unto him shall ye hearken."[6] We are thus ordered to trust and rely on the prophets. They predicted the coming of the Messiah. Hence, one who denies the Messiah casts doubt upon the prophets and transgresses the clear command, "to hearken to the prophets' word." This is the extent of the infidelity of one who negates the Messiah, and it is indeed very far from nullifying the whole Torah.

In presenting the Messianic doctrine in its proper niche in the mansion of Biblical theology, Albo discusses at

---

[6]*Ibid.,* p. 367.

length views contrary to his own. He defends the Biblical
sanction and purity of the doctrine against scholars who
assume that it evolved after the close of the canon, as
mere Cabala, tradition. These scholars find no allusion
to Messianic events in the Mosaic or prophetic books, but
maintain that the first to mention the tradition was
Onkelos, who in translating the verse (Gen. 49:10) : "The
scepter shall not depart from Judah, . . . as long as men
come to Shiloh" explicitly mentions the Messiah.[7] No
doubt, Onkelos inherited the teaching from his masters,
Shemaya and Abtalyon. The doctrine has, however, per-
sisted down through the ages and it is as binding upon us
as any of the precepts of the Written Law.

Very candidly the theologian asserts that "Although
the commentators admit his advent, they differ as to the
prophecies that point to him." He cites, somewhat ap-
provingly, a certain school of thought which countenanced
the theory that the Messianic event was a *fait accompli*
which had been fulfilled in the time of the historic kings
or in the Restoration under Ezra. Perhaps the earliest
scholar to state such views was R. Hillel[8] (3rd cent.), who
declared, "Israel has no Messiah, because they have
already consumed him in the days of Hezekiah." Of the
same import is the legend that God desired to make
Hezekiah, the ideal, long-heralded redeemer, but did not
do so on account of the monarch's vanity. The view that
the glorious promises of the prophets, especially of Isaiah,
were consummated in the second commonwealth, was
grounded on the fact that the term Messiah is used to
describe Cyrus the Persian ruler. (Is. 45:11.)

The eternal existence of Israel, which Isaiah and Jeremiah declared to be as certain as the eternity of the sun,

---

[7]Targum Onkelos, Gen., 49:10 reads, "When the king shall arise from
Jacob and the Messiah wax great in Israel, he will slay the hosts of Moab
and rule over all mankind."

[8]San. 99a.

moon, and stars, excludes the possibility of the people ever disappearing, and, in fact, renders necessary Israel's advancement to power and a peaceful regime. Other nations of antiquity either have lost their racial strain and become extinct, or their names have fallen forever into oblivion. Nations spring up, flourish, and decay. Not so with Israel; she will never end. It is assured that both her glorious name and holy strain will persist everlastingly. She is ever new, as the stars that shine above. These thoughts lead to the comforting conclusion that a future of supernal joy is awaiting Israel—else the continued exile, past and present, is a curse and not a blessing. How can we suppose that God has doomed the chosen ones to endless misery and banishment.

Unlike Crescas, to whom the appalling length of the dispersion was an inexplicable mystery, Albo takes the frequent protests in Psalms against Israel's affliction not as tokens of despair and agony, but as expressive of the people's yearning that He will fulfill His early promises and that He will, for the sake of His great renown and honor, bring redemption. In this connection, Albo adds that the divine mercy must be manifested toward mankind through the Messiah, "through whose power the human species will be perfected and attain its purpose."[9]

4—Views of R. Hayyim Galipapa: All Millennial Promises Referred to Past Historical Events.

Albo cites particularly the conclusions of a certain Spanish scholar, R. Hayyim Galipapa,[10] who is typical of a group of critics who did not indiscriminately refer all prophetic utterances to the millennium, but ascribed them

---

[9]Ikkarim, p. 380.

[10]Rabbi at Huesca and Pampeluna, born about 1310, liberal, who fought the severities of the Talmudists and denied the Messianic dogma. Albo cites his "Epistle on Redemption", not extant. See Responsa of Isaac ben Sheshet, Nos. 349 et seq. for Galipapa's laxity in ritual matters.

to persons and events of the second commonwealth. They took into account the fact that the prophecies were spoken before and during the captivity in Babylon, and would logically apply to a period within the historical perspective of the sacred writers.

By this rationalistic school the famous promise in Gen. 49:10:

"The scepter shall not depart from Judah,
Nor the ruler's staff from between his feet;
As long as men come to Shiloh (until Shiloh come).
And unto him shall the obedience of peoples be"—

is variously explained to predict (a) the uninterrupted ascendancy of the tribe of Judah, (b) that the lion tribe will become great until David (Shiloh) come. The substitution of gold and silver in lieu of wood and stone, promised in Is. 60:17, is in Midrashic and geonic literature taken to indicate the opulence that will prevail in the Messianic era.[11] The critics, however, take it to describe the affluent situation of Israel in the Hasmonean period, in contrast to the poverty of the community when it returned from Babylon. The splendor of the Hasmonean times is evidenced by the Talmudic story that King Jannai ate with the Pharisees at golden tables.[12] So too, the temple of Herod was said to have been more magnificent than the Solomonic temple.

Is. 66:20: "They shall bring all your brethren . . . for an offering unto the Lord," refers to the gifts and the aid which the Babylonians offered the returning Hebrews in accordance with the proclamation of Cyrus, and not to the legendary idea that Gentiles would transport Hebrews as gifts to God. The prediction that universal worship would be rendered unto the Lord, expressed in Is. 66:23

---

[11]In Yalk. Shim., the entire chapter, Is. 60, received Messianic coloring and interpretation.
[12]Kiddushin, 66a.

and Ezra 1:4, applies to the entirety of Israel only. Ezek. 37:22: "And I will make them one nation in the land upon the mountains of Israel, and one king shall be king to them all; and they shall be no more two nations, neither shall they be divided into kingdoms any more"—does not relate to the Messianic future but to the second common-wealth, according to these scholars, and they corroborate this view with Akiba's declaration: "The ten tribes are not destined to return."[18] If Ezekiel intended the re-union of the two kingdoms for the Messianic era, it is hardly probable that Akiba would venture to contradict him and deny the return of the northern tribes. Hence, they assume that the prophet had in mind a restoration in the near future. The "one king" may refer to Zerubabel, to Nehemiah, or to one of the Hasmonean rulers.

So also Zech. 9:9:

"Rejoice greatly, O daughter of Zion;
Shout, O daughter of Jerusalem;
Behold thy king cometh unto thee;
He is triumphant and victorious,"

deals with the accession of Zerubabel to power and glory. Malachi 3:3—"And he shall sit as a refiner and a purifier of silver, and he shall purify the sons of Levi and purge them as gold and silver, that they may offer unto the Lord an offering in righteousness"—does not refer to the Messiah, but to the activity of Ezra in segregating Israel from the neighboring influences and prohibiting inter-marriage.

Galipapa also interprets Daniel historically instead of Messianically. Dan. 7:25—"And he shall speak words against the Most High . . . he shall think to change the seasons and the law; and they shall be given into his hand until a time and times and half a time"—does not refer

---

[18]Mishna, San. X, 3.

to the final wars, or the Anti-Christ, but to Antiochus Epiphanes, who instituted a reign of terror and a persecution of Israel. Dan. 7:18—"But the saints of the Most High shall receive the kingdom and possess the kingdom for ever and ever"—points to the Hasmonean leaders. The last phrase, *ad olma, ve-ad olam olmaya* denotes the limited Maccabean rule, for *olam* here means a Jubilee period. Dan. 7:9, "the ancient of days," does not mean God, but Mattathias, the aged priest of Modin and instigator of the rebellion against Antiochus. The vision of the four beasts is similarly explained as symbolizing the four powers which flourished successively during the second commonwealth: Babylon, Media, Persia, and Greece.

Despite these views Albo feels confident that the foundation and sanction of the Messianic doctrine is not tradition but Scripture. "The truth is that there are in the Torah and in the words of the prophets, writings that necessarily prove the sprouting forth of Israel and their elevation, which have not been realized in their entirety or in part."[14]

He quotes with approval the rabbinic inference of the Messiah's coming from Numb. 24:17. The clause: "shall smite through the corners of Moab", refers to David's exploits, while "break down all the sons of Seth" alludes to the Messiah. It is known that David did not rule over all Seth. It must be supposed, then, that the subjugation of Seth, a task which parallels the conquest of Moab, would be the achievement of one equal to David or possibly greater than he, the Messiah. The epochal event foreseen in Is. 24, which will show God's mercy, can be none other than the redemption of the future.

The temple contemplated and described by Ezekiel was not erected during the second commonwealth, as the second Temple did not embody the details and measurements set

---

[14]Ikkarim, p. 369.

forth by the prophet. That Ezekiel's temple is Messianic is implied in the opinion of Rabbi Johanan, which states that Elijah would expound the section dealing with the new temple sacrifices.[15] Many other matters which this prophet projected, such as the division of the land among the tribes, and the wars to be waged by the unknown and formidable Gog, did not relate to the time of Ezra, but to the Messianic drama. It is erroneous to suppose that the conflict between Antiochus and the Hasmoneans is foretold in Ezekiel's description of Gog's wars. Similarly, the theory that the Goths who overran and conquered Rome were the armies of Gog, can be dismissed as unfounded. The assurance given by Malachi that Elijah the prophet would reappear, still awaits realization as he has not yet come. The fourth frightful beast in the vision of Daniel also points to extraordinary events still to occur in the millennium.

In conformity with tradition, Albo regards Isaiah 53 as referring to Israel. When the prophet says, "Surely our diseases he did bear—whereas we did esteem him stricken, smitten of God and afflicted," he implies that when one sees sufferings falling upon the righteous, one must think that they are thus stricken because of their own failings and, quite naturally, one is surprised. It is not so in fact, however. They do not fall upon them for any sin they may have committed, but as an atonement either for all the world, for the entire people, or for some single city.

5—*Resurrection.*

a. Not Scriptural.

Resurrection is nowhere clearly promised in the Bible.[16] Its only sanction is tradition—Cabala. Albo

---

[15]Menahot, 45a.
[16]Ikkarim, pp. 353-356.

inclines to the opinion that Dan. 12:12, which tells of the awakening of the earth's slumberers, is not a promise of actual and personal re-existence, but of the rejuvenation of Israel in the Hasmonean era and its elevation to power. If, however, the passage be taken literally to foretell the revival of the dead, we may conclude that the word "many" denotes a part and not all.

"Thy dead shall live, my dead bodies shall arise:
Awake and sing, ye that dwell in the dust,
For Thy dew is as the dew of light,
And the earth shall bring to life the shades."
—Is. 26:19.

The above does not refer to the revival of the dead, but to the poor and the downtrodden, who will be raised out of their lowliness. This metaphorical explanation harmonizes with a Talmudic opinion that Ezekiel's vision of the resurrected dry bones is a parable of the national restoration. (San. 92a.)

The rabbis adduce the doctrine of resurrection from Deut. 32:39:

"I kill and I make alive;
I have wounded, and I heal;
And there is none that can deliver out of My hand."

As the words "I have wounded and I heal" must relate to the same person, it follows that "I kill and I make alive" must refer to the dead. But Albo remarks that this passage is not a promise of resurrection, but an indication that He can perform it.

However, Scripture records that certain children were actually revived by Elijah and Elisha. Hence we may assume that resurrection is possible, and can happen in the future. There can be no doubt that it is mysterious. It belongs to the same chain of mystifying facts as the power of a magnet to attract steel. Hence our intellect need not rule it out, on the ground of its being impossible, because corporeal matter possesses secret properties which will forever remain mysterious.

b. Within the Realm of Possibility.

As the miracle does not involve a new creation but a rebirth of what once flourished, it would seem, then, that it should not be beyond the realm of possibility. The body, now lifeless, was once permeated with the divine spark of life. It throbbed with emotion and was quickened by intellect. Although it turns into a clod upon the cessation of spiritual activities, it is still susceptible to the return of the spirit. This entire line of reasoning is contained in the Talmudic aphorism:[17] "If what was non-existent can flourish, how much more logical is it to conclude that that which once existed and died, can return to life once more?"

Resurrection is also a postulate derived from our faith in the goodness and omnipotence of the Lord. His universal mercy extends to the dead. He will not utterly destroy them, but he will grant unto the faithful a new existence of joy and bliss. Who shall question His ability? Is it not possible for him who laid the foundation of the earth and set the planets and stars on their courses in the immense space, to restore the dead? This trust in God's mercy and power to revive the departed has been embodied in our prayer book, a fortress of Jewish tradition. "Thou, O Lord, art mighty forever; thou quickenest the dead with great mercy.—Who is like unto thee, O Lord of mighty acts, and who resembleth Thee, O King, who killest and quickenest and causest salvation to spring forth? Yea, faithful art thou, to quicken the dead. Blessed art thou, O Lord, who quickenest the dead."

Our sages have declared by what means resurrection will be effected. God will drop his vivifying dew upon

[17]San. 91a.

the earth, which like potent semen will fertilize the dead and cause them to grow to full life.[18] Will the resurrection be universal and comprise all the generations that once breathed upon this mundane sphere? Albo assumes that there will be a special resurrection for the righteous at the commencement of the Messianic era. This theory is corroborated by Dan. 12:13 —"But go thou thy way till the end be, and thou shalt rest, and shalt stand up to thy lot, at the end of days." The end here signifies the redemption. "Thou shalt rest"—is death, and "shalt stand up"—is the new life. At this time saints like unto Moses and Aaron, and righteous persons will return to earth to be living witnesses of the all-powerfulness of God and to enable them to perfect themselves to a further degree. This grand miracle will draw the world to the altar of Judaism and the worship of the one true God. Another resurrection, for which there is no support in Scripture, will be held on a larger scale on the day of judgment. If we maintain, as we necessarily must, that the motive of re-existence is compensatory to reward the good and punish the sinful, then that is the appropriate time for it. Retribution will then be meted out to all the earth. This thought, that resurrection will occur in the remote, eschatological future, harmonizes with the assertion in the Talmud that there is no distinction between this world and the Messianic state, save that the latter will bring freedom from persecution.[19]

c. The Resurrected Body.

An insurmountable difficulty of the resurrection is that of the restored body. The organism of man is constantly undergoing physical changes. Its substance and appearance vary from time to time, and man passes through

---

[18]Is. 26:19; San. 90b; Yalk. Shim. Is. 26:19.
[19]San. 99a.

several marked stages. In each, he presents quite a different personality. The question is, which body will be restored. Since re-existence is to reproduce the earthly person, the whole, continuous man must be favored. Nor would it be fair to create a new body from substances similar to those which make up the perished body, because the original body would not share in the regained bliss.

A further difficulty arises from our uncertainty as to the mode and fate of the new life. Will it be a repetition of our present existence? Will we eat, drink, procreate, and die, as now? These quandaries, says Albo, have inclined Maimonides to believe that the dead will be resurrected to a corporeal existence. Physical death will again overtake them. Thereupon their souls will enter the future world of endless bliss and communion with God. But the real reward of the future is spiritual, not corporeal. The spirit and not the body will be freed from all impediments and vestments in order to reach perfection. Nahmanides on the contrary, holds that the dead will be revived physically, but that in course of time their bodies will evolve to a condition of purity, in which the senses will be atrophied, and there will no longer be a need to satisfy any physical desire or proclivity. They will not perish. In the words of Solomon Schechter, "Nahmanides assigns even to the flesh an almost spiritual importance—The soul may have such an influence over the body as to transform it into so pure an essence that it will become safe for eternity."[20] Both Moses and Elijah reached this state of physical purity and spiritualization on earth. For long stretches of time they abstained from gratifying the sensual demands of the body. The view of Nahmanides accords with the Talmudic statement that "the righteous whom God will revive will not return to dust."[21]

---

[20]Schechter, Studies in Judaism, First Series, p. 116.
[21]San. 92a.

Chapter XI

ISAAC ABRABANEL

1—Introduction.

a. Mystic and Man of Affairs.

In the year 1492 the Spanish expulsion of the Jews occurred. Don Isaac Abrabanel (1437-1508) endeavored in vain, through his official position as Minister of Finance as well as by the offer of his wealth to the royal treasury, to have King Ferdinand revoke the edict.[1] To Abrabanel the event was of the same sinister significance as the destruction of the Temple on the Ninth of Ab. In the beginning of his commentary on Deuteronomy he writes: "And they, the Jews, said to one another, let us gather strength for our religion and the Torah of our God. If we survive, 'tis well, and if they see fit to put us to death, then let that be our fate. We will not violate our sacred covenant with God. We will not turn back our hearts. We will go in the name of the Lord our God." As Jeremiah rejected the proffers of the Assyrian commander to abide in safety in the Holy Land and chose to cast his lot with his brethren in exile, so Abrabanel preferred the wanderer's staff to the Spanish court.

The healing balm of this disintegrating influence upon Jewish life was the faith in a redeemer enjoyed by scholars and pious men, among these being Abrabanel. Like many other families in Spain, he claimed descent from the royal

---

[1]Abrabanel gives an account of the expulsion in the preface to his commentary on Kings. His prefaces to Joshua and to his Messianic writings contain much biographical material as well as information on the spiritual and political state of the Jews of his day.

lineage of David.[2] He was the last representative of that trend of religious thought in the Middle Ages which required of its votaries the knowledge and the acceptance of science and Scripture, of philosophy and tradition. Nor did he belong to that category of men, who, in their attempt to adjust themselves to things so discordant outwardly, proved to be neither philosophers nor traditionalists. Luzzato says of him: "This great pious soul freed theology at last completely from the yoke of Aristotelian philosophy."[3] Abrabanel, zealous for the Torah, severely censured the Jewish rationalists who made of religion the hand-maiden of Aristotelianism. Gersonides[4] was the special object of his scorn for belittling the miracles of the Bible. Crescas and Albo, who failed to include the belief in the Messiah among the dogmas of Judaism, were likewise denounced very sharply.[5] The Bible was his first and second premise. He cherished a fervent and unquestioning affection for every word of the Torah and every utterance of the rabbis. This reverence was not diminished by his familiarity with general history, nor by his official position as Minister of Finance in Portugal, Spain, and Naples. The two strands of his character, the devout commentator grieving for his lost manuscript, and the sagacious official administering the complicated financial affairs of a medieval state, these two strands were carefully blended in him and made him the most fascinating personality in the late Spanish Jewish era.

---

[2]Abrabanel in many places repeats the fact of his Davidic lineage. See comm. on Zech. 12:6—"Rabbi Isaac B. Giat wrote that to Spain at the destruction of the first temple came two families of the dynasty of David. One, the family of the Davids, settled in Lucena, and the other, the family of Abrabanel, settled in Seville, and from the latter am I".

[3]Jost's Annalen 1840, p. 17.

[4]French philosopher (1288-1344), author of Milhamot Adonai (Battles of the Lord) and a Bible commentary.

[5]Rosh Amanah (The Pinnacle of Faith) is a defense of the dogmatics of Maimonides against Crescas and Albo; Chapter 14 of this book deals with the Messianic doctrine.

Though in the differences that arose over the existing liberalism and the creed of Maimonides, Abrabanel was inclined to favor the sage, yet, fundamentally, he disagreed with him. Solomon Schechter characterized his position truly in these words: "Abrabanel must not be considered a Maimunist. It is only a feeling of piety toward Maimonides or perhaps a fondness for argument, that makes him defend Maimonides against Hasdai and others. His own view is that it is a mistake to formulate dogmas of Judaism, since every word in the Torah has to be considered as a dogma in itself. . . . On this and similar grounds Abrabanel refused to adopt the dogmatic articles for Judaism and thus became the head of the school that forms a class by itself among the anti-Maimunists, to which many of the greatest Kabbalists also belong. . . . To him and the Kabbalists the Torah consists of at least 613 articles."[6]

b. Messianic Writings.

The belief in the Messianic advent, insists Abrabanel, is a basic and essential doctrine of Judaism. The predictions regarding it form an integral part of the Torah. He who denies them denies the validity of the Torah. Were Abrabanel to have formulated the Messianic dogma, it would undoubtedly have been identical with Maimonides' twelfth article of faith.

Don Isaac closes the Ateret Zekenin[7] with this pious wish for the restoration: "I entreat God, I beseech His Presence that he may behold the oppression of His people; be mindful of our affliction and abasement, and bring us up from amongst all nations to the place of justice, the chosen land. As in days of yore, may He establish us

---

[6]Schechter, Studies in Judaism, Macmillan, 1911, first series, pp. 173, 174.

[7]Ateret Zekenin (Crown of the Ancients).

forever upon our soil, and raise up unto us a faithful shepherd. May he fulfill the words of the prediction, 'As in the days of thy coming forth out of the land of Egypt will I show unto him marvellous things.' "[8]

Abrabanel's treatment of the doctrine stands out boldly from that of earlier authorities in sheer size, thoroughness of detail, polemical argumentation, and in the full-rounded discussion of every aspect of the question. He wrote three books: "The Wells of Salvation," December 26, 1496; "The Proclaimer of Salvation," December 20, 1497; and "The Salvation of His Anointed," February 26, 1498.[9] In these works his Messianic views are profusely and exhaustively given. The first volume is an exposition of Daniel's prophecies; the second, of all Messiological utterances in the Mosaic and prophetic writings; and the third deals with rabbinic Messiology. No one before him had attempted this task on so large a scale. In the last book the writer enumerates a large number of Agadahs and Midrashim that are appropriated by Christians to demonstrate: (a) that the Messiah has already come; (b) that he has been born and is now existent; (c) that he is divine; (d) that the Mosaic Law will be abrogated in the new era; (e) that the redemption is spiritual and not material or political.

In the preface of "The Salvation of His Anointed," he castigates the Jewish apostates who bring disrespect and alarm upon Israel by denying the Jewish doctrine, and who summon Israel's leaders to disputations before kings and popes and vast multitudes. The traitor, Joshua Lorki, who opposed the most illustrious rabbis in the religious disputation at Tortosa, in 1413-1414, is singled out as the special target of the writer's odium.[10] Although the sages

---

[8]Micah, 7:15.
[9]Mayene ha-Yeshuah ed., Amsterdam, 1647. 2. Mashmia Yeshuah ed. 1644. 3. Yeshuot Meshiho ed., Konigsberg, in 1860.
[10]Joshua Lorki is the author of Tractatus contra Judaeos, ed. Lyon, 1677.

succeeded in adroitly overcoming their opponents, since the truth was on their side, yet in the opinion of Abrabanel they failed to explain various legends properly. He believed that the common sense interpretation of Talmudic legends and Midrashim had been well begun by Solomon ben Aderet and Jedaiah Bedarshi,[11] and he proposed to follow in their footsteps.

Other writings which furnish us with material are Abrabanel's commentary on the Bible; his commentary on the Ethics of the Fathers,[12] as well as the small but valuable books, the Rosh Amanah, a critique of the dogmatics of Maimonides, Crescas, and Albo, and the Ateret Zekenin. No doubt the destruction of Jewish life in Spain and the life-and-death struggle in new countries challenged the faith of Jews and brought forth the noteworthy defense of Abrabanel. It was not now a question of saving Judaism by harmonizing it with Aristotelian philosophy as did Maimonides in the "Guide of the Perplexed." The exigency of the times demanded the sustaining of the Jewish will to survive against the diabolical plan to destroy the race. Abrabanel answered this demand with enthusiasm.

c. Aims.

Abrabanel definitely sets out to controvert the Christian interpretation of Messiological passages in the Bible and Talmud.

First, he wished to show that the promises of redemption are not to be understood as purely spiritual and moral. Thus it was charged that the deliverance of which

---

[11]Rashba (Spain 1245-1310) ; see Graetz, Gesch. VII p. 150, on Rashba's polemical writings, and rational treatment of Agadah. He wrote a refutation of Raymond Martin's Pugio Fidei, also a commentary on the Agadot. Jedaiah, poet, author of Behinat Olam, also wrote philosophic commentaries on various Midrashim and Agadot—some of which are still extant in manuscript, see Jew. Enc. Vol. VI. p. 626.

[12]Nahlat Abot (Heritage of the Fathers).

the prophets speak does not mean liberation from physical distress and servitude, but liberation from sin. Christians claimed the term "Israel" in the prophecies did not refer to the descendants of the historic nation, but is supposed to represent "the church," the regenerated mankind of the future. In the opinion of Abrabanel, the charge was preposterous. He held that the specific and realistic language of the predictions, and the distressing circumstances that evoked them, force us to ascribe the promises to the physical and material release of Israel.[13]

Second, he offered evidence that Jesus was not the accepted Messiah and denied the allegation that our sages accepted him as such. Nothing, he said, was further from the truth. As a matter of fact, Israel rejected his teachings, and turned a deaf ear to his apostles. It was these very sages who tried and adjudged him guilty. Instead of following him, our leaders strengthened Judaism and built it up more firmly than ever. The best proof that they did not accept him as Messiah is the fact that they continued to ask and ponder the question of the future coming of the anointed one.

Third, he essayed to show that the Biblical anticipations were neither wholly nor partially fulfilled at the return of the exiles from Babylon and in the establishment of the second commonwealth (536 B. C.-70 C. E.). This was the contention of many Jewish authorities.[14] One cannot help but feel that the aims stated above were subsidiary, as he felt most acutely his people's burden of

---

[13]Mashmia, p. 50a.

[14]Yeshuot, p. 16b; *et al.* Abrabanel censored R. Moses Ibn Gikatilla, Spanish exegete, second half of 11th century, for his untraditional leanings,—"It is surely lack of faith on the part of R. Moses ha-Kohen and his followers concerning the precious principle of the Messiah's advent that constrains him to pervert the words of the prophets and to consider the prospective and the future, things of the past." Comm. on Joel 3:1; See Posnanski, Ibn Gikatilla, Leipzig, 1895.

misery; his chief purpose was to reanimate their forlorn hope in a Messiah.

At this point it is well to note Abrabanel's remarks concerning the Agadah, the non-legalistic writings of the rabbis. The question as to what attitude we should take toward the Agadah tantalized many of the medieval scholars. It was one of the issues fought out in the controversy over Maimonides. He states freely that he disagrees with the rationalizing tendencies of the Jewish thinkers. He has no quarrel with them on the problems of metaphysics —that is not within his province. But he does not like their manner of allegorizing, or discarding altogether, Biblical and rabbinical data, especially such as do not fit into their *a priori* systems. Since the Agadah is used so freely by Jews and Christians to form the Messianic picture, the character of one's Messianic concept will depend upon his attitude toward the Agadah. For this reason, Abrabanel took pains to define his position towards the rabbinic legends and dicta. He classified them in these six groups:[15] (a) Where there is more than one opinion on the question. (b) Where the same scholar gives conflicting views. (c) A statement of detail at variance with the general belief or scheme. (d) An inference which is not Sinaitic (authoritative) and does not accord with the context. (e) Tales used to stimulate the interest of the scholars or a prominent opponent. (f) Worldly wisdom and science.

There are some who affirm that Talmudic passages which fall in any of the above classes need not be accepted.[16] They are discounted as unessential. Another attitude is to allegorize the legends and rationalize the views, as did Maimonides, Abraham ibn Ezra, Levi b. Gerson, and Levi b. Abraham. Abrabanel also assails

---

[15]Yeshuot, p. 17.
[16]*Ibid.*, p. 17a. He criticized Nahmanides, who, when confronted with a legend by Pablo Christiani replied, "I do not believe this legend."

the Cabalists. All of these observations he rejects. He urges a sympathetic study and acceptance of rabbinic opinion. One must read between the lines and understand the point of view of the ancients. If we find difficulty in comprehending their teachings, it is due to our deficiency, not theirs. His line of defense, when confronted by Christian polemicists who presented Hebrew legends that seemed to favor their view, was to argue from the correct and actual meaning of the text that their deductions were erroneous and that Jesus was not the fulfillment of the Jewish Hope.

d. Biblical Exegesis.

The author follows the Talmud and the Midrash in his Messianic explanations of numerous passages in the Pentateuch, Prophets, and Psalms.[17] The vision of Abraham narrated in Gen. 15 disclosed to the patriarch the subjection of his progeny to the four world empires and their eventual liberation by the Messiah. The heifer symbolizes Rome; the she-goat, Greece; the ram, Persia; the turtle dove, Islam (Babylonians); the young pigeon, Israel; the bird of prey is the Messiah.

Jacob's blessing to Judah (Gen. 49:10) contains an assurance that the tribe of Judah will always be in the ascendant. It will produce foremost teachers and leaders both in the Holy Land and in the diaspora, for Israel in exile belongs chiefly to the tribe of Judah. Accordingly, the promise regarding Shiloh, the Messiah, is that the tribe of Judah will retain its supremacy for ever so long a time, even until the Messiah's advent.

The first clear enunciation of the destruction of Israel's foes and her triumph is found in the utterances of Balaam, Num. 24:17-24, the first of the seventeen

---

[17]The following analysis of Messiological sections in the Bible is based on the Mashmia.

messengers to proclaim the Messianic future. Abrabanel refers this entire passage to the Messianic future, disagreeing with Rashi and Maimonides, who assign it partly to the fortunes of King David and partly to the King Messiah. The passage predicts that Edom will be vanquished and become forfeit to Israel. Abrabanel gives a clever turn to the clause, "There shall step forth a star out of Jacob," when he says that the constellation which, under God, holds Israel in exile, will decline and give way to the Messiah in the Messianic epoch.[18]

According to the expounder, the following verses in Deuteronomy are futuristic: 11-21; 19:8-9; 30:1-10; 32:34-43. The first declares that the Holy Land is given to Israel as a permanent possession; the second speaks of the apportionment of three additional cities of refuge when the country is enlarged by the annexation of the lands of other races. This had not been done in the first conquest. On the basis of the other two passages, Abrabanel adduces several essential features of the Messianic belief.[19]

1. God Himself will deliver Israel and not an agent like Cyrus in former times. Hence the deliverance will not be transitory.

2. The deliverance will include all Israel, while formerly only a fraction of the population, the lowest element, returned from Babylon.

3. All who belong to the seed of Israel, even sinners and apostates, will be redeemed.

4. The Shekina, prophecy, and other holy functions will be restored.

5. This time Israel will be supreme over the nations.

6. Israel will be secure against exile and disintegration.

---

[18]do-rak—to step out; Mashmia 4c.
[19]Mashmia, pp. 5c-6.

7. Israel's foes will meet deserved punishment.

8. God has determined the "end," and has not divulged it to any prophet.

9. The merit of the fathers will not influence the redemption.

10. Before the redemption, Israel's sins must be atoned for either through repentance or through affliction.

11. Redemption is not conditional on repentance. God will afflict Israel for its sins and will forgive them when the chastisement is completed.

12. Resurrection will occur soon after the ingathering.

13. As certain promises regarding the fertility of the soil and national happiness were realized, so will the promises of future redemption come true.

Isaiah is rich in Messianic material. The following sections give familiar features to the glorious event: Is. 2:1-4; 10:33-34; 11:1-16; 12:1-6, 8, 19, 24; 26:7-end; 27; 34; 35; 40; 41:1-5; 54; 55; 60; 61 until 63:6; 65:8; 66.

Verse 9:5 is best applied to Hezekiah. The title Pele-joez, El-gibbor, Abi-ad are apposites of God, the subject of "and He called." The only title given Hezekiah is Sar-shalom. With surprising clarity Abrabanel summarizes the Messianic elements derived from the Isaianic prophecies in the following fourteen principles:[20]

1. Vengeance upon Israel's foes, who will suffer ignominy and ruin while engaged in the invasion of Palestine. Plagues, disasters or international war will wipe them out. Christians knowingly will ascribe this colossal defeat of Gentile nations to the machinations of Anti-Christ, whom they cunningly adopted from the Jewish Messiah ben Joseph.

---

[20]Mashmia, pp. 32c-34. In Yeshuot, p. 26a, b, Abrabanel groups all the Biblical Messianic predictions under the following ten heads: 1. Rise of a Davidic Redeemer. 2. Ingathering. 3. Vengeance. 4. Prosperity of Palestine. 5. Spiritual Eminence. 6. Return of Prosperity. 7. Enactment of Miracles. 8. No More Dispersion. 9. Universal Monotheism. 10. Resurrection.

2. Edom (Rome) will be the worst sufferers. Those who survive the destruction of Rome will be deemed unworthy of accepting Judaism.

3. At this time a complete ingathering will take place in contrast to the return from Babylon which was limited.

4. The ten tribes will be restored. Scriptural references to them do not signify the conversion of distant nations to Christianity.

5. Deliverance will be modeled after the Exodus from Egypt in all its particulars.

6. There is a definite period for the deliverance. Although there is a possibility of an earlier end, depending on the people's merit, the prophet knew that it would not occur before the inevitable year.

7. The redemption will occur after a very long dispersion.

8. At the redemption, the Shekina will reappear with greater perfection than at Sinai. Prophecy will return; knowledge and wisdom will be widespread. The claim of Christians that the purpose of prophecy was to proclaim the coming of the man-God-Messiah, and that therefore it ceased at his birth, is false, because prophecy actually stopped several hundred years before his birth.

9. Sinners and apostates will return. They may have strayed afar, but they ever remained the sheep of God's fold. Threats of violence, enticements, or other extenuating circumstances may have accounted for their relapses.

10. A descendant of the Davidic family will rule over Israel.

11. Israel never again will suffer dispersion, because wickedness will cease and they will not incur the divine wrath.

12. Most nations will adopt monotheism. Christendom cannot claim the distinction of having converted the world to monotheism, because it represents only a minority of mankind. Asia and Africa are still idolatrous.

13. Universal peace will prevail.

14. Resurrection will occur during the deliverance or soon thereafter.

The peculiarity of tabulating his ideas or arguments which Abrabanel appears to overdo is certainly a virtue in his expositions of our theme.

Abrabanel proceeds to analyze microscopically the rest of Scripture and, of course, finds support for the above mentioned views of Isaiah.

The Messianic sections in *Jeremiah* are: 3:22-4; 1-2; 23:1-8; 30; 31; 32; 36-41; 38; and *Lamentations* 4:21-22. Additional elements in the Messianic vista of Jeremiah are (a) the enlargement of the city of Jerusalem. It is wrong to assume that the promise is of the heavenly Jerusalem since actual places and boundaries are stated. (b) The name of King Messiah will be the "Lord, our Righteous One," or the "Righteous Sprout."

The Messianic parts of *Ezekiel* are: 11:15-25; 30:22-44; 35; 37:1-15; 38; 39; 45; 47:13 *et seq.;* 32:17-32; 34:11-end; 36:16 *et seq.;* 37:16-28; 46:1-15. Abrabanel discovers variations from the Mosaic code in the priestly ritual of Ezekiel. The latter will be adopted in the Messianic state. The variations are: 1. Enlargement of the temple and the city. 2. Teruma offering will be given to the nasi or ruler. 8. Special sacrifice will be offered on the first day of Nisan. 4. Other changes in sacrificial rites.[21] 5. Directions regarding the entrance of the nasi into the Temple and the closing and opening of the gates.

---

[21]The cause of these changes from the established order raised difficult questions. Hence R. Johanan declared that Elijah will in the future (Messianic) era expound it (Menahot 45a).

More than any other prophet Ezekiel stresses the war of Gog and Magog, and the horrible fate that will overtake them.[22]

Abrabanel finds that all of the minor prophets save Jonah spoke of the Messianic end. He mentions the following passages: *Hosea* 1, 2, 3; *Amos* 9:7-15; *Micah* 4, 5, 7:8 *et seq.; Zephaniah,* 3:8 *et seq.; Zechariah* 1:7-21-17; 7, 8, 9, 10, 11:1-2; 12 and 13; *Malachi* 2:17 and 3.

In his discussion of the Psalms, Abrabanel first singles out those which complain of the bitterness of the exile and pray for deliverance. Such are Psalms 44, 72, 74, 77, 79, 83, 89, 94, 99, 119, 120, 122, 123, 124, 128, 129, and 136. The distinctly Messianic psalms are 42, 43, 46, 47, 48, 74, 75 to 80, 117, 118, 126, and 129.

The Messianic portion of Daniel are chapters 2, 7, 8, 9, 10.

At the end of "The Proclaimer of Salvation," Abrabanel writes: "I have not seen fit to offer proofs from the books of Proverbs, Canticles, Ruth, and other Hagiographa, for they are not clear and compelling in their simple meaning. Yet they are true proofs, as the sages have interpreted in accordance with tradition. Verily, I was not induced to write this treatise except to bring verification for our deliverance and redemption from the necessary meaning of the verses in their simple interpretation, in order to refute the heretic."

2—*The Why and Wherefore of Redemption.*

a. Necessity, Cosmic and National.

As in his entire theology, so in the Messianic concept, Abrabanel was an eclectic. He gathered up the thoughts of many and let them pass through the alembic of his own

---

[22]Mashmia pp. 48-49. For critical views of Gog and Magog see Jew. Enc. Vol. VI, pp. 19, 20.

mind. That is why his treatment of the doctrine is so complete. This fact becomes clear in his writings about the need and the purpose of the redemption.

Redemption is a double necessity. First, it is a necessity of the cosmic order. The belief that the world's duration is divided into seven millenniums corresponding to the six days of creation and the seventh of Sabbath, was prevalent in Talmudic times. At the end of the seventh millennium the world will be destroyed. At the completion of the sixth epoch, before the final cataclysm, all mankind must return to God.[23] For the Almighty had a purpose in creating the world; it was, that mankind should learn and accept His principles of peace and righteousness.[24] Neither mankind in general, nor Israel in particular, have lived up to His sovereign purpose. Since the sin of Adam, we have sinned; we have belied God and creation. The world has become alienated from Him. Therefore, that His work shall not have been in vain, and to vindicate Himself, He must redeem mankind through Israel.

Redemption is also necessary for the nation Israel and for the Holy Land. God has vouchsafed Israel's imperishability. The doctrine that God, who is eternal, will never suffer His chosen seed to become the prey of hostile powers, is the undercurrent that nourished the fertile minds of the prophets and revivified the dried bones of the people.[25] God has willed that Israel should aspire to eternity and has made her strong against the vicissitudes of time and place. As for the exile, it is the consequence of the people's deviation from the Almighty, and does not mark His severance from them.[26]

This double necessity gives rise to a two-fold purpose. The first is the national purpose, which can be viewed from

---

[23]Mashmia p. 23ab: "The world order will end at the termination of the sixth millennium." Mashmia p. 73c.
[24]Jer. 33:25; comp. trans. of J. P. S.
[25]Jer. 31:36
[26]Prov. 3:12.

two aspects. In relation to Israel, the redemption will be ameliorative. The Lord will compensate His people for the intolerable affliction, which prevented their consecration to His service. Following from this is the penal purpose in relation to other nations. God will wreak vengeance upon them for their rejection of the Torah, and their ill-treatment of the Jews. The nations violated the fundamental laws of universal morality as contained in the seven Noahic laws.[27] One of the prophets predicted the utter ruin of Damascus and Amon for cruel treatment of the Gileadites; of Phoenicia and Philistia for engaging in the barbarous slave trade; and lastly of Edom for faithlessly violating a brother's oath. But the redemption has a larger, a universal side to it. God is the God of all the world and all mankind. He does not desire a temple home in Zion, for Heaven is His throne, the earth is His footstool, and the whole earth is full of His glory. His aim is to benefit mankind ultimately. Through Him the redemption of all humanity will be effected. At last they will accept His decrees of justice and peace.

b. Repentance as a Condition of Redemption.

For the sake of clearness, the author divides time into three intervals. During the first period the Messiah cannot and will not come. During the second his advent is possible, depending upon the repentance of the people. Then there is the period in which the Messiah must necessarily appear.[28] Whether redemption can be hastened by repentance is an ancient moot question as appears from a

---

[27]These laws are directed against 1, idolatry; 2, blasphemy; 3, murder; 4, adultery; 5, stealing; 6, against eating flesh from a living animal, and the laws commanding the establishment of courts of justice. These universalistic precepts were binding upon all mankind before revelation and still are binding upon non-Jews.

[28]Yeshuot, pp. 11b-12a; Mashmia 28d. The repetition of the word "Nahmu" in Is. 40:1 has reference to the possible and inevitable ends.

controversy between R. Joshua and R. Eliezer.[29] The
latter asserts: "If Israel repent they will be redeemed, but
not otherwise." Said R. Joshua to him: "According to
you, if they do not repent, they will not be redeemed at
all?" To this R. Eliezer replied: "The Holy One, blessed
be He, will appoint for this purpose a king whose decrees
against Israel will be as severe as Haman's. This will
bring them back to the better side." Abrabanel adjusts
the two conflicting views to his own division of conditional
and unconditional periods. In the conditional period, redemption may be achieved by expiation and pious deeds.
As in the realm of nature water extinguishes fire, so in
the spiritual world repentance can wash away the stain
of iniquity and accelerate the Messiah's advent. And repentance, according to the Spanish rabbi, does not consist
in flagellation and self-mortification, but in heartfelt recognition and avowal of God. In the unconditional period,
the Messiah must appear whether Israel repent or not.
If we accept the traditional view, the order of events will
be as follows: sin will be followed by punishment, punishment by repentance, and repentance by redemption. But
after the pre-ordained "end" had arrived, repentance is
not a condition *sine qua non*. Deliverance must inevitably
ensue, even though there be no repentance.

The Messiah's advent must not be abortive like the
early bloom of spring that is followed by frost. In so far
as the advent is potential in the conditional era, we are
justified in affirming that it is delayed by the unworthiness of the people. However, just as fruit which ripens
naturally and in season is preferable to fruit that matures
sooner by the application of artificial stimuli, so Israel
should wait uncomplainingly for the decreed end and not
hasten his advent before the ordained time. Were the
Messiah to appear in the conditional period, he would

---

[29]San. 98b-99a.

come as an unripe fruit and the deliverance of the people would not be complete. Israel would be emancipated from her oppressors, but there would be no vengeance, no ingathering of the exiles, nor any of the other miraculous events. Aside from these considerations the Messianic era proper cannot be inaugurated during the period when the nations are still exercising their sway. The merits of the patriarchs, which helped to reduce the duration of the Egyptian servitude, will not foreshorten the future redemption, nor conversely will the activities of sinners prevent or hinder it when the decreed "end" arrives. The counsel of Abrabanel to prostrate Israel then is not even to accelerate the end, but simply to wait for the time appointed which is sure to come.

There is a very interesting legend which makes the advent contingent upon the nation's regeneration and which, according to Abrabanel, refers to the conditional era. The story is that Rabbi Joshua ben Levi visited the Messiah at the gates of Rome and asked him when he would come. He answered, "This day." When Joshua met Elijah, the latter questioned him as to what the Messiah had said. Joshua replied that the Messiah had said, "Peace be with thee, son of Levi." Said Elijah, "He assured thee of a share for thyself and for thy father in the world to come." Joshua rejoined, "He mocked at me by saying that he will come *this day.*" And Elijah answered, "This day means as in Ps. 95:7: "To-day, if ye would but hearken to his voice."[30]

The statement that the anointed one will not come unless the whole generation be either righteous or wicked means that in the conditional era, he can only appear if the generation is righteous, but in the unconditional era

---

[30]San. 98a. See I. Rahlin, "Bar Livai", New York, 1906, pp. 68-90 on eschatological legends in which R. Joshua b. Levi figures.

even the wickedness of the people will not retard his advent.[31]

c. Year of the "End."

Abrabanel sets a definite period for the predestined end which has not been divulged to the prophets. The fact, to the contrary, that the terminations of the Egyptian and Babylonian exiles were announced was because they were of brief duration and the people could expect relief from their tribulations without falling to despair. The truth is that the Babylonian captivity did not serve as a punishment since the Jews enjoyed a fair measure of prosperity in Babylon. This is evidenced by their reluctance to return to Palestine. No expiation for Israel's misdeeds took place and many more sins had been committed during the second commonwealth. The present dispersion had been decreed by God, says Abrabanel, for the atonement of the nation's wrongs and will extend over a long period, but will not be of infinite duration.

The intensity with which the people visualized the advent lent to it a reality greater than the occurrences of their daily life. It was a *force vivante*, which buoyed up their dispirited hearts in times of trouble, and in time of backsliding deterred them from further sin and reminded them of their filial responsibility to their Heavenly Father. To Abrabanel, as to the pious soul in every generation, the anticipation of the Messiah was an imminent ideal. The anointed one might come today or tomorrow. The Spanish scholar had faith that he himself was living in the appointed time of visitation and recompense, and that the troublesome events of the day were the "Woes of the Messiah". Moreover, the Messiah was already born and on his mission to redeem Israel. In his

---

[31]*Ibid.* Saadia Gaon taught that repentance is essential for redemption and if need be the repentance will be compulsory.

efforts to calculate the "end", Abrabanel does not pass
unnoticed the many rabbinic passages which disparage
such attempts "because the calculators usually err, and
when the appointed time comes and the Messiah does not
appear, they say he will not come any more." Samuel b.
Nahmani says: "What do the words, 'it declareth of the
end' mean? (Hab. 2:3). They mean the souls shall be
blown out of those who are sitting and appointing times
for the arrival of Messiah."[32] In another passage we
read that the day of vengeance is a deep secret with the
Almighty.[33]

d. Apology for Computing the End.

Abrabanel finds it necessary to defend himself against
those who twit him for engaging in a quest so generally
prohibited, in a task so enigmatic.[34] He is aware that he
treads on forbidden ground. In order to ascertain the
exact Messianic year one must be able to penetrate the
very mind of the all-knowing One. Even Daniel, who received an oracle that contained the coveted information,
admitted that he heard, but understood not. Abrabanel
thus appears presumptuous in his own eyes in venturing
to publish with any degree of assurance the "year of
wonders." But there is another horn to the dilemma.
Would the great saints and authorities like Saadia,
Rashi, Abraham b. Hiyya, and Nahmanides have made
Messianic announcements if Judaism really forbade it!
Hence, it must be that the antagonism is directed against
those only who compute from the false science of astrology, the figures which mislead the people. There can
be no reasonable objection to deriving the end from
Holy Writ and Abrabanel's own efforts are directed to a

---

[32]San. 97b.
[33]*Ibid.*
[34]Mayene, p. 11b.

sincere and earnest elucidation of Biblical and rabbinical passages of Messianic import. Thus he stands on firm ground. But bearing in mind the fruitless results of earlier calculations, he refuses to vouch for the absolute veracity of his deductions. He can only speculate not prophesy. Neither is his putative "end" a tradition from the time of Moses. His calculations may even prove fallacious; nevertheless his trust in God to deliver Israel remains constant. An investigation, such as he undertakes has dangers, but it is worth while. He concedes that the year of wonders will be unknown and unknowable during the dispersion and will be disclosed only near its termination. The state of affairs will then prove clearly that the blissful hour has struck.[35]

Abrabanel's computations as that of all others was governed by the archaic belief that the world will endure six thousand years. As he was living in the sixth millennium, he had to fix the date for that epoch. We shall soon see that he was forced to shift the beginning of the sixth chiliad into the future in order to make it coincide with his own age. According to the creation calendar, Abrabanel lived between 5197 and 5268.

The redemption must occur in the sixth millennium— to be exact, 5263 after creation, or 1503 C. E.[36] The fifth millennium was the conditional era during which the Messiah might have appeared.[37] Thus we read that the school

---

[35]*Ibid.*, p. 12.

[36]Yeshuot p. 13b; "As the Shemitta drops one year out of every seven, so the universal time drops 1,000 years for each 7,000 years." In the seventh millennium the world will be desolate. See Yeshuot 19a. Whether the cataclysm at the end of the sixth chiliad will be cosmic or terrestrial only, "like a flood in which disembodied intellects, heavenly beings, and the souls of the esteemed will survive", Abrabanel confesses he does not know. Prof. Ginzberg in an article on "The Flood of Fire", in Ha-Goren, 1912, pp. 35-51 treats it as an eschatological conception. He shows that the idea prevailed among the Jewish masses, but not among scholars. The latter compromised by transforming the legend to refer to the punishment of the wicked by fire.

[37]Yeshuot p. 20a. The Messianic possibilities of the fifth chiliad is evidenced by Messianic movements which showed a groping toward

ISAAC ABRABANEL

of Elijah taught: "Two thousand years the world will exist without Torah, two thousand years with Torah, and two thousand years will form the Messianic age; and because of our sins which are many the latter era is belated."[38] The last two thousand years Abrabanel divides, making the fifth millennium the conditional, and the sixth millennium the unconditional period. However, the Messianic regime will not flourish for the full 2000 years, for the fifth millennium will commence four hundred years after the destruction of the Temple by Titus. Therefore, 3828 (Temple destroyed by Titus) plus 400 equals 4228, at which time the conditional era will begin. This computation is obviously based on the statement of R. Johanan, "If 400 years after the destruction one should offer a field worth 400 dinars for one dinar, do not buy it."[39] For in the Messianic era the purchase would be of no consequence.

A corroborating passage which offers the initial period of the conditional era is found where Elijah says to Judah: "The world will continue for no less than 85 Jubilees, and in the last Jubilee the son of David will come." And to the question whether he would come at the beginning or the end of the Jubilee, he answered: "I do not know." "Has this period passed already, or will it come?" Again he answered: "I do not know." R. Ashi, however, said Elijah informed him thus: "Until the above mentioned

---

the truth and light. Jesus, Bar Kochba and Mohammed made their appearance in that millennium. Abrabanel cited Maimonides' Letter to Yemen on the various pretending redeemers who appeared in Maimonides' day. He says: "already the great rabbi wrote at the end of the Mishneh Torah that these false Messiahs did not come into the world except to make a straight path for the King Messiah."

[38] San. 97b.

[39] Abodah Zarah, 9b. Incidentally, Abrabanel points out that the division of universal history into three equal parts cannot be taken too literally. The first two thousand years were not completely Torah-less, for the generations between Adam and Enoch, which lasted 235 years, declared their faith in God. It was after Enoch that the practice of idolatry began. In the third and fourth millenniums there was a period lasting 232 years, from the selling of Joseph to the Revelation on Mt. Sinai, which must be excluded as a part of the Torah-age. So a corresponding number of years must be deducted from the two Messianic chiliads.

time you shall not hope for him. But after that time you may hope for him."[40] The conditional epoch then will begin in the year 4250 (85x50) from creation, or 490 C. E.

e. Daniel a Fertile Source.

The book of Daniel is a fertile source for Messianic calculations.[41] From it Abrabanel derives the first year of the unconditional era. Verse 7:25 reads: "And he shall speak words against the Most High and shall wear out saints of the Most High; and he shall think to change the seasons and the Law; and they shall be given into his hand until a time, and times and half a time." Abrabanel controverts the Christian interpretation of this verse and chapter as applying to the Anti-Christ, who will flourish for three and a half years and will then be slain. For the Christian interpreters understood "time" to mean one year. Abrabanel takes it to be 410 years, the period of the first Temple. His computation therefore, is as follows: 410 (time) plus 820 (times) plus (½ time) 205, equal 1435. These many years Israel will be subservient to Rome and the nations. The year 1435 added to 3828 (when the second Temple was razed) equals 5263 or 1503 C. E., which will mark the termination of the hostile empires and the supremacy of Israel. In this year, Abrabanel expected the Messiah. He gives an identical calculation for verse 12:4.

Another calculation is based on 8:13-14: "Then I heard a holy one speaking; . . . : 'How long shall be the vision concerning the continual burnt offering and the transgression that causeth appalment, to give both the sanctuary and the host to be trampled under foot?' And he said unto me: 'Unto 2300 evenings and mornings then shall the sanctuary be victorious.'" The expression "evenings and mornings" does not mean days, for if so, the word "yom" should

---

[40]San. 97b; Yeshuot, p. 21a.
[41]Mayene, pp. 51, 56-57.

have been used. Neither can we say that "erev" and "boker" mean one day, because in verse 26—"And the vision of the evenings and mornings"—the expression is a figure of speech redolent of sorrow, *erev*, and of joy, *boker*. Therefore in verse 14 it cannot be taken literally either. Abrabanel understands the number 2300 to signify years. He adds to it the year of Solomon's death, which marked the division and eventual dissolution of the Kingdom, and thus ascertains the year of the reunion and the re-establishment of the monarchy.

        2448 (Exodus from Egypt)
         480 (erection of Temple after Exodus)
          36 (years Solomon reigned after erection of the
               Temple)
        ————
        2964 (Solomon died)
        2300
        ————
        5264
          —1 (deficiencies between lunar and solar year)
        ————
        5263 (the end of wonders or 1503 C. E.)

Another supporting passage from Dan. 12:12, reads: "Happy is he that waiteth and cometh to the 1335 days." Taking "yomim" to mean years and adding the numerical value of its letters yod, mem, yod, mem, which amount to 100, to the 1335, he gets 1435; this added to the year 3828, when the second Temple was destroyed, equals 5263.

Abrabanel offers the following legend,[42] which seemingly refutes his deductions, to reinforce them. R. Hanan b. Tahlipha sent a message to R. Joseph: "I met a man who possessed a scroll, written in Assyrian characters and in the holy language. And to my question where he obtained it, he answered, 'I hired myself to the army and among the treasures of Rome I found it.' And it was

---

[42]San. 97b; Yeshuot, 21b.

written therein that 4291 years after creation the world
will be orphaned; many years will be the wars of the
whales (the avaricious nations), and many more will be
the wars of Gog and Magog, and the remainder will be
the days of the Messiah. But the Holy One, blessed be
He, will not renew the world before 7000 years will have
elapsed; and R. Aha b. Rabba added, after 5000 years will
the world be orphaned." Abrabanel construes the altered
view of R. Aha to mean the existing state of affairs will
terminate in the year 5291 of creation and clears away
the discrepancy with his own date (5263) by making the
latter mark the commencement and the former (5291)
the termination of the Messianic era.

By employing gematria, which was not uncommon with
a certain class of commentators, Abrabanel adduces the
year 5291 from the phrase "time of the end" (Dan. 12:4).
"But thou, O Daniel, close up the words and seal the
book until *the time of the end:* many will roam about, yet
shall knowledge be increased." Abrabanel adds the
numerical values of the letters *es kez,* letting *ayim* stand
for 70, *tav* for 400, *kof* for 100 and *zadi* for 900. The total
being 1470. This year added to the year 3821 when Titus
besieged Jerusalem equals 5291.

3—Controversial.

a. Refutation of the thesis that the Messiah had already
come.

Abrabanel's book the Yeshuot Meshiho has a rare value
as a compilation of rabbinic data and legends used by
apostates to prove the authenticity of their Messiah.[43] At
this point I will cite several of these proofs that the Messiah had already come, in order to illustrate the claims of
the antagonist and the method of Abrabanel.

---

[43]Yeshuot, pp. 18-47.

Genesis 49:10—"The sceptre shall not depart from Judah, nor the ruler's staff from between his feet, as long as men come to Shiloh," is offered as evidence of the Messiah's advent. The Christian argument is built out of the following catena of passages. The Talmud observes that forty years before the destruction the Sanhedrin was dispersed from the Chamber of Hewn Stones and convened in the Market Place.[44] Another statement emanating from R. Moses ha-Darshan quoted by the apostate Lorki reads as follows: "The rod shall not depart from Judah,"—this is the Chamber of Hewn Stones, situated in the territory of Judah. "And a lawgiver from between his feet"—these are the inhabitants of Jabez who teach the law to Israel in the great Sanhedrin.[45] And so it is claimed Jacob predicted that the Sanhedrin that convenes in the Chamber of Hewn Stones shall not depart from the territory of Judah to try capital cases until Shiloh, who is the Messiah, shall come. The following statement is also offered as corroboration. Rabbi Nachman said: "When the great Sanhedrin was abolished from the Chamber of Hewn Stones, the trial of capital cases was abolished; they wore sackcloth on their skin and tore the hair of their heads and said, 'Woe is us, for the rod of Judah has departed and the son of David has not come.' "

Upon the basis of this the apostate concluded that since the Sanhedrin had ceased, the Messiah had already come, thus upholding the Christian claim that the cessation of the Sanhedrin synchronized with the appearance of their savior. Abrabanel refuted this proposition as follows. The apostate wilfully misquoted the foregoing statement, which originally included the added section that the lawgivers of the people of Jabez will not cease to teach the laws to Israel until Shiloh, who is the Messiah, shall come.

---

[44]Abodah Zarah 8b; Sabb. 15a.
[45]Comp. Yalk. Shim. I, par. 160.

THE DOCTRINE OF THE MESSIAH

The part omitted by the apostate conveys the view that even if the Sanhedrin had ceased to function, so long as the lawmakers, represented by the sages of subsequent ages, still flourish and continue to shepherd Israel in dispersion, the time is not ripe for the veritable Messiah to appear. Furthermore, the view that the rod of Judah symbolizes the Sanhedrin is an individual one. Other opinions have it that the rod refers to the exilarchs of Babylon, and the lawgiver to the descendants of Hillel of Davidic lineage, who disseminate Torah.[46] Thus the prediction relates to the long succession of future scholars and leaders, and the gist of the verse is that Judah will not lack spiritual leaders prior to the Messiah's arrival. This interpretation is in accord with an opinion that the Messiah will not come until judges and officers cease to function in Israel. The passage may also mean that when the Messiah arrives the Sanhedrin, with its decrees and adjudications, will be a thing of the past. It will not be needed, for unanimity and perfection of religious practice and belief will prevail. In his Bible Commentary Abrabanel ingeniously interprets the word "ad" not as a limitation of time but as denoting a long stretch of time. The meaning will then be that Judah will not cease to wield authority as long as the Messiah may come.[47]

The author refutes an implication of the Messiah's arrival made from the statement that the fifth and sixth chiliads are Messianic.[48] The apostate holds that since we are living within those intervals, it follows that the redeemer has come. But Abrabanel explains that the statement does not necessarily prove the fact. It does mean that the time is ripe for his coming.

---

[46]San. 5a. Where Gen. 49:10 is also taken Messianically. The rod is "the Messiah, son of David, who is destined to rule the empire with a rod." "Until Shiloh comes,"—for all the nations are destined to bring gifts to Israel and to King Messiah.

[47]*Lo l'haqvil z'man, elo l'haflih ha-inyan.*

[48]San. 97a; Abrabanel's answer is identical with that given by Albo to his disputant.

Another inference is extracted from Deut. 30:5—"And the Lord thy God will bring thee into the land which thy fathers possessed and thou shalt possess it." R. Jose concludes that Israel was promised only two possessions of Palestine.[49] This is ammunition to Christian propagandists, who conclude that since the two possessions are those of the conquest under Joshua and the return under Ezra, hence there will be no third possession. This, affirms Abrabanel, is plainly contrary to Jewish belief, and he disposes of the Christian surmise by declaring that the return of the Jews under Ezra cannot be regarded as a possession, since it was too short-lived. Besides, they were continually under the heel of other races. The second acquisition of Palestine by the Jews, therefore, must occur in the future.

The following curious and fanciful legend tells of an incident that happened to a certain Jew who was engaged in plowing. An Arab passed and heard the ox bellow. Said the Arab: "Son of a Jew, loose thy oxen, loose thy plows, for the Temple of the Jews is destroyed." The Jew did so. As he was doing this the ox bellowed a second time. Said the Arab: "Yoke thy oxen, yoke thy plows, for the Messiah has just been born." But the Jew asked: "What is his name?" The Arab said: "Menahem." "And what is the name of his father?" "Hezekiah." "Where was he born?" The Arab answered, "In Bethlehem-Judah." The Jew then sold his oxen and his plows and became a trader of infants' swaddling clothes. He went from city to city until he came to Bethlehem-Judah. There all the women gathered to buy clothes for their children. Said he to them: "Does the mother of Menahem dwell among you?" "Yes," they replied. And when he had found her he said to her: "Why dost thou not come and buy for Menahem, thy son?" She replied: "Luck has been

---

[49] Yebamot 82b.

bad, for on the day that he was born the Temple was laid waste." He said: "But we trust that as through him it was laid waste, so through him it will be rebuilt." She answered: "I have no money." Then he said: "It matters not; take the clothes, and you will pay me at another time."

Some days later he returned to that place and went to the mother and said: "How is the child doing?" She answered: "Did I not tell you the last time you were here, that luck was bad. It has continued to be bad. Winds and tempests have come and snatched him away from me."[50]

This legend is used to bolster up the argument that the Messiah had been born, and that he is identical with the Christian savior, who was born about the time of Jerusalem's downfall. Abrabanel explains this metaphorically, and among other things says that the legendary birth of the Messiah on that disastrous day means that God conceived a plan for Israel's deliverance at that time. That the Messiah will come as successor and by virtue of David, is suggested from the word Bethlehem, the birthplace of David. He will be a comforter, (Menahem) and will be like unto Hezekiah in good deeds. The Jews will become itinerant traders. The nations of the earth will recognize their usefulness as merchants and will patronize them. The sinister spirits which snatched the infant away are the sins and evils which retard the Messiah's advent.

b. Isaiah 53. Critical Treatment of Christian Interpretation.

In his commentary, Abrabanel considers Isaiah 53 very minutely, and marshals many reasons to prove the fallacy of non-Jewish theologians who interpret the entire chap-

---

[50]Ekah Rabbati 1, 57; Yerush. Ber., 17b; Yeshuot, pp. 39-42. This legend is the theme of the play, "The Eternal Jew," by D. Pinski; see Israel Levi, The Revue des Etudes Juives, Vol. 74, pp. 113-117, and Vol. 75, pp. 113-118 discusses this legend.

ter as testimony of the divinity of their savior. Actually the contents of the chapter are incompatible with the history of Jesus.

In his customary way the author poses several questions along which his investigation proceeds; the answers to these queries furnish the exposition of the chapter.

1. Who is the subject of the chapter: "The learned among the Nazarenes expound it as the man who was crucified in Jerusalem at the end of the second Temple, and who, according to them, was the son of God and took flesh in the virgin's womb, as is stated in their writings"?

2. How is the Messianic interpretation of Is. 52:13-15 by the Midrash to be justified?

3. Why does the prophet use the term "man", which implies a single individual rather than a collective individual?

4. What notion is involved in the subject's suffering,— verses 4, 5, 11?

Abrabanel avers that he can choose between two alternative interpretations; the more likely one is to refer it to Israel, as in other passages where "my servant" means Israel. Moreover, the chapter under discussion is intermediate between two such sections, 52:12 and 54:1; both of these treat of the nation. Israel is conceived as a unit; the term, man, may denote the genus man collectively, rather than a specific person. "Our sickness" and "our pains" need not mean the sicknesses borne by the nations but those inflicted by them upon Israel. The nations will confess that they were the agents of Israel's affliction. They had thought that "by his stripes they were healed"; that by harassing Israel they would obtain healing and peace for their souls. Hence they were bent on Israel's destruction.

THE DOCTRINE OF THE MESSIAH

The sage attacks the salient doctrine that the acclaimed Messiah had for his mission the salvation of mankind from original sin.[51]

1. It is argued that Jesus saved man's soul from eternal punishment imposed for the original sin of Adam. Abrabanel refutes this proposition as ungrounded, for nowhere does Scripture state that Adam's soul was doomed to hell.

2. Even if Adam had sinned and was punished spiritually, why should his sin and doom be inherited by subsequent generations? It is true that the mortal body can inherit sin and weakness, but the soul being divine, comes from a pure source, untainted, and therefore should not be liable for Adam's disobedience.

3. Granting that mortals inherit sinfulness from Adam, are we to believe that it is impossible for the Almighty to forgive? Must he become incarnate and endure suffering? Logic and justice demand that the sinner be punished and not the one who is sinned against.

4. If it appears plausible that one being should bear the sin of mankind and suffer for all, then that being might conceivably be a prophet, or a saint, but not a God. Moreover, the Christian doctrine is based on an impossibility, namely, that the Deity is corporeal.

Further difficulties encountered in the chapter show that it cannot refer to Jesus.

1. 52:13: "Behold, my servant, yaskil (shall prosper)." If we translate, yaskil, "shall become wise", it would imply that God-Jesus had previously lacked wisdom. This is inconceivable, as God's wisdom is eternal. If we translate, "my servant shall prosper", it becomes absurd, for how can a condition of prosperity or success

---

[51]See Abrabanel Comm. on Is. 52:13, ed. 1641, p. 78b.

be predicated of the Godhead? Even humanly speaking, it cannot be said that Jesus prospered, because of his tragic end.

2. How can the term servant be applied to one who spiritually and intellectually is supreme, a God?

3. The words "He shall be exalted and lifted up, and shall be very high", cannot describe him humanly, because of his unhappy life. If the words are construed metaphorically they must refer to God.

4. "He had no form nor comeliness that we should look upon him. Nor beauty that we should delight in him", cannot be said of Jesus, for history reports him to have been attractive in appearance. If the verse describes his condition at death, there is nothing singular about it, because it is true of every dead person.

5. "Surely our diseases he did bear . . ." cannot refer to Jesus' release of the wretched souls imprisoned in gehinnom for the sin of the first parent, because spiritual penalty is never called sickness.

6. "Lamo", v. 8, is plural, "to them", and indicates that the subject spoken of in the singular throughout, must be a virtual plural, the nation Israel.[52]

7. "They made his grave with the wicked". His grave, says Abrabanel, was not molested. Interest centered only in his death. The other expression: "And with the rich, his tomb", shows conclusively that reference is not to him, for history records nothing about his tomb.[53]

---

[52]Kimhi was the first to note that the plural form excludes reference to a Messianic redeemer, see *Fifty-third Chapter of Isaiah according to Jewish Interpreters.*

[53]Abrabanel cites Psalm 88:6—"free among the dead"—in connection with Is. 53:9; and says bitterly that Israel was not even free, meaning unmolested, in death; the persecutors dragged the dead from the tombs, especially if the departed was sufficiently wealthy for them to imagine that his riches might be buried with him.

8. "Yet it pleased the Lord to crush him by disease". If Jesus wished to save the wicked from perdition, then he assumed responsibility for his sufferings, and it is wrong to argue that God willed it.

9. "That he might see his seed, prolong his days". Jesus died young and left no descendants. The verse cannot refer to his adherents and disciples, because "zera" (seed) is never used metaphorically but always of physical offspring.[54]

10. "And he shall divide the spoil with the mighty". Nowhere do we read that he plundered.[55]

Consistently with this method of interpretation, the sage disagrees vehemently with the Midrash and a host of expositors who identify the chapter with the Messiah, son of David. He exonerates them by supposing that the earlier authorities merely applied the traditions they had received respecting the Messiah to the present passage, without in the least imagining such to be its actual meaning. For although our rabbis explain the first verse, "Behold my servant shall prosper", of the King Messiah, yet the remaining verses are applied exclusively to Israel. He is compelled to take cognizance of the Messianic elaboration of Is. 52:13 in order to keep the heretics from seeking shelter therein. The Midrashic paraphrase is: "Behold my servant shall prosper"—this is the King Messiah; "He shall be exalted"—above Abraham; "lifted up"—above Moses; "and shall be very high"—above the ministering angels.[56] He observes that the *mem* prefixed

---

[54] See Kimhi, *ibid.*

[55] Other arguments against the divinity of Jesus, the Messiah, derived from Is. 53 are: 1. He ought to have removed temporal death. 2. To have repaired Adam's sin entirely. 3. To have made mankind sinless. 4. If he is God, with whom could he intercede? 5. How could he "be exalted"?—God is always exalted. 6. If he were God it could not be said, verse 10: "The pleasure of the Lord shall prosper in his hand," since it would be God's own hand.

[56] Yalk. Shim. on Is. 52-13.

ISAAC ABRABANEL

to "Abraham" and "the angels" does not indicate the
derivation of the subject "my servant", but is the *mem* of
superiority or comparison. It means that the Messiah, in
the opinion of the homilists, will be vastly more eminent
in his vindication of Israel than either the patriarch, the
law-giver, or the angels.

c. Daniel, Chapters 7 and 9.

The unusual interest of Abrabanel in this subject is
seen in the fact that he wrote a fair-sized book on the
visions of Daniel, the core of which he found to be the
successive sway of the world empires of Babylon, Persia,
Greece, and Rome, and the permanent Messianic state.
Many of the millennial ideas found in Abrabanel's exposition of Daniel have been given in other parts of this work.
Herewith are added certain detailed explanations along
historical lines.

The "small horn" in Dan. 7:8 refers to the first Pope.

The "three horns", v. 8, that were plucked, may represent the three systems of Roman rule—kings, consuls, and
emperors, who were later displaced by the papal power;
or they may refer to the three Roman rulers who died
before Jesus was born, Julius Caesar, Augustus, and
Tiberius.

"Eyes, like the eyes of a man", and "a mouth speaking
great things", v. 8, characterize Rome. The first denotes
wisdom or sophism, and the second, oratory, for which the
Romans were noted.

"Ancient of days", v. 13, is God; "and one like unto a
son of man", is Israel. Israel's salvation will then follow
upon the overthrow of Rome, and in contrast to the sup-
planted monarchies, it will be imperishable.

Abrabanel combats the interpretation of this section,
according to which the birth of Christ is foretold at the
end of seventy weeks of years, or 490 years, and that the

phrase, "to finish transgressions", means that he will bring forgiveness and everlasting righteousness to mankind throughout the world.[57] Accepting the traditional chronology he figures that the 490 years covers the interval from the first destruction to the second destruction in 70 C. E. and declares that a new dispersion will commence for Israel at the expiration of the 490 years, or at the destruction of the Temple in 70.

9:24—"To finish the transgression, to make an end of sin and to forgive iniquity" relates to the necessity of a longer exile to enable Israel to expiate the frightful iniquities committed during her long stay in Palestine.

"To bring in everlasting righteousness", so that by the time Israel is ultimately delivered, the world will have become converted to the Torah of righteousness.

"To seal vision and prophet", means not that the activities of the prophets will be terminated, but that there will be an extraordinary fulfillment of their prophecies.

9:24—"And to anoint the most holy" (kodesh hakodoshim) may mean that either the Temple, the Torah, or Israel will be re-sanctified.

9:25—"Unto one anointed a prince", most probably refers to some distinguished person who figured in the return from Babylon. Josephus thinks it means the priest Joshua son of Jehozedek. Rashi refers it to Cyrus; Ibn Ezra and Nahmanides to Zerubabel. The seven weeks (forty-nine) refer to the Babylonian captivity; the sixty-two weeks (434 years) to the troublesome time under Greece and Rome.

9:26—"An anointed one shall be cut off", this connoted the high priest whose ministry will end, or the death of Agrippa II.

---

[57]Mayene, pp. 66-67 give the refutation; pp. 59c-66 present Abrabanel's theories.

9:26—"The people of a prince that shall come shall destroy the city and sanctuary", refers to the destruction of the Temple by Titus.

4—*Age Preceding the Advent.*

a. Description of Its Degeneration.

As though the baleful career of the Jews did not warrant their faith in a redeemer, the people felt constrained to color with the most livid and somber hues the age preceding the advent. The gulf between now and the hereafter was widened to such a degree as to magnify the benevolence of God, when He would intervene in their behalf. More, the darker the night, the brighter must the morrow be. All their adversities were intensified a thousand fold. The coming age would beggar description.[58] Mankind would have reached the lowest pitch, the abyss of deterioration. The earmarks of the age would be social debasement, the expansion of heresy all over the world, the impairment of sacred family ties, and acute physical anguish because of the lack of the simplest necessities. These inevitable predictions, known as the "Birth Travails of the Messiah", would be ephemeral. According to the Talmud which Abrabanel follows they were to last for seven years. As the blackness and gloom of the night are dispelled by the first rays of the dawning sun, so shall the dazzling radiance of the light (Nehora) of the Messiah penetrate and gladden the heart of Israel. The evils of the sinister prelude to the Messianic era are of an economic, political, moral, religious, and cosmic nature. Under the political aspect is included the expansion of the wicked empire, Rome, over the entire world for nine months, and the collapse of Jewish communal life in Palestine and in

[58]San. 97a; Yeshuot, pp. 33b-37 discusses the dreadful prelude of the Messianic era.

the diaspora. No semblance of Jewish independence or jurisdiction will survive. Thus we read : "The son of David will not come until the two patriarchal houses perish from Israel. These are the Resh Galuta in Babylon and the Nasi in Palestine."[59] R. Simlai also said that there would cease to be judges and officers in Israel. To those who contended that the Messiah had not appeared in spite of the abolition of the two patriarchal offices, Abrabanel replied that the Nagid of Spain is the successor to the Nasi of Palestine.

Abrabanel felt that many of the rabbinic word pictures of chaos, penury and degeneration in the pre-Messianic era fitted his own times. We can surmise then how insufferable Jewish life was. The statement that the whole world must be converted to "Minuth", heresy, before the Messiah's arrival was corroborated by the spread of heresy in Judaism. More especially did he see these ominous predictions come true in the heretical Protestant reformers.

The hypocrisy and the worldliness of the higher clergy and the common monks of the Catholic church did not escape his observation. During this time "Ecclesiastical Rome offered a spectacle of moral corruption and spiritual downfall which has been compared to the corrupt age of the Roman Empire". Little wonder then that he believed he was living in the Age of Woe.

The following are a few of the descriptions that Abrabanel culls from the Talmud. R. Nehuria taught that in "the generation in which the son of David will come, young men will make pale the faces of old, old men will rise up before youth, a daughter will rebel against her mother, a daughter-in-law against her mother-in-law, the leaders of the generation will have the nature of dogs, and a son

---

[59]San. 38a; The Resh Galuta was the civil head of the Jews in Babylon up to the end of the geonic period. The Nasi in Palestine presided over ecclesiastic and communal matters.

will not be ashamed when his father reproaches him". R. Judah says: "In the generation in which the son of David comes, the houses of study and assembly will be converted into brothels. Galilee will be destroyed. Gaulan will be desolated. The men of the border of Palestine will travel from one city to another, but will meet with insolence. The wisdom of the scribes will be corrupted. Men who fear sin will be hated. The leaders of the generation will have the nature of dogs, and truth will be missing. Scholarly men will decrease, and of those who remain, their eyes will protrude from sighing and sorrow. Many chastisements and evil decrees will be renewed. One will not yet cease, while another will have come". The prediction of the rabbis that prior to the Advent informants would increase, he saw materialized in the activities of the Spanish inquisitors and spies against professing Jews. He gives a metaphorical explanation of the curious remark that the Messiah would not come until a small fish will be needed for a sick person and it will not be found: murder will be rampant in the pre-Messianic era. As the large fish devour the small ones, so the powerful will mercilessly destroy the weak. Another interpretation is that the fish is symbolic of Egypt. That country will be so utterly destroyed that no living thing will survive in the great river.

In another passage the dark and bright side of the seven year prelude to the new era is described thus: In the first year, the woes of the prophet Amos will come to pass, "And on one city I caused it to rain, and upon another city I caused it not to rain"; in the second year the arrows of famine will be sent out; in the third year there will be a great famine from which men, women, and children, pious men and men of good deeds will die, and Torah will be forgotten by the disciples; in the fourth year,

there will be abundance, and not abundance; in the fifth
year there will be abundance and people will eat, drink,
and enjoy themselves, and the Torah will return to her
scholars; in the sixth year voices will be heard saying:
"Messiah is near"; in the seventh, will come the wars;
at the end of the seventh, the son of David will appear.

Though Abrabanel refuses to be counted among the
Cabalists, and throughout his writings disclaims any lean-
ing toward their mystical theories, he nevertheless mani-
fests sympathy for several of their views. He quotes
the statement that the son of David will not come until
the Treasure House had been emptied of its souls.[60] The
assumption of the mystics is that the number of souls
that were to enter earthly bodies had been fixed at the
creation and that they had all been created simultaneously
with the soul of Adam. In the course of time these souls
are to take up their abode in the "lower world", the earth.
As long as some souls remain in the depository, the Messiah's advent is prevented. Just as the generation that
left Egypt could not enter the Holy Land but perished
in the desert as expiation for their sinfulness, so in the
next possession of Palestine, all souls destined to inhabit
earthly bodies must leave the Treasure House before redemption occurs. Good deeds and repentance can hasten
the arrival of the Messiah by emptying the storehouse of
souls more rapidly. For the souls that inhabited the
bodies of worthy and repentant people will not be condemned to transmigrate. Hence the supply of original
souls in the Treasure House will be duly exhausted.

b. Messiah ben Joseph and the Anti-Christ.

The Messiah b. Joseph should properly be considered
a pre-Messianic figure, because his activity would be con-

---

[60]Yeb. 62a; Ber. Rabba 24:4; Yeshuot 36b-37. Abrabanel mentions
the Cabalistic notion that Adam's soul migrated to David and is destined
to enter the Messiah.

fined to the seven aforementioned years. He would be a precursor of the Messiah b. David. His other name, Ben Ephraim, denotes more clearly that his origin is to be of the tribe of Ephraim.[61] During the war of the nations he will arise in Rome, reassemble the Jews in the sacred land, and re-establish the Hebrew state. He will distinguish himself on the fields of battle. After much suffering he will meet death in Palestine at the hands of the enemy. His successor will be the son of David, to whom he will be inferior in every way; in the possession of an ideal character, in the performance of miracles, and in the organization of a political state. The belief in an Ephraimitic Messiah arose out of the doubtfulness inherent in the conception of a political and a spiritual emancipator. The Messiah b. Joseph can only be conceived in the former light. This explains why Akiba (120 C.E.) proclaimed Bar Kochba, though not of Davidic descent, the Messiah. Bar Kochba enacted the role of a military political champion.

Abrabanel is the only writer in this series who alludes to the Anti-Christ. He propounds the ingenious theory that the Jewish belief in a Messiah b. Joseph has been appropriated by Christianity with only a single modification, the change in name.[62] Christian expositors find the latter-day antagonist of the church pre-figured in Dan. 7:7-14; 11:36-*et seq.*; and 12. "The little horn", mentioned in Dan. 7:8, is an anti-Christian power destined to arise in the future. His activity will extend over three and a half years, for "time" is taken to signify one year. His

---

[61]Mashmia, 74a; see Prof. Ginzberg on "Anti-Christ" in J. E. Vol. 1, pp. 625-627, and Bousset "The Anti-Christ". Bousset sees the source of the Anti-Christ legend as a simple reincarnation of the old dragon myth which had in the first instance nothing to do with particular political powers and vicissitudes. For the dragon is substituted the man armed with miraculous power who makes himself God's equal—"a man who in the eyes of the Jews could be no other than the false Messiah" (p. 144 of Peake's translation).

[62]Mashmia, p. 13c; Mayene, pp. 45 and 74.

functions are all those of the Messiah b. Joseph and the latter's function as an avenger upon the powers hostile to Israel. Declaring that the Messiah had already come in the person of Jesus, the early Christians still had serious apprehensions that the redeemer awaited by the Jews might appear and frustrate the Messiahship of Jesus. To discredit the Jewish Messiah they formulated a belief in an anti-Messiah who would antagonize the dominant faith and wage war upon their countries.

5—*Features of the Redemption.*

a. God the Redeemer.

The future deliverance will not be effected by the capricious will of an earthly monarch whose decree may be rescinded by a successor. It will be absolute. In this respect it will be singularly distinguished from the many times Israel had gained release from tyrannous rulers. The liberality of Cyrus permitted Israel to return to Babylon, only to be undone by the despotism of succeeding monarchs. But future redemption carries with it the intrinsic stipulation that God himself will be the Redeemer. He will be as expeditious as He was in the deliverance from Egypt and in the revelation on Mt. Sinai. So we read: "And the Eternal brought us forth from Egypt not by means of an angel, not by means of a seraph, nor by means of a messenger, but the Holy One, blessed be He, in His glory."[63]

Of the same train of thought are the following striking illustrations: "In Thy light do we see light."[64] The meaning of this verse can be illustrated by a parable. A man was walking by the light of a candle at night. As often as he lit it, the light went out. Then he exclaimed: "How

---

[63]Yalk. Shim. on Ex. 12:12.
[64]Ps. 36:10; Mid. Tehilim on that verse; also Pesikta R. Kahana ed. Buber, ch. XXI, p. 257.

long shall I weary myself? I will wait here until sunrise
and will proceed by the light of the sun". Thus it happened with Israel. When they were enslaved by Egypt,
Moses arose as redeemer; when exiled in Babylon, Daniel,
Hananiah, Mishael, and Azariah redeemed them; when oppressed by the Medes, Mordecai and Esther redeemed
them. Then they were enslaved by Rome, whereupon
Israel exclaimed: "We are wearied by the intermittent
redemptions and enslavements; we do not desire the light
brought by man, but from now on we will wait for God to
light the way." A similar passage reads: "The Holy One,
blessed be He, said, In this world I delivered Israel
through the children of man; in Egypt through Moses
and Aaron; from Sisera, through Deborah and Barak;
and from the Midianites through the Judges. Because
these deliverances were wrought by man they were not
lasting. But in the future, I alone will deliver you and
you will not be enslaved again; as the verse reads: 'O
Israel, thou art saved by the Lord with an everlasting
salvation.' "[65]

b. The Ingathering.

The principal feature of the redemption is the ingathering of the exiles.[66] In the minds of the rabbis it was
tantamount to the work of creation. The clearest statement of it is given by Isaiah 43:5-6, "Fear not, for I am
with thee; I will bring thy seed from the east, and gather
thee from the west; I will say to the north: 'Give up'; and
to the south, 'Keep not back', bring My sons from far, and
My daughters from the end of the earth." The work of salvation will not be complete until all Israel has been sifted
from among the nations, so that no Israelite will remain
in dispersion. Those who have abandoned the faith and

---

[65]Is. 45:17; Yalk. Shim. on Zech. 9:9.
[66]Yeshuot, p. 26.

others who have removed the traces of circumcision in order to be known as Gentiles will, if they renounce their Godless ways, share in the redemption. The mere commission of sin does not eliminate one from the Jewish fold. Impenitent sinners will perish in the Age of Woe, very much as the generation of the desert had to be consumed before the people's entrance into the Holy Land. The heathen population will be decimated as a consequence of the final wars. Those surviving annihilation will acknowledge the sovereignty of God, who will bestow upon them a share in the joys of the bliss-spreading era.

The lost ten tribes surely will be included in the restoration. The dissenting opinion of the Tannaitic authority Rabbi Akiba, does not infringe upon the doctrine of a universal Jewish ingathering. According to Abrabanel,[67] Akiba denied the return of those Northern exiles who settled in Halah, Habor, and on the River Gozan, for the obvious reason that they were extinct; either they perished from unfavorable climatic conditions or because they had become part and parcel of the indigenous population. However, the progeny of the ten tribes who fled to Judah, to Egypt and to other surrounding states, would be included in the general ingathering.

c. The Exodus as an Analogy.

The deliverance from Egypt is the archetype for the future redemption which, unlike the former, will embrace all mankind.[68] The prophets and sages felt very profoundly the similarity in scope and nature between the two events. The Exodus came at the beginning of Israel's career, when for the first time it was subject to a foreign power; the future deliverance will witness the final emancipation of Israel and its sway over all nations. The

---

[67]San. 110b; Yeshuot, pp. 31-33 treats also of Bar Kochba's Messiahship.

[68]Mashmia, 10a and 31b.

Messianic figure at his noblest and best is but a replica
of the grand personality of Moses, whose prophetic intuition, divine attachment, prudence in practical affairs,
and self-sacrifice he will embody. The future redemption
will be actual and physical, as was the Exodus, and not
as the Christians hold a salvation from sin. Like the
Exodus, the future deliverance will be in Nisan, and the
dissenting view that it would be in Tishri, applies to the
victory over Gog and Magog, which will complete the
pageant of redemption.[69] The miraculous events connected with the Exodus will be repeated at the redemption, as the prophet Mic. (7:15) says: "As in the days
of thy coming forth out of the land of Egypt, will I show
unto him marvellous things". The Euphrates will be dried
up, so that the exiles who are in farthest Assyria, or even
those of the ten tribes who survive in other lands, may
pass dry-shod into the sacred land. Then also, as formerly, Israel will acclaim the kind providence of God,
and chant a paean of victory to Him, their Redeemer.

Because the return from Babylon was not comparable
in its marvels to the Exodus and fell short of it in many
respects, it could not have been the final deliverance en-
visioned by the prophets.

6—*The Messiah.*

a. No Redemption without a Messiah.

A distinction exists between the advent of a personal
Messiah as the key to the millennium, and the attainment
of national and universal perfection without his instrumentality. To Abrabanel, the Messiah was indispensable.
Unlike the view of skeptics, that the Messiah would not
come, and the Christian view that he came in the person

---

[69]Rosh Ha-Shana 11a; Abrabanel cites Hai Gaon to the effect that
the resurrection would occur at Passover, and the wars of Gog and Magog
at Succot.

of Jesus, a fundamental principle of our faith asserts that
the Messiah is still to come and that he will inaugurate the
millennium. He must appear, because God had vowed to
David to perpetuate his dynasty.[70]

R. Hillel's categorical statement to the effect that
Israel has no Messiah because they had already consumed
him in the days of Hezekiah (723-694 B. C.) is explained
in two ways by Abrabanel.[71] One is that the sage had
reference to the conditional period when the Messiah
could not be expected as a reward for the merits and good
deeds of the generation. Whatever merits Israel possessed
had been rewarded in the time of Hezekiah, in the miraculous overthrow of Sennacherib. Another plausible explanation is that the amora denied the intervention of a
Messianic personality, but not the other conventional features of redemption such as the ingathering, vengeance,
and resurrection. R. Hillel, forsooth, was satisfied that
the ideal character of King Hezekiah was the perfect em-
bodiment of the Messiah. Hezekiah was a sprout of the
branch of Jesse. He possessed the spirit of wisdom and
judged the poor with righteousness. He was humble,
placing his reliance in God. Hence one of the names of
the Messiah is Menahem ben Hezekiah. In a beautiful
legend we are informed that because of the ingratitude
and pride he exhibited on several occasions he forfeited
the Messiahship. He failed to praise God when the latter
vanquished Sennacherib, and he showed vanity in display-
ing to the embassy of Baladan his treasure, instead of the
holy vessels. At any rate Hillel assumed, explains Abrabanel, that the Messianic type of leader had already appeared and that the distinct liberation of Israel will be
consummated without a Messianic advent.

---

[70]II Sam. 7:16.
[71]Yeshuot, 25ff. Rosh Amanah. Ch. 14. Hillel, the author of the statement was an amora of the 3rd century.

b. His Function as Restorer of Pristine Blessings.[72]

The coming Messiah will be of the royal lineage of
Solomon and David, and will trace his ancestry still
further back to Ruth the Moabite. As Moses was born in
Egypt and Zerubabel in Babylon, so the Messiah of the
future will be born of Jewish exiles in the Roman imperium. Where mention is made of Bethlehem as his
birthplace, it refers to his origin from the Davidic dynasty.
As soon as he sees the light of the world, his father will
die. For a long time he will live unknown, unrecognized,
ridiculed, and then he will make a sudden appearance. His
functions are not attenuated or formal. First and foremost, he will emancipate Israel from the yoke of oppressors. He will bring light to those in the darkness of affliction. The rabbis, in recognition of this activity, call him
"Menahem"—Comforter; "Nehorah"—Light; "Huliah"—
"he will save from suffering."[73] Israel, scattered to the
four ends of the earth, will gather about his standard, and
he will lead them to the sacred land. The nations which
had harassed Israel and cruelly subjected her, will suffer
extinction at his hand. He will cast down from their
"celestial abodes" the tutelary powers who heretofore
acted as intermediaries for their earthly clients.

The Messiah's advent will affect not only Israel, but
all mankind as well. Analogous to the creation of man
on the sixth day, will be the advent of the Messiah in the
sixth millennium; and the lordship of man over all previously created, symbolizes the sovereignty of the Messiah
over all nations. His imperium will be as extensive and
all-embracing as that of the world conquerors. He will

[72]Yeshuot, pp. 48-49b; Mashmia 8c-10.
[73]San. 98b; Ekah Rabbati 1:56; Ber. Rabba 1:8; see Schilo, Posnanski, p. 38, note 2. For the names Hivra (San. 98b) and Hulia (sick one)
applied to the Messiah read *M'kadmoniot ha-Yahudim*—A. Epstein, pp. 111
seq. Our Talmud mentions only Hivra. Both names are given in a quotation in the Pugio Fidei, by Raymond Martin, ed. Leipzig, p. 862.

not live forever as sovereign; it is the perpetuity of his dynasty that is vouchsafed. He will restore to his age what previous generations had forfeited through Adam's fatal sin; heavenly radiance, strength of life, stature, plentiful harvests and the pristine brightness of the luminaries.[74] He will renew prophecy, which has been discontinued since the dispersion.

c. His Pre-existence.

The soul of the Messiah, as the souls of all mortals, came into being on the first day of creation. Rabbinic passages which tell of the Messiah's pre-mundane existence prove the teleological object of God in the universe. The world is a purposive, ever-developing organism. At different stages the manifold designs of God are unfolded and come to fruition. So also the manifestation of the Messiah is an event pre-destined in the plan of the Creator. The passage stating that seven things were created before the world was made: Torah, repentance, reward and punishment, the throne of God, the Temple, and the name of the Messiah,—means that the underlying religious principles of these were determined before creation.[75] We can, therefore, affirm that the birth of the Messiah preceded creation not actually, but in the purpose and will of God. A legend which assumes extraordinary longevity for the anointed one tells of his birth on the day the second Temple was destroyed.[76] Abrabanel explains this in two ways. One, that he was not actually created at that time, but that the intention to send him rose at the time in God's mind. The other is that the Messiah may have been born on the day of the destruction, but that he was transferred to Paradise to await the propitious hour because of the

[74]Ber. Rabba 12:5.
[75]Pes. 54a, Yeshuot 47a. Mention is also made of six who were called by name before they were born: Ishmael, Isaac, Moses, Solomon, Josiah, and Messiah. Comp. Ber. Rabba 1, 4.
[76]See Note 50 in this essay.

unworthiness of the generation to receive him. Abrabanel finds corroboration for this possibility in the Agadot statement that nine entered Paradise alive, and among them were Elijah and Messiah.[77]

d. His Character not Transcendental nor Divine.

The Messiah will not be a "transcendental figure coming from an extraneous source." He will be neither a God, nor a son of God; he will be the holiest of the holy. Our author stresses the human birth of the redeemer. Though earthly in every respect, (adam gamur) he will be a superman, for he will have attained the acme of perfection possible to a mortal. The Messiah will best exemplify the true spirit of loving kindness and godliness. The supreme virtues of the great men of the Bible will be his. He will be master of himself, over-riding his sensual impulses. In judicial insight and fairness, in support of the defenceless, and in the fearless espousal of truth, he will be a second Solomon. In magnanimity he will excel Abraham, and in faithful leadership of the people he will surpass Moses. In prophetic power, however, he will fall short of Moses. Intellectuality, physical prowess, and piety, qualities which are not frequently found in one person, will be combined in him. Abrabanel strongly combats the view of certain scholars that Isaiah 11 describes King Hezekiah. "And the spirit of the Lord shall rest upon him, the spirit of wisdom and understanding, the spirit of counsel and might, the spirit of knowledge and of the fear of the Lord," means that the Messiah will possess the wisdom of Solomon, the valor of David, and the divine awe of Hezekiah. His ties of attachment to God will prove unbreakable and unassailable. While as a political figure he will rank with David, in his reliance

---

[77]Derek Eretz Zuta; end of Ch. 1; Yeshuot 39c; Higger, Massektot Zeirot, pp. 74, 129-131.

upon God, Hezekiah will be his prototype. His noble character and exalted station are attested in the high sounding names that our rabbis gave him. So the school of Shilah taught that his name is Peace; the school of Yannai, Dignity; the school of Hanina, Grace.[78] Abrabanel rejects the opinion of Christians that the Messiah is divine, that he has already appeared, and that the Old Testament has been abrogated by a new one. The latter two points are treated in other sections of this study.

e. Alleged Proofs of the Divinity of the Messiah.

At this time may be stated some of the "evidence" offered by the opposition, to prove his divinity and the refutations by the author.[79] Abrabanel refers to collections of rabbinic legends and statements made by apostate Jews for the purpose of showing that the Messiah had come and that Christianity was the true religion. He cites also the counter-arguments of Jewish authorities, and criticizes them for crediting the opposition with honesty and taking them too seriously. He also thinks that the logical arguments to which the Jewish scholars resorted were unnecessary. Often he finds that the opponents maliciously tampered with the text, or, in their ignorance, misunderstood its import. His refutation of Christological interpretations consists in giving the true meaning of Talmudic passages, which may be figurative or poetic. At other times the thought may be in accord with the ideals and principles of Israel and Judaism.

The citation from Genesis Rabba Rabbati, to the effect that the ten kings who ruled the earth were God, Nimrod, Joseph, Solomon, Nebuchadnezzar, Darius, Cyrus, Alexander, Augustus and the Messiah, is offered to show that

---

[78]San. 93b. Yeshuot, 47a, "Names", says Abrabanel, "are immaterial. It is what they denote that counts." These three appellations ingeniously accord with the names of the school: Shilah-Shiloh (Shalom); Yannai-Yinon derived from Ps. 72:17. Hanina means grace.
[79]Yeshuot 51-67.

the Messiah will be divine.[80] Here God is mentioned first, and the Messiah last. In Is. 44:6 God declares: "I am the first, and I am the last." Therefore God and the Messiah are one. Abrabanel regards the quotation as erroneous and cites a parallel passage in the Chapters of R. Eliezer which gives the following order: God, Nimrod, Joseph, Solomon, Nebuchadnezzar, Darius, Alexander, Messiah, and God.

There is a comment in the Midrash on Cant. 3:11— "The crown wherewith his mother hath crowned him." God called Israel daughter, then sister, and lastly mother.[81] From this it is supposed that God had a mother and was partly mortal. According to our sage, the three female relationships are given in a parable of a king. But he also cleverly observes that the relation of motherhood must be taken figuratively, else we must believe that He also had a daughter and a sister.

The word "vine" in Gen. 40:9 is taken by the Midrash to refer to Israel, or to the Messiah. It goes on to say that there is a planting below, and a planting from above and below. The planting below is Abraham; the planting below and above is the Messiah.[82] The latter thought leads the apostate to conclude that the Messiah is constituted of a dual nature, divine and human. To our author it merely means that the power of the Messiah will overwhelm the celestial "patrons", the protecting gods of the nations as well as all earthly rulers.

The phrase "other seed" and "seed" in Gen. 4:25 and 19:32 is referred by the Midrash to the Messiah, whence the apostate derives support for the Messiah's mystic and

---

[80]The passage is not found in our present Ber. Rabba. It is cited in the Pugio Fidei and there its source is given as the Ber. Rabba Rabbati of R. Moses ha-Darshan, French Rabbinist, middle of 11 cent. Rashi makes citations from this Midrash which unfortunately is lost. See Jew. Enc. v. 9, p. 64 and A. Epstein, "Moses ha-Darshan aus Narbonne", Vienna, 1891.

[81]Yalk. Shim. 3:11; Shir ha-Shirim Rabba, 3:21.

[82]Yeshuot, p. 53b; quoted from Midrash of R. Moses ha-Darshan.

divine origin.[83]   Says Abrabanel: "The rest of the Midrash clearly shows that 'other seed' is expounded to mean that the Messiah will come from the inter-marriage between Boaz and Ruth the Moabite."

"The thrones" mentioned in Dan. 7:9, according to the Talmud, are designed for God and David.[84]   Rashi adds for the Davidic Messiah. If so, argues the apostate, the Messiah is placed on a plane with God and is divine. Abrabanel explains that one cannot take the idea of actual thrones too literally. The conception of a throne is that it is a seat of judgment. One throne indicates the judgment of God at the time of the deliverance over the celestial powers, and the other denotes His judgment over the mundane sphere.

Is. 9:5, in which the Messiah is described as "Mighty God, Everlasting Father, Prince of Peace," does not show that the Messiah was divine. A rational view offered by our writer is that "El" is an attribute used in connection with holy objects. Jacob called an altar "God of the Gods of Jacob."[85]   Ezekiel called Jerusalem "The Lord is there."[86] In Hebrew a judge is called a God because of the sacredness of his office. So the Messiah could receive the name because of his great purpose and mission.

The statement that the Messiah will be superior to Abraham and Moses and above the ministering angels, is offered as evidence that the Messiah was angelic and even divine.[87]   In accordance with a current view that the nations have celestial representatives and that they will be overthrown in the deliverance Abrabanel asserts that the statement refers to these guardian angels of the nations which the Messiah will overcome.

---

[83]Ber. Rabba 51:10 and 23:7.
[84]Hag. 14a.
[85]Gen. 33:20; Yeshuot 49a.
[86]Ez. 48:35.
[87]Yalk. Shim. Is. 52:13.

ISAAC ABRABANEL

Is 45:17—"A people saved by the Lord" is thus expounded by the homilists: In the past Israel was saved by Moses, Aaron, Sisera, Deborah, Barak, and the Judges. In the future God will save them.[88] Hence the Messiah traditionally regarded as the Redeemer, is identical with God. In defense, Abrabanel replies that the last redemption will not be effected without an intermediary. Even in the case of the Exodus, where the Talmud says that God alone delivered Israel: "I and no angel, I and no seraph", Moses was the actual deliverer. The significance of the above homily is merely an indication that the last redemption will be so effective that it will appear as though the Lord Himself had consummated it.

There is a quaint legend that in the future God will walk with the righteous, and that he will hold a dance for them in Paradise.[89] He will stand in the center and they will point to him with their fingers. This indicated that God is corporeal. The language, remarks Abrabanel, is human, but the thought is figurative. The appearance of God walking and dancing amongst human beings expresses the notion of His providence and attachment to Israel. In another sense, Palestine may be conceived as the land of Paradise. The dance may refer to the redemption, and as at the Red Sea, so in the future luminous era the pilgrims will exultingly point their finger to God and praise Him for His goodness and greatness.

Ps. 2:2—"Nashku bar", according to the apostates, means "embrace the son," the divine Messiah, son of God.[90] Even if "bar" meant "son", notes Abrabanel, it would not

---

[88]Yalk. Shim. Zech. 9:9, compare Meg. 24b.
[89]Taanit 31a; Wayikra Rabba XI, 9.
[90]The following note from Psalms I, International Critical Commentary ed. C. A. Briggs, p. 17 is enlightening. The reading in the English versions "kiss the son", the Messiah, cannot be justified by usage or context and is based on a misinterpretation due to Syriac and Aramaic influence. The translation of the Jewish Publication Society is "Do homage in purity," with a pure heart. The Peshitta also reads son; the Targum and the Septuagint translate "bar" by instruction.

apply to the Messiah, but to Israel, so frequently called my son:—as "My son, my first born son is Israel" and "Ye are children of the Lord your God." But the word, as the Midrash further explains, connotes the spiritual food of the Torah, to be received by Gentiles in the Messianic future.

Proof that the Messiah had no human father, and hence shared a divine nature, is based on the following Midrash of R. Moses ha-Darsham.[91] R. Berachya said: "God said to Israel, Ye have said before me; we are orphans and have no father,—so the deliverer, whom I will raise among you, will have no father." So the Scripture reads—Zech. 6:12: "Behold a man whose name is the Shoot and who shall shoot up out of his place," and Is. 53:2 reads: "For he shot up right forth as a sapling"—from which it is concluded that the Messiah had no male parent, and hence was divine. Abrabanel offers several solutions to this dilemma. One is that the Messiah will be a posthumous child, a view in line with R. Eleazar's statement that as soon as the Messiah sees the light of day his father will die.[92] Hence he will grow up alone. The usual and sensible explanation of the verses is that the Messiah will be "self-made". He will not inherit his throne. His wisdom will be innate. He will require no aid or stimulus to arouse his prophetic and spiritual gifts. Great renown and mastery over life will come to him through his original qualities and self-energizing efforts. Another view which commends itself to our author is that the Messiah will be helpless, as an orphan without a protector, and like Israel he will undergo distress and oppression, before he reaches the stage of independence.

An interesting and unusual Midrash is offered to show that the Christian Messiah was conceived of a virgin.

---

[91]Found in Pugio Fidei, p. 594; A similar homily occurs in Ekah Rabbati 5:4; where a redeemer in Media is mentioned, who will be bereft of both father and mother; Esther is clearly named the redeemer.
[92]Yeshuot 50a.

Israel sinned through a maiden, for "There their virgin breasts were pressed," (Ezek. 23:3). Israel was smitten through a maiden, for "They have ravished the women in Zion, the maidens in the cities of Judah," (Lam. 5:11). It will be comforted through a maiden, "For the Lord hath created a new thing . . . , a woman shall court a man," (Jer. 31:22). R. Huna declared that the last passage implies the birth of the Messiah, and offered Ps. 2:7 in support; "This day have I (God) begotten thee."[93] All of which, maintains the apostate, shows that the mother of the Messiah was conceived of God. Such a conclusion betrays a mistaken view of Biblical style and thought. The word "maiden" is used figuratively of Israel. It describes the purity of Israel's attachment to God. As long as Israel does not bow down or compromise with other gods, she is a "virgin." But she has sinned and become corrupted by her intercourse with other religions. Before the redemption she will relinquish her evil associations and with her former fidelity pursue her lover (God).

f. Legend of the Suffering Messiah.

The superhuman nature of the Messiah and his suffering was derived by the Dominican from a legend in the Bereshit Rabba of R. Moses ha-Darshan, based on the verse, "In the beginning God created."[94] This alludes to the "light sown for the righteous," (Ps. 97:11). R. Abba commented that this is the light of the Messiah, for Scripture reads: "For with Thee is the fountain of life; in Thy light do we see light," (Ps. 36:10). We infer that the Almighty anticipated the Messiah and his light and concealed them beneath the Celestial Throne. The legend mentioned is as follows: Said Satan before the Holy One,

---

[93]Yeshuot, p. 50b; Pesikta Rabbati ed. Friedmann, p. 157a; cited in Pugio Fidei, pp. 354-355.

[94]See Yeshuot, pp. 62-64; Pesikta Rabbati, p. 161b; see chapter on Nahmanides for his interpretation of these legends. Pugio Fidei, p. 416.

blessed be He, "O, Lord of the universe, this light which is concealed beneath Thy Celestial Throne, for whom is it?" God replied: "For the Messiah and his generation." Satan then said: "Allow me, and I will foil the King and his generation." The Holy One, blessed be He, answered: "You will not overcome him." To which Satan replied: "Permit me and I will overcome him." Whereupon the Holy One blessed be He, spoke: "If that is your intention, I will destroy Satan from the world and one belonging to that generation." Thereupon God stipulated with the Messiah and said: "O my righteous Messiah, the sins of those who are concealed with thee are destined to bring thee under a severe yoke. Thine eyes will not see the light, thine ears will hear scorn from the heathen world, thy nostrils will inhale ill odors, thy mouth will taste bitterness, thy tongue will cleave to thy palate, thy skin will be fast on thy bones, thy soul will faint in sorrow and sighing. What is thy pleasure? If thou acceptest them, well; if not, forthwith will I annihilate thee." The Messiah replied: "I will rejoice and assume the sufferings on condition that thou wilt revive the dead that died in my day, and from the time of Adam to the present. And not only such as are interred but even those that have been devoured by wolves and lions, and those who have been drowned, also the Nephilim, (fallen angels) aye, even those who have not yet been created but whom the Lord intends to create." The Holy One, blessed be He, acceded. Forthwith the Messiah assumed all sufferings in love, as Scripture reads: "He was oppressed, though he humbled himself." Is. 53:7.

Abrabanel impugns the veracity of the legend in this form, and quotes a similar one in the Pesikta Rabbati with several important variations. In the Pesikta version, Israel addresses God and anticipates the blissful future in return for loyalty to the Torah. Again the Ephraimite

Messiah is definitely alluded to. As for the sufferings of the redeemer, they are described in a word or two, whereas the antagonist's citation dwells upon them more fully and acutely. Finally, this version relates that the redeemer will endure affliction for one week. Abrabanel discerns in this unusually fantastic Midrash, the metaphorical presentation of certain well-known features of the Messianic drama. Light in religious imagery is everywhere the symbol of knowledge and wisdom, and in this instance the wide-spread prevalence of these two blessings is betokened. The concealment of the light under the divine throne indicates that the Almighty had preordained the spiritual and intellectual illumination of the human race at the advent. The Satan in the story personifies the evil inclination of man, which because of its materiality and allurements will be loath to relinquish its hold upon man, and will thus impede the perfection of the race and the sway of the Messiah. The characterization of Satan as trembling and prostrate, is an imaginative way of expressing the extirpation of evil.

The reference to the Ephraimite Messiah excludes the possibility of identifying the founder of the Church with the subject of the tale. The sufferings mentioned may then be connected with the traditional accounts of the wars and the death of the Messiah, son of Ephraim. Abrabanel argues that the antagonist obviously distorted the story by expatiating upon the supposed Messiah's personal affliction, in order to bear out the New Testament story of his maltreatment.

The one week of affliction is the week preceding the great advent, which the Talmud and the Midrash fill with the "birth travails of the Messiah". The stipulation between God and the Messiah is to be taken figuratively. The inevitable concomitant of the Messiah's advent will be the resurrection of all Israel, so that the entire nation might share in the ingathering in Palestine. The Nephilim are those who have fallen away from the faith, and at that time they will be reclaimed. "Those who had ascended into the divine Mind, but had not been created," are the unknown descendants of the Jewish stock, born and nurtured in Christendom, who will retrace their steps and be included in the Restoration.

7—The Final Wars.

Israel and the Christian nations are hereditary foes. Whether on his own soil or in exile, "the sin of Edom is the unrelenting blood-feud with which he follows his brother of Judah." Christendom, or Roman power, grew out of the Biblical race of Edom.[95]

The soul of Esau, father of the Edomite race, passed into Jesus.[96] The hostility can be traced back to the dim past. In the womb of their mother the twin progenitors of these races vied with each other. The pre-natal encounter between Jacob and the Prince of Edom presages in miniature the prolonged contest between the nations. But the time will come when the inveterate rancor of Edom will be requited and Israel ultimately will prove the victor. This will be at the redemption, for the rule of God is incompatible with that of Caeserea. "The existence of one necessarily involves the destruction of the other." So God at the making of the covenant with Abraham revealed to him the four world-monarchies, Babylonia, Persia, Greece, and Rome, which were to tyrannize over Israel, and the ultimate supremacy of Abraham's descendants. The statue of different metals, and the four beasts that Daniel saw, symbolize the four

---

[95]Yeshuot, p. 15,—"Edom mentioned here does not apply to dwellers in the land of Edom near Jerusalem, but to Christians and all inhabitants of Italy."

[96]The author notes the identical letters ESIW and ISWE, Mashmia, p. 19d.

empires. Each represents a different stage in the "downward progress" of mankind, and at the last, even the powerful fabric of the Roman state will be shattered and replaced by the rule of God's chosen people.[97]

Abrabanel maintains that, by the irony of fate, the Christians and Mohammedans will execute the designs of God upon themselves in an exterminating war.[98] The final conflict will be precipitated by the altruistic eagerness of the Ishmaelites, including the Persians, to requite Edom for its destruction of Egypt. This will be Egypt's penalty for having enslaved Israel at the beginning of her career. The forces of Gog, King of Magog, will constitute a great part of the Ishmaelite armies, and they will plunder and slaughter from a selfish motive.

A more real and plausible cause for the final war will be the claim of Rome to the land of Ishmael, especially Palestine, as containing the sepulchre of their divinity. Rome will succeed in subjecting the world, including Palestine, for nine months. Then Ishmael will wage a counter war to dispossess Rome. They will subdue Italy, destroy its capital, the seat of the Church, and invade the Holy Land. The clash between Rome and Ishmael, (Christianity and Mohammedanism) Abrabanel found hinted at in Dan. 11:45 and clearly spoken of in the two Talmudic passages.[99] One statement reads: "Rav says, 'Persia will be conquered by Rome.' Said R. Kahana sceptically, 'The builders (allud-

---

[97]Mayene, p. 13ab. The pivot upon which traditional Messiology hinges is the sway of the four successive empires and their supplanting by Israel. Abrabanel makes the induction from (a) Four kings overthrown by Abraham; (b) Four rivers of Paradise; (c) Animals in covenant with Abraham; (d) Balaam's four oracles; (e) Ps. 42; (f) Hosea II, 21-23; (g) "Three years shall it be forbidden." Lev. 19-23. "These are the three kingdoms when you shall not expect the Messiah"; (h) Zech. Four horns, four craftsmen, four chariots. "Who are they? R. Simeon Hasida says, Messiah ben David and Messiah ben Ephraim, Elihu, and the righteous priest." (Sukkah 52b.)
[98]Yeshuot pp. 34b, 35; Mashmia, p. 17.
[99]Yoma. 10a; Yeshuot p. 15.

ing to Cyrus' permission to the Jews to rebuild the Temple) delivered into the hands of the destroyers?' Rav answered, 'It is the decree of the King.' Some say he answered, 'Rome too is to be destroyed.' " The other statement is, "Rome is destined to be conquered by Persia." The conflict will rage in the sacred land, near the very city of Jerusalem; Ishmael, descendant of the ancient Babylonians, will be vanquished, for they will bear the guilt of the destruction of Samaria and the Temple of Solomon. Armilus, the captain and exponent of the allied Roman forces, will be slain, as will Gog, who is represented as leader of the Asiatic army.[100]

The war will immediately *precede* the final redemption and at its termination the new Jewish State will be inaugurated. During the war, the Messiah b. Joseph will establish his rule in Palestine, but will meet death at the hands of the enemy. Then the Messiah b. David will arise from Rome and completely and finally divest the nations of their prestige. The Messiah b. Joseph, as well as Elijah and the righteous priest, will participate in the work of extermination. The armies of Gog and Magog will be mown down by internecine warfare, by pestilence, hunger and fire. Their chastisement will therefore be swift, and not protracted nor long-suffering, as that of Israel. Their weapons will be of no avail. All people will participate in the interment of the enemy's slain, an occupation which will consume nine months. The great pit will be known as the Valley of the Army of Gog. Rome, the mightiest and most wicked of nations, will receive condign punishment, particularly for her guilt in scattering Israel and razing the sanctuary. As the "black sheep" in the family of nations, no mitigation of her sorrowful fate will be offered to her. While the people of some countries

---

[100]Yeshuot 15—As the term Edom includes all Latin and Christian races, so Ishmael comprises the Asiatic, Mohammedan people. The ancient Babylonians survive in the modern Arabians.

will accept the monotheistic creed, Edom will be deemed unworthy of this privilege. For the vengeance upon Christian nations will be severer than upon the Mohammedan.[101] Ruination will come upon these two races representing two-thirds of the family of nations, while the remaining third, Israel, will be further sifted to find those who profess belief in God.[102] The glory of God will not suffer from the decimation of these races; as the prophet says: "Behold, the nations are as a drop of a bucket, and are counted as the small dust of the balance; behold, the isles are as a mote in weight." Israel and the residue of mankind will then realize that God alone is supreme.

8—*The Messianic Age.*

a. Character and Duration.

There are several views as to the chronological place of the Messianic age in the sequence of the millennial drama. According to a very early conception, there are two antithetical epochs—present and future. The Messianic era will be part of the future world. Another view places the Messianic era within the duration of the present world, after which a complete disrupting change will ensue, followed by the renewal of the world. In a third view, held by Abrabanel, the Messianic era is the interlude between the present and the future world.[103] It will extend from the redemption, specifically the ingathering of the dispersed, to the resurrection. The latter event will inaugurate the supremely blissful era. It is therefore an intermediate and very necessary step in preparing mankind to receive God's highest boon. At no time does Abrabanel give the exact duration of this golden era, but

---

[101]Mashmia 48b.
[102]Mashmia, p. 75a—Abrabanel obtains this idea from Zech. 13:8, 9. "Two parts" means the two dominant races of Edom and Ishmael and "the third" means Israel; so called because of the three patriarchs.
[103]Yeshuot 57b.

it can be surmised from his computations that it will last about thirty years.

Abrabanel criticizes Maimonides for holding that nature, human and cosmic, will continue in its wonted ways in the Messianic era. The statement of Samuel that there is no difference between the present and the Messianic age, save in Israel's subjection to the nations, is on the surface contrary to the plain promises of the Bible that the state of affairs will be of a supernatural order.[104] It contradicts what we believe about the superhuman perfection of the Messiah, the excessive fertility of the soil, extraordinary vengeance upon foes, the innocence of mankind, and resurrection. In Abrabanel's opinion, Samuel did not deny the transcendental things predicted by the prophets but relegated them to an epoch beyond the Messianic interim. The latter period will be simply a repetition of the times when Israel lived on her soil and was governed by God's appointed ones. The lands, which in ancient years flowed with milk and honey, will in the future enjoy an equal degree of fertility. Then there was great affluence, as is evidenced by Scripture: "And the king (Solomon) made silver to be in Jerusalem as stones and cedars made he to be as the sycamore trees, for abundance."[105] God will manifest Himself through miracles and signs as he did in bygone days through Moses, the judges, and seers. Prophecy will be restored to those qualified to receive it. Poverty will not be uprooted; but as Moses declared for his own generation: "The poor shall never cease out of the land."[106] Nor will the earth produce woven garments and baked cakes. The marked distinction, however, between the transitional Messianic age and Israel's past his-

---

[104]San. 99a. Yeshuot, p. 56b—Abrabanel criticizes Maimonides who holds that no miracles will occur in the Messianic state, a view that involves a denial of resurrection.

[105]I Kings 10:27.

[106]Deut. 15:11.

tory will consist in the subjection of all nations to Israel. As glorious as were the times of David and Hezekiah, yet Israel did not rule the nations of the earth. This hegemony the reinstated people will enjoy in the Messianic state. Thus Abrabanel does not interpret Samuel's declaration to mean that Israel will be free from foreign subjection, but that she will dominate all the nations.

That Samuel did not gainsay altogether the transcendental features but ascribed their fulfillment to a real future world, is deduced from several passages.

An instance in point is the following:[107] R. Hisdai asked if there is a contradiction between Is. 24:23 "Then the moon shall be confounded, and the sun ashamed"; and Is. 30:26: "Moreover the light of the moon shall be as the light of the sun and the light of the sun shall be sevenfold, as the light of the seven days". The apparent difficulty is resolved by referring one verse to the luminous future world and the other to the Messianic era. However, according to Samuel, who says there is no difference between the present and the Messianic age except in the emancipation of Israel, both must be referred to the future world. And in that case one refers to the abode of the righteous, and the other to the place where Shekina dwells.

Abrabanel's own belief is that the Messianic age will be an age of miracles; as for Samuel he merely expressed an isolated opinion. He declares that the authorities appear rather to share the view of his disputant, R. Johanan, who anticipates the consummation of all predictions with the advent of the Messiah.

b. Fourteen Generalizations Concerning Resurrection.

The doctrine of resurrection is treated by our author in the fourth chapter of the Nahlat Abot, as he called his commentary on the *Ethics of the Fathers,* and in the *Rosh*

---

[107]Pes. 68a; Rosh Amanah Ch. 16.

Amanah, Chapter 24. In the latter he justifies Maimonides for including the belief in resurrection among the thirteen cardinal principles of Judaism. It is distinctly taught in the written and oral law. It constitutes a large and significant part of Torah teaching. Moses, Isaiah, Daniel, and Malachi predicted it in unmistakable language. Although he is uncertain whether to accept Ezekiel's vision of the revival of the dry bones as a reality or a parable, it most assuredly teaches resurrection. Another factor that raises this belief to the rank of a cardinal principle is that it belongs to the category of reward and punishment, an indispensable and central teaching of Judaism. Resurrection is one of the ways in which God will bestow reward and punishment. Abrabanel states the pragmatic viewpoint that circumstances and the trend of the times determine which Jewish teachings should be stressed and raised to dogmatic importance. Thus he argues that Maimonides made the belief in Providence, with its corollaries of the Messianic advent and resurrection, dogmas, because of the failing contrary belief in divine Providence, caused by the obvious injustice in the world and Israel's misery. When resurrection and redemption are accomplished, the teachings of the Torah concerning them will fall. Apparently this involves a change in the totality of the Torah, and challenges the Maimonidean doctrine that the law is immutable. But Abrabanel clears the fog by stating that these doctrines only involve the belief that these events were predicted by the prophets of Israel, and that they occurred in the precise manner taught by the Torah.[108]

Abrabanel seized upon the eschatological statement in the *Ethics of the Fathers,* IV, 29 to expatiate upon the subject of resurrection. At the outset he expresses his divergence from Maimonides, who took the tannaitic state-

---

[108]Rosh Amanah *ibid.*

ment to refer to the condition, the judgment, and the recompense of departed souls. He himself is certain that
the principle of resurrection is involved. Fortunately,
Abrabanel's method of enumerating his views on a subject
enables us to set forth the principal elements of the doctrine in the following systematic manner:

1. At death, the body decomposes and is reduced to its
elements. The spirit survives, entire. It does not deteriorate. "The dust returns to earth as it was, the spirit
returns to God, who gave it."

2. Resurrection will occur in the last flourishing era
of the earth's duration and not at a period when the world
will be destitute of life. It will take place when all the
souls still remaining since creation in the depository of
souls, will at last have left to inhabit earthly bodies.

3. Fundamentally and actually, resurrection means
that the same earthly bodies will receive the same souls.
This precludes all other theories, such as transmigration
or that the new person will be an ethereal creature composed of rare celestial matter.

4. The revived body will be the original person as he
appeared before death.

5. Only a portion of Israel will be revived. At death
it is decreed who will merit re-existence.

6. The purpose of this great miracle is to judge the
complete person (body and spirit) fairly for his deeds.

7. The generation living at the time of the miracle will
continue to live, but will be tried on the Day of Judgment,
together with the resurrected. Then will ensue the true
enjoyment of rewards in the soul-world.

8. Another purpose is to enable a large part of Israel,
who through the ages succumbed to Gentile bestiality, to
behold the ultimate triumph of their people and the

benevolence of God. It would be unfair if the joys and victories of the new era should be witnessed only by those who happened to live at the redemption.

9. The revived will recognize each other and be reunited to their families and tribes.

10. One effect of the resurrection will be the conversion of Gentiles to monotheism.

11. The reawakened life will not be wrought by a prophet, or by God's messenger, or through the influence or incidence of the stars, but by God Himself.

12. Man is judged at three different moments. a. Every New Year for his earthly fortune. b. At death the soul is judged for admittance into the soul world. c. On the Day of Judgment in the eschatological future for his eternal state.

13. Resurrection will occur among all classes of Israel and as for the other races of the earth, only the extremely righteous and the extremely wicked will be revived. "And thou seest that this faith is rooted in all Gentiles. They all believe that their dead will arise. Hence I maintain that at the coming resurrection our own people will arise to be associated with the salvation of God, to stand up at judgment, and for the other purposes I have mentioned. And there will also arise from other nations in their lands, in every territory, domain, province, and city, not only the righteous among them but also the wicked and the sinful, and they will be the more notorious among them. And it must be so in order to know and to make known, to broadcast throughout the world, the faith in God, blessed be He, that their sages, priests, and prophets be witnesses of this fact."[109]

14. The revived will live a complete physical existence on a plane of innocence and righteousness. The notion

---

[109]Nahlat Abot end of Ch. 4.

that they will be spiritualized beings, although retaining their corporeal substance and frame, is contradictory to accepted Jewish views. This theory was entertained by Nahmanides, Crescas, and Albo. Abrabanel also differed from Maimonides, who taught that the resurrected life will not be corporeal.

Towards the end of his discourse on the fourth chapter of the Ethics, there is a discussion as to the exact connotation of "the world to come"; whether it means the spirit-world, or the world of the resurrected. Abrabanel groups the views of the following leading scholars. A. Maimonides, Ibn Ezra, Gabirol, Judah Halevi, Alfasi, hold that it denotes the state of souls after they leave the body at death. B. Rashi believes that it is the world of resurrection.

c. Regeneration of Mankind.

In the Messianic interim, three fundamental changes will occur; the inward regeneration of man, the restoration of the religious and political life of Israel, and the sovereignty of Israel over all the world. The new age will mark the perfection of mankind. The world will appear as though recreated in all freshness and fecundity. The innocence of childhood and the perfection of Adam before he sinned will be upon everyone.[110] All impediments to right thinking and clean living will be uprooted. Man will be morally transformed and renovated. The rabbis say: "And days shall come when thou wilt say, 'I have no desire in them'—these are the days of the Messiah, in which there will be no righteousness and no wickedness.[111] Man will find himself in a state of purity. His carnal propensities will be subdued. His evil nature will be purged. There will be no impulse to sin. The best in him

---

[110]Mashmia 6b.
[111]Shabbat 151b.

will seek spiritual harmony. The conquest of one's inmost and invisible enemy, the "evil inclination", will be the first step in attaining universal peace. For, declares Abrabanel, the two chief causes of war are religious differences and the selfish instinct to appropriate what does not rightfully belong to us. The purification of men's hearts, coupled with the universal acceptance of a common monotheistic creed, will assure the establishment of perfect harmony among individuals and nations.[112] Even the beasts will outgrow their rapacity, and peacefulness and friendliness will mark their attitude toward one another and toward man. It is Abrabanel's opinion that the last condition will prevail only in the Holy Land.

d. Restoration of the Religious Life; Mosaic Laws Will not Be Abrogated.

God is the life-principle of the Jews. He is to Israel what rain is to the plant, the vitalizing force. He is indissolubly bound up with Israel. In Him and through Him, Israel finds spiritual sustenance. Regarding the Almighty in this light, the future restoration of the exiled people and the rehabilitation of their priestly life become an assured fact. The divine glory will resanctify the land, and God will rejoice over Israel as a bridegroom rejoices over his bride. The Torah will never fall into oblivion, for He Himself will impart its teachings and will make a new covenant with the people that they violate not His commands.[113] The reasons for the inexplicable precepts of the Bible will be revealed. Such reigns of idolatry as obtained under Ahab and Jeroboam will never be repeated. Because the next redemption will eclipse the miracle of the Exodus, the obligation of making special mention of it will have passed away, but the Passover festival will be retained. The Agadic statement that all festivals except

[112]Mashmia, p. 9b.
[113]Ibid., p. 23a.

Purim and the Day of Atonement will be suspended in the time of the Messiah cannot mean that they will be completely abrogated because every scriptural law possesses an eternally binding power.[114] It does mean that special remembrance of them will not be made, because the marvels of Israel's early career will be overshadowed by the transcendental character of the redemption. However, the Day of Atonement, which is the judgment day of Israel and of mankind, and Purim, which symbolizes the miraculousness of our history, will retain their full significance.

Abrabanel refutes the proposition that the laws of Moses will be abrogated in the Messianic era.[115] There is nothing in Scripture nor in the Oral Law to establish that proposition. The ceremonial, the sacrificial, and the agricultural laws will continue in force in the future. The observation that the third and fourth chiliads will be the age of the Torah, should not lead one to infer that it will be abolished after that time.[116] The Torah is perpetual. The broad statement of R. Johanan to the effect that one may perform whatever a prophet commands even if contrary to Torah, except idolatry, seems to give a basis to the charge that it was possible and permissible for Jesus to abolish the law.[117] Incidentally, through Christian efforts idolatry has receded and has been superseded by the "new dispensation". Abrabanel retorts that the provision of R. Johanan applied only to an exceptional case or to an exigency where certain laws might be violated or held in abeyance. But it could give no sanction for the

---

[114]Midrash Mishle, beginning of Ch. 9. Yerush. Megillah I, 4; Yerush. Taanit II, 12, mentions Hanuka and Purim as the two holidays that will not be abolished.

[115]Yeshuot, 67b to the end.

[116]See note 39, p. 245.

[117]Yeshuot 71a. The statement cannot be located; the nearest to it is Bekorot 45a, where R. Johanan says, the words of the Sages are as revered as those of the Prophets. On this Rashi comments—words of a prophet must be given unquestioned obedience.

complete or permanent suspension of the Torah. And any prophet who would venture to advocate the abolition of Judaism, *ipso facto* rules himself out of the fold, and thus loses his authority. As for idolatry, it still persists in a large part of the world.

The apostate cites Rashi's comment on Is. 2:1-4, about the mountain of the Lord's house being established firmly and raised up above the hills. Rashi stated that a greater miracle than the one on Sinai will occur on that day. This signified to the opponent the superiority of the Christian Testament over Sinaitic revelation. Abrabanel answers simply that the next verse mentions Jerusalem as the chief religious center of the future, implying that the law and life which were fostered in Israel's historic capital will survive. As for Rashi's remark, it conveys the gladsome thought that the new and greater revelation will consist in the extension of the Torah's sway over all mankind.

The statement of R. Hanina, that King Messiah will promulgate two new laws unto the nations, Succah and Lulav, is exclusive of the Torah, which will remain in force in Israel forever.[118]

Midrash Canticles, on 1:2—"Let him kiss me with the kisses of his mouth"—says in part that the people asked God to reveal the law directly to them, in order that it should never be forgotten and ever fixed in their hearts. But Moses replied: "Not now, but in the future; as the verse reads: 'I have set my Torah in their inward parts and will write it upon their hearts.' " In the same vein, Jeremiah spoke: "I will make with the house of Israel and Judah a new covenant." From these statements, it is surmised that a new, a different law, will be promulgated. Abrabanel denies the logic of such a conclusion. The word "brith" (covenant) does not connote law, but means an

---

[118]Yeshuot 67b to the end. Midrash on Psalms says that Messiah will give six new Mizwot to Gentiles; but it mentions only Succah, Lulav, and Tefilin. Cf. Abodah Zarah 3ab.

oath, an agreement. God will renew His ancient covenant with Israel. The same Torah will be followed, but
with greater scrupulousness and instinctive submission.

A strange claim of the apostate is that the priesthood
was removed from the tribe of Levi and its prerogatives
transferred to the church and its followers. It is contended
that the present-day church communion, a former function
of the Hebrew priesthood, has replaced the ritual of old.
This claim is based on a midrashic exposition of Gen. 14:18
which tells of the meeting between Abraham and Melchizedek. The latter, as a priest, offered up bread and wine
to God.[119] Abrabanel regrets that he has not the source
of the Midrash to verify the quotation and suggests that
the original has been tampered with. Earlier authorities
denied that the part which reads: "Melchizedek offered up
wine and bread to God", was in the Midrash. The correct
meaning of the verse is that the bread and wine were used
to refresh the battle-sore troops of Abraham, and as a
priest it was natural for Melchizedek to inform the patriarch on priestly matters.

e. The New Temple and the Abodah.

The patriarchs Abraham, Isaac and Jacob symbolize
the first, second, and third temples respectively.[120] As
Abraham surpassed Isaac in many virtues, so did the
Temple of Solomon, built by the behest of God, possess
more sacredness and external grandeur than the second
Temple. Isaac's failing vision in old age is analogous to
the desecration of the sanctity and glory of the second
Temple by pagan rulers. The first Temple was raised by

---

[119]Yeshuot 69ab; the apostate according to Abrabanel draws from the
Midrash of R. Moses ha-Darshan. Ber. Rabba 43:7 has two opinions on
what happened. One opinion is that Melchizedek transmitted to
Abraham the laws of the high priesthood. "Bread" is the shew-bread,
and "wine" is the libation. The rabbis say he revealed Torah to him as in
Prov. 9:5; where bread and wine are used allegorically for Torah.
[120]Mashmia, p. 8bc.

the Babylonians, descendants of the "children of Ketura", one of Abraham's concubines; and the second Temple was built by the descendants of Esau. The third Temple will last to eternity, for among the sons of Jacob there was none who left the patriarchal family to intermarry with the "daughters of the land".

The joy at the erection of the last sanctuary will exceed that of the days of Solomon and Ezra. This time its inviolability and perpetuity are vouchsafed. The dedication will extend from the first day of Nisan to the twenty-first of Tishri, marking the interval from the ingathering of the exiles to the victory over Gog and Magog; while the dedication of the tabernacle in the wilderness lasted seven days, that of the Temple of Solomon fourteen days, and that of Ezra, twenty-one days.[121] The Holy of Holies, with all its sacred paraphernalia, the ark, the tables of the covenant, scroll of the Law, and the oil of anointment, will be restored. The Abodah, or priestly service, as set forth in the Pentateuch, will be re-instituted. The sacrificial order mentioned in Ezekiel XLV, XLVI, which differs from the Pentateuchal prescriptions, will be in vogue during the dedication period only, in addition to the regular daily and festival sacrifices prescribed in the Pentateuch.[122] Priests and Levites will serve in their respective functions, and will be recompensed by the customary sacrificial portions and sacerdotal revenues. The offspring of daughters of proselyte families, who intermarry with priests or Levites, may serve in the Temple. Not all forms of sacrifices will be retained.[123] The atonement and sin-offerings, for instance, will be discontinued, for the heart of man being purified there will be no occasion for such sacrifices. Aye, the Temple will have lost its character

---

[121]Mayene, p. 51a.
[122]Mashmia, pp. 50-51ab. The changed order in Ezekiel cannot refer to the second Temple, for there it explicitly says, Ezra 3:2, "To offer up upon it burnt offerings, as it is written in the law of Moses, man of God."
[123]Yeshuot 69.

as a place where expiation is to be made. Beside the regular offering from the wine-vat and the threshing floor, which the Bible enjoins to be offered to the priest, freewill, animal and wine offerings will be given to the Nasi (King Messiah). He will devote part of it to the requisite daily and holiday offerings, and the rest will be in the nature of a fund upon which he may draw for communal or private purposes. After the restoration mankind will make a pilgrimage to the Holy City twice a year instead of three times, in the seventh month and in the interval between Passover and the Feast of Weeks.[124]

f. Rehabilitation of the Political Life.

The enchanting but illusive hope of the Jews to return to the sacred soil has continued from the Middle Ages down to modern times, and has exerted a most salutary influence on their preservation as a people. God has bound Himself to bestow the lands as an abiding patrimony to the descendants of the patriarchs, who despite their banishment, are destined to repossess it. The future regaining of the land through the activity of the Messiah will be the second time that Israel has possessed Palestine, the first being under Joshua. The return under Ezra by the privilege of Cyrus vassalized Israel. As the return was not prompted by divine intervention, the Jewish community in Palestine was no different from other Jewish settlements, as for example the one in Alexandria. In the future, however, Israel will be restored by God and will regain permanent freedom. Royalty and priesthood will again be vested in the descendants of the original incumbents.

The usual antithesis between earthliness and heavenliness will not exist, for the Kingdom of God and the House of David will become one and the same. Israel will no

---

[124]Mashmia, p. 32b.

THE DOCTRINE OF THE MESSIAH

longer form a schismatic state. The prophet Ezek. 37:19-22 exquisitely expresses the union of the two kingdoms thus: "Behold, I will take the stick of Joseph, which is in the hands of Ephraim and the tribes of Israel his companions, and I will put them unto him, together with the stick of Judah, and make them one stick, and they shall be one in My hand.—And I will make them one nation in the land, upon the mountains of Israel, and one king shall be king to them all; and they shall be no more two nations; neither shall they be divided into two kingdoms any more at all."

The land will be equally divided among the twelve tribes, not as in the time of Joshua, when division was based on population. Equal apportionment will be necessary particularly in order to have sufficient room in the smaller tribes for the resurrected dead. Pre-redemption converts to Judaism will receive portions in the tribes to which they became attached. No proselytes will be received. The apportionment will be in thirteen equal parts, twelve for the tribes and one for the city of Jerusalem, including the sanctuary, dwellings for the priests and Levites, and other necessary appurtenances. Of this thirteenth portion, an allotment will be made to the Nasi (Messiah), which must remain in its entirety in the ruling Davidic dynasty from generation to generation. The enlarged unwalled boundaries of Jerusalem will inclose an area of thirteen square miles. The sanctuary and temple will occupy one and a half miles.[125]

The anticipated felicity of Israel will be in proportion to the magnitude of her suffering in the diaspora. The future will be as sweet as the past was bitter. God will evince his special predilection for Palestine in concrete ways and will extend over it His special Providence. Copious restitution will be made of all sacred vessels

---

[125]*Ibid.*, 51cd, 52.

borne away from Jerusalem by the destroyers. Secure from foreign attacks, and with no cause to fear expulsion, Israel will enjoy uninterrupted peace and happiness. God will enter into a covenant with nature respecting the seasonal rains and the productiveness of the earth, so that there will be neither drought nor famine. The fecundity of woman and the fruitfulness of the fields will be extraordinary. The span of life will not be increased to what it was after creation, but none will die young. The "new heavens" predicted in Is. 66:22 has reference to the grand conjunction of Saturn and Jupiter in the constellation Pisces, in the year 5224. This strange phenomenon, which has occurred only once before, at the Exodus, portends the deliverance of Israel and the joys of the new age.[126]

g. The Sovereignty of Israel.

Israel, hitherto the weakest, the worm among nations, will gather strength and become mistress of the world.[127] One of the first and chief features of the new state, without which any picture of the Utopia is incomplete, is the enlargement of the boundaries of Palestine proper. The territory of the Keni, Kenisi, and Kadmoni, corresponding to Amon, Moab, and Edom, which together with the land of the seven states was contained in the ancient promise of God to Abraham's seed, will be annexed to the Holy Land. Israel will supersede the former world-monarchies, and her imperium will extend from sea to sea, that is, from the Euphrates to the Mediterranean. Unlike her predecessors, she will not aggrieve the surviving races and governments by the imposition of taxes and other severities.

---

[126]Mashmia 24d; also last section of Mayene: Abrabanel follows the method of Abraham b. Hiyya. To Abrabanel, astrology is an asmachta, used merely as corroboration of an accepted view.

[127]Thus he explains, "A woman shall court a man"—Jer. 31:22. Israel (woman weak and passive) will dominate her former masters (man) the nations.

Indeed, Israel will enjoy not only political, but also spiritual hegemony. The city of Jerusalem will be the heart of humanity. The supreme sacredness of the Ark in relation to the other parts of the Temple will be analogous to the central position which the Temple will occupy, politically and spiritually, in relation to the world. The Temple's chief significance will lie in its sanctified character, rather than in its architectural preeminence. It will be a central and universal court of justice and arbitration. The King Messiah will be a "light", radiating justice, peace, and truth for the guidance of men and nations. He will dominate not by the sword, but by "his word." Men will no longer ascribe divinity to the sun, moon, and stars, nor deny Providence, for His presence and operation will be visibly manifest.

The sage glorifies, in fantastic imagery, the eminence of Israel in the new day. Israel will be unique among the nations, and her phenomena will be comparable to those of supermundane bodies. The chosen nation will receive illumination direct from God and not from the sun: "For the Lord shall be thine everlasting light."[128] Israel will be like a celestial sphere which revolves but does not deteriorate in the process. So Israel may undergo motion and change, but not decline. Jerusalem will be the desire, the joy, the supreme attachment of every heart: "For behold I create Jerusalem a rejoicing."[129]

Although at the dawn of history the nations rejected God's proffer of the Torah, after the redemption they will crave His knowledge and will make pilgrimages to the Holy Land. The King Messiah will give the foreign peoples two commands, Succah and Lulav, to commemorate his people's victory over Gog, King of Magog, the last of Israel's foes.[130] Gentiles will be exempt from the Biblical

---

[128]Is. 60:20.
[129]Is. 65:18—see end of Ateret Zekenim.
[130]Yeshuot 67b.

injunctions regarding abstinence from the food of unclean animals, and the prohibited degrees of marriage. They will be in the same status as "The Generation of Noah," who, while they acknowledged God, heeded only the seven obligatory laws.

The nations will display their indebtedness to Israel in many ways. Multitudes of converts will wend their way to Jerusalem, bringing with them gifts of gold and spices, and cattle for sacrifices. A beautiful legend illustrates the underlying thought of the future relations between Israel and the world at large. "A king was once provoked to anger by his population, and they entreated the prince to intercede in their behalf. When the prince had reconciled his royal father, the people hastened to the palace of the king to sing his praises. Then exclaimed the king: 'Is it to me that you sing praises? To my son are praises due; for were it not for him who entreated me, I would have laid waste the entire land.' So does the verse read: 'All nations clapped their hands.'—Said the Holy One, blessed be He: 'Is it to me that you sing praises? You owe them to Israel, for were it not for Israel, this world would not exist'."[131]

---

[131]Yalk. Shim. Ps. 2:12.

Chapter XII

SUMMARY

Most of the authorities here studied lived during the
full blaze of the creative cultural activities of the Jews
in Spain and nearby countries, and represent, from the
point of view of the Synagogue, a homogeneous group.
They were the standard-bearers of Biblical and Talmudic
Judaism. They gave full hearted devotion and punctilious
observance to their inherited faith. Yet when we approach them analytically we see glaring variations in
their concept of Jewish dogmas and their methodology.
They were divided in their views toward the synthetic
rationalistic movement among the Jews of the middle ages,
that flowered most beautifully in Moses, son of Maimon.
The keen argumentative Saadia contrasts with the mystic
Nahmanides; the unsophisticated and naive Rashi, with
Maimonides the rationalist; the effusive and poetical
Judah Halevi, with the dogmatic Albo; and the discriminating and metaphysical Crescas with the discursive and
enthusiastic Abrabanel.

Touching the Messianic theme, we have seen that in
general there prevailed among the sages of the Talmud
two divergent views: the one mystical and Midrashic; the
other quite natural and historical. The many-sided gaon,
Saadia, carried on the Midrashic tradition and created a
rather romantic picture of the advent which retained certain fantastic features, such as the final adversary
Armilus, the ethereal transportation of the Hebrews to
Palestine, and the use of precious jewels and stones as
building material for the new Jerusalem. The Talmudist,

SUMMARY

Rashi, breathed a like spirit into his commentaries. Abraham bar Hiyya, Nahmanides, and Abrabanel were akin to Saadia in their Messiological exegesis as well as in their fantastic characterization of the advent. These theologians employed an identical technique in unearthing intimations and prognostications of the advent, of resurrection, and of other requisites of the final redemption, not only from the familiar eschatological passages of "the end of days," but also from other colorful and prophetic sections of Holy Writ. They placed a Messianic interpretation even upon the least obvious eschatological parts. Their authority for this hermeneutic method is evidently the theory held by the exponents of the Talmud, that the words of the Torah possess both a literal and a hidden meaning. When the simple reading did not convey the interpretations of the scholar or school, the desired views were obtained by esoteric interpretations. Hence, taken by and large, their deductions are similar. They all agree on the traditional elements of the Messianic drama, and differ only in particular phases. Holy Writ offers abundant and accurate details concerning it, and in order to obtain these details they utilize certain mystical and artificial methods, such as homiletic deduction, gematria and the deciphering of the dates given in the Book of Daniel. Abraham bar Hiyya even goes to the extreme of reconciling the major events in universal and biblical history with astrology, and firmly believes that his conclusions concerning the Messiah are substantiated by astrological computations. This shows to what a great extent some rabbis were influenced by the current false sciences. In this use of astrology he is followed with more moderation by Abrabanel. Some scholars, like Ibn Ezra, are skeptical about the usefulness of astral science for this purpose, and therefore censure those who have recourse to it. Maimonides rejected it altogether.

THE DOCTRINE OF THE MESSIAH

Maimonides was the first synagogue authority to deviate from the Midrashic path trodden by Saadia, and boldly ventured into new fields. He liberalized the Messianic concept and made the advent the final stage in the progressive spiritual unfolding of humanity. The sage of Cordova differed in the following salient points from the more traditional writers on the doctrine:

1—First of all he disclaims candidly any knowledge of the details and sequence of events of the redemption. This attitude may be due partly to his rationality and cool-headedness. He admitted that one cannot formulate objectively the scheme of things in the Messianic regime because it is shrouded in mystery. Much of what has been written on the subject is subjective. The enthusiasts, the mystics, had projected their own pious aspirations on the stage of a remote future; the literalists had utilized Scriptural texts to furnish a description of Messianic events. Being neither a literalist nor a mystic, Maimonides viewed those observations pertaining to the Messianic time with the clear judgment of a philosopher. Accordingly we find that:

2—He divested the Messiah of supernatural powers.

3—He agreed that the Messianic age would not witness any alterations from the normal course of natural phenomena.

4—He stressed the religious motives behind the Messianic expectation more than did the other authorities. Israel's ambitions are not chauvinistic, aiming at a political world imperium, as that attained by Greece, Rome and Islam; her hopes are rather toward national independence and security, so that she may devote herself, unmolested, to the service of God.

5—We look in vain, therefore, in Maimonides' writings for any Jewish vindictiveness toward the Gentiles, an attitude observed among some writers. He sought rather a reformatory and corrective outcome to the dramatic struggle between the two religions.

6—Maimonides went further than Saadia, Abraham bar Hiyya and others in placing man's highest aspirations in the future world rather than in the restored state. It is true that the resurrected life is a requisite and inevitable step in the eschatological scheme and in human destiny, since the resurrected life will receive either reward or punishment. The resurrected life will be fundamentally a physical existence; but the real and lasting bliss will be spiritual, to be enjoyed by the souls of the deserving in the Hereafter. Nahmanides, also, places the *summum bonum* beyond the Messianic epoch.

Save for Crescas and Albo, who challenged the indispensability of the doctrine as set forth by Maimonides in his commentary on Mishna Sanhedrin, Ch. X, all the authorities valued this belief in the future life as a cardinal teaching of Judaism. They all regarded the doctrine as Scriptural and not rabbinic, as inherent in the grandiose promises of God, and not emanating from Israel's unhappy history. This doctrine was authentically taught by Moses and the prophets and hence is binding upon all Jews. Its acceptance appeals forcibly also to us because it involves the basic belief in divine retribution; the requital of Israel in the Messianic regime for all her sufferings, and vengeance upon other nations for their persecutions of Israel; and the credibility of the prophets' words and teachings. The fountain of our faith and knowledge in the blissful future is in the Scriptures.

The Messianic doctrine descended to medieval Jewry as one of the great legacies of Biblical and Talmudic Judaism. Usually we think of a legacy as an inert although precious inheritance. The belief in the advent, however, was a legacy that pulsated with magic life. It had a definite, functional use in the organization of

THE DOCTRINE OF THE MESSIAH

Israel's religious life. It was not the desiccated and cloistered teaching of Israel's schoolmen; it was rather a yearning that eventuated from the gruelling experience of the people at large. The fervor and vitality of the redemptist hope is evidenced by the popular poetry of Israel's immortal bards, Solomon ibn Gabirol, Judah Halevi, and Abraham ibn Ezra who found a motive for their exuberant espousal of the national yearning in the frightful persecutions of the Jews by Islam. The poetry of the Middle Ages, as the newspaper and periodical of our day, reflected public opinion and sentiment. Their piyyutim and reflective writings voiced the ever-living faith of the people in the swift overthrow of Islam and Christendom and in their own inevitable salvation. Both as poets and religious authorities they found it natural to infuse into their poesy many of the motifs and elements that are standard in Jewish Messiology, such as the imminent appearance of the Son of David, the ingathering, love for the sacred land, reliance upon Divine mercy, restoration of the ancient commonwealth, and the political ascendancy of Israel. In addition, Judah Halevi has bequeathed to us a fascinating apologetic work, the Kuzari —in which he treats of the two obvious facts of the Messianic doctrine—the divine preferment of Israel and its inalienable possession of Palestine. The Messianic opinions voiced by Ibn Ezra in his commentaries vacillate between the homiletic interpretations of Rashi and the advanced critical views of Maimonides.

Many elements seem to have fused together to form the distinctive Messianic doctrine of the Jews. Viewed genetically there is in it a vestige of the political hope, born at the dissolution of the united kingdom of Solomon, for a legitimate successor of the divinely favored dynasty of David to occupy the throne in Jerusalem. This is the significance of the Messiah's appellation, the Son of David.

SUMMARY

The nation will have many kings and saviors but a genuine Messiah must trace his descent from David. However, one may surmise that the hope of a coming blissful era preceded, in time and in the people's emotional experience, the hope for a redeemer. Some scholars are inclined to locate the genesis of the entire Messianic expectation in the period of decline that ensued upon David's brilliant rule. For the disunion of the tribes and the precarious state of Israel, due to the belligerent attitude of their neighbors, called forth the grandiloquent eschatological utterances of the prophets. Biblical Messianism might have remained forever a vague idealistic wish, preserved by reason of its exquisite prophetic expression, had it not been for the destruction of the Temple in 70 C. E. and the provocations of Rome and early Christianity that turned the prophetic hope into a real political necessity.

All these theologians subscribed to the view that the purpose of the dispersion was to expiate the sins of the people incurred during the Second Commonwealth. The Messiah, they held, will not arrive until full atonement has been made. Another deterrent was the straying of Israel in exile from God and His law. Instead of contracting the breach between God and Israel, the dispersion had widened it. When the nation amends her ways the people will be redeemed. The mystics injected other speculations in determining the "end". According to them, a time-limit, set by the grace of God and known to' only a few chosen persons, will inevitably be reached. Some of them even made the Great Fulfillment coeval with the end of this world and the swift inauguration of a new universe.

Saadia, Rashi, Abraham bar Hiyya, Maimonides, Nahmanides and Isaac Abrabanel yielded to the temptation and the task of computing the "end". These computations must be understood in the light of an underlying belief that this world will endure for 6000 or 7000 years. Upon its dissolution, it may be either reborn and other worlds may be created, or life on this earth may assume new physical forms altogether unlike what they are at present. The limitation of this earth to the period stated, certainly represents a short-sighted view of history and restricted the authorities to fix the end in a definite era. The redemption must be enacted on this earth and since they were drawing near its close, the authorities set the end during their own lifetime or in the immediate future.

These scholars differed in their stand toward the practice of calculating the end, between the apathetic attitude of Maimonides and the passionate searching and compiling of Abraham bar Hiyya. Nahmanides, for example, foresaw the advent with crystal clearness. He even presaged that the Messianic date was a Sinaitic tradition conceived by Moses, which had to be rediscovered at the propitious hour. They were cognizant of Talmudic opposition, but their hypersensitiveness to the anguished situation of Israel and the confidence that they were living in the pre-Messianic milieu, made each one proceed, oblivious of the Talmudic prohibition, to calculate the end. Possibly the scholars eased their minds with the knowledge that certain doctors of the Talmud also conjectured the "end". Others essayed to unravel the secret believing that the prophets and sages withheld the "year of wonders" because it was too far in the future. A few understood the prohibition to refer to astrological speculation and not to Biblical deductions.

The writings of Abraham bar Hiyya, Nahmanides, and Abrabanel fairly teem with Messianic mathematics. The *locus classicus* was Daniel, Chapters 8, 9 and 12. Because the putative "ends" in many cases fell within the lifetime of the calculator, they surmised that the persecutions of the day were the "Birth Travails of the Messiah". It is remarkable to see the patience and fortitude of the people when these dates pregnant with hope arrived, only to pass away like transient dreams. The ingathering of the tribes, resurrection, the renaissance of the Hebrew state in its ideal form, and the restitution of the sacerdotal system were anticipated by these scholars. Some who were mystically inclined, injected into their vision preternatural elements such as exceeding longevity, universal prophecy, and cosmic changes. In the expected event all of them saw not only the fulfillment of Israel's national desire but also the attainment of cosmic perfection. The Messiah would consummate all the struggles of the human race and all the plans of God for a perfect world. Man will at last become a perfect human being, divested of all sinful impulses.

The awakening of the dead will feature the Messianic age. Ethically considered, it will compensate man for the inadequacy of his present existence. Theologically, it is connected with the belief of a Day of Judgment and individual reward and punishment. Saadia Gaon places this miracle at the very beginning of the Messianic era. Others, like Crescas and Albo, remove it to a more remote future. Albo speaks of two resurrections, an early one at the redemption for the select righteous leaders of Israel, and a later one, for all Israel and mankind. The source for this doctrine was the Scriptures, reinforced by Talmudic utterances, and belief in the possibility of miracles. The question of the nature of individual life in the world to come divided the theologians into two groups, best represented by Maimonides and Nahmanides. The former believed in an incorporeal, and soul-like existence, and the latter in a spiritualized corporeal life.

A striking feature that characterizes the medieval Messianic literature is the apologetic treatment of the Messianic doctrine. Although the scholars we have studied lived in the golden age of the dispersion, it was golden only in so far as it described the brilliant literary productiveness of the race. As citizens, they were *personae non gratae*. They were exposed to all manner of physical torment and insecurity of life and property. These centuries were a nightmare. The widespread conversionist efforts of Christianity and Islam placed Jewish leaders on the defensive and evoked innumerable justifications of the holy faith. In their commentaries, and at public disputations, they persistently and boldly expounded the faith that the "end" was still to come and hence neither Jesus nor Mohammed was the veritable Messiah. The logic underlying the doctrine and the stark reality of contemporary life aided the Jews, for the advent must synchronize with the inauguration of universal peace, justice, virtue, and monotheism, besides bringing freedom and security to Israel. The absence of any and all of these conditions belied the alleged messiahship of these two teachers.

The church authorities have, through the ages, relied much on Isaiah, 52:13 to 53:15, as decisive evidence of the historicity of their redeemer. Their zeal and imagination even discovered for them in Isaiah the details of his career and end. Suffice it to say that medieval Jewish interpreters came closer than their opponents, the church authorities, to modern critical commentators in identifying the "Servant of the Lord" which is the subject of the chapter, as Israel, the nation. It is simply a case of the personification of a nation. Everywhere else in Isaiah the term "servant" is addressed to Israel and the Jewish authorities very sensibly equate its use in chapters 52 and 53 with the identical use of the term elsewhere. The rabbis also had to grapple with the numerous stories, and references to the redeemer and the "end", found in the Talmud, in Targumim and in Midrash, which Christian polemists cited to prove their case.

SUMMARY

To counteract the Christian belief in the redeemer's divinity, it is worth noting that all the scholars vehemently stress the human origin of the anointed one, although some ascribe to him mysterious endowments and thaumaturgical exploits. He will be a descendant of the royal line of David, will equal his namesake in fortitude and piety, will match Solomon in wisdom and will approach Moses in the possession of the prophetic spirit. He will redeem mankind in this world, unlike the Christian Messiah who will save mankind from doom in the world to come. One Messianic aspect stressed in Christian theology is the vicarious and atoning power of the redeemer. In the Hebrew conception this thought is entirely absent. The Messiah, it is expected, will perform a great political and spiritual service. But his unique goodness will not bring about the deliverance of Israel or of mankind from their present state of guilt. The people must attain by their own efforts the innocence and rewards of the Messianic era.

They all take for granted the appearance of the Ephraimitic Messiah who will be slain in battle after a brief and impetuous career. The revengeful note that all non-Israelitish nations are to be exterminated does not occur in the expositions by our authors. Only the armies of Gog and Magog, a legendary designation for the host that will contest Israel's right to Palestine after the ingathering, will be vanquished. Abrabanel has the most to say on the final wars and vengeance and he, as well as the others, looks upon Israel as only one nation among many that will be influenced to turn in worship and submission to God.

Another task to which the rabbis applied very serious efforts was the refutation of a certain critical school of Jewish interpreters which applied all Scriptural prophecies to the second commonwealth instead of to the final release from our present dispersion. These men were either anti-messianist; or, if they shared the hope of the Advent, they were reluctant to find for it a scriptural basis in the usual messiological passages. Although the rabbis here considered occasionally identified certain enigmatic allusions in the Bible with historical persons or events, they generally shifted the predictions to the Advent.

In spite of the fact that they were unalterably opposed to the Christian Messianic doctrine, certain theologians like Maimonides and Halevi yielded a point in admitting that the hand of Providence was evident in the spread of Christianity. They consoled the people, telling them that the dominant religion is, at least an advance beyond heathenism and tends toward the purer God-idea of the Hebrews.[1] The conquest of idolatry and paganism by the Christian Church is regarded as a forward step in the progressive march of Scriptural teaching, that will some day culminate in the appearance of the Messiah. This tolerant attitude and estimate of Christianity has been manifested by many rabbis in other situations where Christians are placed in a higher category than heathens.

The Messianic doctrine does not fascinate and enthrall the modern Jew, as it certainly did the Jew of the past. Together with the entire ancestral order of belief, its credibility has been impugned in certain quarters. Concerning the teaching of redemption through a Messiah it is argued that the amelioration of Israel's status in Europe and throughout the world, has taken from it its poignancy. Those who desire to retain inherited Jewish concepts but find it difficult intellectually to do so, resort to elastic interpretation by retaining part of the doctrine and discarding the other. In the case of the Messianic doctrine the emphasis is placed, in certain quarters, not on the

---

[1] See I. Abrahams, Jewish Life in the Middle Ages, pp. 413-415.

advent but on the millennium, not on the Messiah but on the blissful age. Possibly the shift from kingship and autocracy to democracy in political and social life and the increasing spread of inter-racial and international good-will accounts for the altered conception of the doctrine. However, it cannot be gainsaid that the history of the world is the biography of its great men. In the history of the United States, the martyr President of the Civil War, quite normal and commonplace in so many ways, has been greatly idealized. Posterity has surrounded his person with the aureole of an almost religious sanctity. Likewise, every nation has its dominating figures to whom the eminence of the nation is ascribed. Israel, the priest-people, the servant of God, has not outgrown the spiritual concept of a person who will be measured in terms of universal and eternal greatness, and will effect a final and lasting transformation of society. This redeemer will be a conquering personality who will possess intuitive wisdom and superb piety, the vision and buoyancy of the prophets, and the stamina and power of a formidable champion. He will be acclaimed for his ability to win for Israel the decisive possession of Palestine. He will administer a final rebuke to the Gentile world for its irreligious and uncharitable conduct. He will summon all mankind to pay homage to the covenant announced at Sinai.

After following the course of this doctrine as taught by the leading medieval thinkers for 500 years, we find that Abrabanel cherished the same ideal as Saadia, and if we were to record the range of views on the Messianic doctrine within the circle of believers today, it would no doubt be the same as that reflected in these pages. The virile heart of our people even now expects the great fulfillment. The need for our salvation and the salvation of mankind is as exigent to-day as in yester-years. The world that environs us may change, we may be able to penetrate and ascertain the secrets of the physical universe, but the internal life of man and the spiritual potentialities of humanity are still to be understood and controlled. Man needs to be reconditioned. Society needs reconstruction. Israel must emerge from her lowly position. The creed of the Synagogue expresses through the Messianic doctrine its awareness of human infirmities and fallibilities and offers the vehicle of faith and good deeds for the eventual triumph of the virtuous.

Appendix

ABRAHAM BAR HIYYA

1—*The Megillat-ha-Megalleh.*[1]

a. Its Peculiar Methodology.

The Megillat-ha-Megalleh of Abraham bar Hiyya of Barcelona, Spain, 1065-1136, astronomer and philosopher, is historically noteworthy for several reasons. It is the first eschatological work of an European rabbi and the forerunner of the abundant Messianic literature of the medieval rabbis. Its author exerted a very marked influence, particularly in astrology, on Nahmanides and Abrabanel. Then again, it is the key to the metaphysics and mysticism of the author and of his school, which represented a distinct tendency in Jewish scholasticism. The book is a peculiar conglomeration of esoteric exegesis, astrological history, and number-worship, with, of course, certain rationalistic parts which render it of unique value in the variegated development of the Messianic doctrine. And how different is the methodology of Hiyya from that of Maimonides or Crescas!

The chief Messianic contributions of this book are:

1. Its concern with the pivotal question of the year of the redeemer's advent.

2. The adaptation of the creation story of Genesis to eschatology.

---

[1]*Megillat-ha-Megalleh* (Scroll of the Redeemer). Ed. by A. Posnanski, for the first time with introduction and notes, by Dr. J. Guttmann, Berlin, 1924.

3. The use of astral science to verify the past history of Israel and the world, and to furnish a clue to the final redemption.

The writer offers no description of the course and character of events of the Messianic age, in the manner of other authorities. His chief desire is to ascertain the apocalyptic "end", and for this purpose he draws upon philosophy to establish the premise that as time had a beginning, so it must have an end—at the expiration of the seventh millennium. He employs Scripture—Mosaic, prophetic, and Danielic verses—to arrive at a definite terminal year. Confidently, he points to the coming grand conjunction (every 2859 years) of Saturn and Jupiter, which will herald the transformation of the cosmos and of humanity.

The reader of this strange eschatological work notes the author's timidity. He always appears on the defensive, almost apologetic. He feels constrained to justify both his anxiety and his unprecedented method in quest of the "end". His rationalization leads him to conclude that any principle based on the Torah, which inspires and strengthens the people, deserves investigation and sympathetic treatment. However, everyone is permitted the widest latitude in conceiving of the advent in his own way, because the Messianic belief, unlike the ritualistic or legislative precepts, must not be accepted according to precise, unchanging rules. He therefore feels free to proceed in his own manner. "When I saw that Scripture allows the multitude to ponder over this thing, I mused, that with them I will ponder and investigate this sealed thing. When we see men, mighty in wisdom and God-fearing, of the present generation, as well as the great men of former times, consider this matter and compute the end, let this not deter nor restrain us from investigating and doing likewise. We do not aver that every seeker will ascertain (the date) beyond peradventure, but we do say that he is worthy of praise; he may be on the right path and with God's help fathom the secret to its depths. The termination of the diaspora will become known, especially when the time mentioned by the Bible approaches. 'For the words are hid and concealed until the time of the end.' "[2]

According to their attitude toward the doctrine, people may be grouped into three classes. There are those who categorically deny that salvation is possible or that the "end" must arrive. These are heretics, and his book does not purport to be a refutation of their negative and un-Jewish point of view. Then there are the Christians who assert that the Messiah has already arrived and that the time of salvation has long since passed. By his calculations Abraham bar Hiyya ventures to prove that both these events must be awaited in the future. Finally there are the believers who retain faith in the Jewish dogma. They will derive strength and consolation from his deductions.[3]

b. Mystical Exegesis of the Creation Story.

Rabbi Abraham, the Prince, adheres very strongly to the mystical exegesis that the seven days of the creation allude to the history and progress of the human race over a period of seven thousand years.[4] Much space is given to an exposition of this theory. He shows how the phenomenal things enumerated in the Genesis story have been paralleled by significant occurrences in the past, and how certain other events, to take place in the future world, are intimated. "It has been strongly maintained among us that the seven days are the days (the periods) of the universe. . . . It is clear that if we could ascertain the measure of one day, as a day of the universe, we could

2*Ibid.*, p. 2.
3*Ibid.*, p. 3.
4*Ibid.*, ch. 3-4.

comprehend the duration of the world."[5] The declarative "he" prefixed to the sixth day—"hayom hashishi"—which is not used in mentioning the first five days, is a presentiment of the sixth millennium.[6] The Sabbath day represents the seventh millennium, which will ensue after the salvation of Israel has been accomplished.[7] Through a midrashic procedure, Abraham bar Hiyya discovers the chronological divisions of man's evolution upon earth in the following sentences: Gen. 2:7: "Then the Lord God formed man"—from the flood to the revelation. Gen. 2:7: "He breathed into his nostrils the breath of life"—from revelation to the Messiah. Gen. 2:7: "Man became a living soul"—from the Messiah ben David to the resurrection.

Several Biblical lines suggest certain characteristics of the future world. "The great lights"—Gen. 1:16—refer to the luminaries in the world to come. "The dust of the ground"—Gen. 2:7—of which man was formed, is the specially selected dust which will be recognizable at the resurrection and will identify the resurrected person.[8] The designation of green herbs as food of wild beasts refers to the tameness of animals in the future world. This is corroborated by Isaiah's prediction—11:7—"And the lion shall eat straw like the ox." The serpent alone will not feed on forage, but is irrevocably doomed to bite the dust.[9] The longevity of man in the world to come will result from the knowledge of how to nourish and sustain his physical and spiritual powers properly. The promise of new heavens in Isaiah signifies that the firmament will possess and radiate its own light, instead of receiving

---

[5]*Ibid.*, p. 19.

[6]Bahya ben Asher on Gen. 2:3.

[7]Moses Hess, Jewish nationalist leader messianized the *Genesis* story in his *Rome and Jerusalem*, published in 1862. See Waxman's trans., N. Y., 1918, pp. 132, *et seq.*

[8]Thus our author explains "Dust thou art and to dust (wherewith thou wast formed) thou wilt return" (at the resurrection). This deduction is made in Ber. Rabba, 7.

[9]For this thought see Mid. Tehilim on Ps. 1:2.

illumination from the sun. Then there will be no darkness. The light of the present day will be the light of the night in the future. With the new earth, predicted by the prophet, will come the cessation of hate and ferocity among beasts. These alterations, marvelous though they be, will not be against the course of nature. They have been prepared and have pre-existed from the time of creation, and await only the propitious hour for their installation. This explanation of the Messianic wonders accords with the sentiment of Eccles. 1:9: "There is nothing new under the sun." The rabbis paraphrased this thought thus: some things will appear to be new at the redemption, which really are not, for they came into being at the creation of Adam.[10] The splitting of the Mount of Olives—Zech. 14:4 —a marvel which many scholars reverentially place in the Messianic era, is dismissed as a simple thing. "It will not be one of the changes, because stones and hills can shatter and divide under present circumstances and there is nothing new in it. I do not include this fact nor other things like it."

c. Defends His Method and Conclusions.

Abraham bar Hiyya had to meet a barrage of objections to his peculiar adaptation of the Genesis story to the coming of the millennium. Nothing daunted, he very frankly lists the grounds of opposition. It is contended that his technique had no antecedents in the writings of the rabbis, who should be the only authorities to follow in this respect. Nowhere, as far as is known, did they arrive at specific knowledge of the "end" from the first chapter of Genesis. Secondly, his exegesis contradicts that of the rabbis. Thirdly, he should consistently expound the entire Scripture in his own peculiar way, and draw his calculations not only from the first chapter but also from those

---

[10]Megillat, p. 57. This also is the view of Maimonides.

that follow. Other critics questioned the philosopher regarding the longevity of the first generation. Finally, there is the criticism that he offers only homilies and allusions. Diverse interpretations of the same passages have been propounded by other scholars, and hence there is nothing decisive in his declarations. In the case of resurrection, for instance, not one indubitable promise that it will occur has been quoted from Scripture.[11]

The author replies to each argument with great lucidity and pointedness. To the first objection he makes the sharp rejoinder that if he, perchance, had not come across any eschatological theories based on Genesis in the rabbis, it is possible that someone else may have seen them. The fund of knowledge in the rabbis is both wide and deep. The very dictum that the world was created for the sake of Israel only—Sabb. 88a—renders it natural for us to seek in the Bible, aye, in the very first chapter, for the key to her history and destiny. Furthermore, he, a philosopher, may differ from the ancient sages, but difference does not involve contradiction. Divergent views on the same subject are permissible, for it is generally emphasized that the Torah is elastic and capable of more than one interpretation. Anyone who desires him to follow the same exegesis of the Holy Writings through succeeding generations, asks too much. The fact is, grants the rabbi, that "every chapter, word and letter in the Bible has a secret connotation. Would that we could grasp a little of this mighty knowledge! But the vastness of the literature should not make us desist. We must search as far as we can." To the opinion that the verses in the Genesis story allow of various meanings, he answers: "This should not stop me from expressing what I believe."

The complaint that his Biblical text is at best a mere allusion to the future, he dismisses on the ground that

---

[11]*Ibid.*, p. 74.

such allusions are not without value, nor do they affect
the soundness of his system, since that is all one can expect
on such matters. Other passages which certainly betoken
the future redemption are also stated in recondite language.[12] It is quite surprising that the blessing bestowed
upon Judah by Jacob—Gen. 49:10—is not taken to be
Messianic by our erudite rabbi. He cannot understand
why Jacob should predict so distant an event as the appearance of the Messiah and not foretell the glorious
achievements of Moses and the magnificent reign of David.
His explanation of the verse, a quite reasonable one, is
that the supremacy of Judah will be limited to his tribe
until the sanctuary at Shiloh is destroyed. Then, through
the ascendancy of David, will Judah's rule spread over
entire Israel. Strangely enough, he finds the Messiah
indicated in the least suspected passage of Gen. 49:11-12:

> "He washeth his garments in wine,
> And his vesture in the blood of grapes;
> His eyes shall be red with wine,
> And his teeth white with milk."

"Wine" and "blood" are reminiscent of the golden age
of David, stained with bloody warfare. The "milk white
teeth" intimates the perfect and peaceful regime of the
ideal future Messiah.[13] The use of the name "Anani" in
I Chron. 3:22-24, which in the Talmud is given as one of
the names of the Messiah, leads him to believe that the
passage is Messianic.[14] "It is obvious", he remarks, "that
the verses in I Chron. 3:22-24 are not for the purpose of
enumerating all those generations, but to serve as an allusion to the advent, which will occur at the end of the
generations."[15]

---

[12]*Ibid.*, p. 74.
[13]In Ber. R. 98:14, references to the Messiah are made from this
figurative language.
[14]Tanhuma, ed Buber, p. 140, the "Anani" in I Chron. 3:24 is identified with "Anani" in Dan. 7:13 where it means cloud.
[15]Megillat, p. 80.

THE DOCTRINE OF THE MESSIAH

2—The "End".

a. Calculations Based on Biblical Verses.

The "end" was revealed to Moses at Sinai and was known to the prophets, sages, and members of the Sanhedrin, as a tradition handed down from the great lawgiver. They did not disclose the "end", because it was so remote. It was imbedded in the Torah, and now that the time is close at hand it may be discovered there and revealed. Most writers exploit the enigmatic figures in Daniel to obtain knowledge of the secret year. Abraham bar Hiyya makes it clear that the visions of Daniel were not written specifically for the purpose of divulging the "end", but that they were given casually. Daniel treats of the course of history and the divine providence over nations in the same way as other great prophets. Many of the calculations made by our author are based on the belief that the world will endure six millennia, corresponding to the six days of creation, and on the tradition that the Torah was promulgated in the middle of the world's history—at the end of the third millennium. The actual dates were obtained by a process of duplication.[16]

(a) The following calculation is based on the traditional chronology, which held that the promulgation of the Torah or the people's entrance into Palestine occurred in the middle of the world's duration—the end of the third day—either 2448 or 2495. Doubling these two periods would bring us down to 4896 (1136 C. E.) or 4990 (1230 C. E.) the threshold of the Messianic era. This does not imply that the Messiah must arrive in these years, but that the period of his possible arrival begins then.

(b) Deut. 28:63: "As the Lord rejoiced over you to do you good and to multiply you, so the Lord will rejoice over you to cause you to perish, and to destroy you."

16*Ibid.*, p. 36.

Hence the period of suffering will be as long as the period of rejoicing. The latter amounted to 1380 years, the interval from the Sinaitic revelation, 2448, to the second destruction in 3828. Accordingly, 1380 years reckoned from 3828 will furnish the most distant year of the advent, 5208, or 1448 C. E.

(c) Is. 40:2 is proof:

> "Bid Jerusalem take heart
> And proclaim unto her,
> That her time of service is accomplished,
> That her guilt is paid off;
> That she hath received of the Lord's hand
> *Double* for all her sins."

Here the calculator doubles the 890 years from the Sinaitic revelation to the first destruction, and arrives at the number 1780. Then, adding this to 3338, the year of the destruction, he finds the total to be 5118, or 1358 C. E.[17]

(d) The Talmudic statement that the world will endure 6000 years, the fifth and sixth millennia of which will comprise the Messianic era, is to be taken literally. The prince expounds the legend that the Messiah was born on the day the Temple was destroyed, not as signifying his actual birth, but the rise of the hope in a restorer. This gives us 3338, the year of the first destruction, or the end of the fourth day, and leaves 2662 for the fifth, sixth, and seventh days. One day is 887⅓ years, or 890 in round numbers. Doubling 890, for the fifth and sixth days of the Messiah, we have 1780; added to 3338, this gives us 5118. Rabbi Abraham sets the earlier date for the advent and the later date, 5163, for the resurrection.[18]

(e) Other calculations are the result of strained Midrashic interpretations of Bible verses. Ps. 90:4:

---

[17]*Ibid.,* pp. 38, 39.
[18]San. 97ab; Megillat, pp. 39-47.

"For a thousand years in Thy sight
Are but as yesterday when it is past,
And as a watch in the night."

Here the calculator takes "a watch in the night" to be
part of the thousand years. One thousand years therefore
equals twenty-eight hours, that is the full twenty-four
hours of "yesterday", plus four hours, which is a watch or
"a third of the night"; consequently the evaluation of a
twenty-four hour day is 857⅐ years. Further, 857 x 2
(two Messianic millennia) equals 1714. This added to the
year 3448 is the precise time when the fourth chiliad
spoken of in the Talmudic statement ended, yielding 5162
for the end. This harmonizes with Daniel's figure 1335,
plus 3828; hence the second destruction is set for 5163.[19]

(f) Lev. 25:10: "And ye shall return each man to his
inheritance and each man to his family, shall ye return",
is an intimation of the final restoration of Israel to its
patrimony, Palestine, and the resurrection—the return
of each person to his family. As the fiftieth year is the
Jubilee of freedom, so the fiftieth generation will witness
the liberation of all Israel. The period of the seven generations from Adam to Enoch is 687 years; seven times
that yields 4809, forty-nine generations. Adding the sum
of the 300 years up to the death of Enoch yields the result-
ant 5109, the date of the redemption.[20]

(g) Another fantastic calculation is based on Deut.
32:8:

"When the Most High gave to the nations their
inheritance,
When He separated the children of men,
He set the borders of the peoples
According to the number of the children of Israel."

19 *Ibid.*, p. 46.
20 *Ibid.*, p. 72.

Abraham bar Hiyya infers from this that God will increase Israel in the diaspora until she reaches the population of the sixty-nine nations which flourished at the time
of the Exodus; and then He will redeem His people. He
arrives at the figure 2760 by multiplying the number of
the nations, sixty-nine, by forty, the number of years
Israel dwelt in the wilderness. 2760 plus 2448, the year
of the Exodus, gives 5208, the year of the resurrection.[21]

Unlike Saadia, R. Abraham does not make the conflicting Danielic figures 2300, 1290, and 1335 terminate
in the same year, but in successive periods.

(h) Dan. 8:14: "Until 2300 evenings and mornings
shall the sanctuary be victorious." The numeration begins
from the erection of the first Temple, 2928. Adding 2300
to this number results in 5228, or 1468 C. E., the "end".
If one reckons from the Davidic conception of the erection of the Temple, then the final date is 5208, or twenty
years earlier.[22]

(i) Dan. 12:11: "From the time that the daily sacrifice shall be taken away. . . . shall be 1290 days." The
scholar identifies the event alluded to with the destruction of the second Temple in 3828; adding 1290 to this
gives an aggregate of 5118, or 1359 C. E. "Times" equals
560 plus 472 years of Mohammedan possession, or 1032.
258 (½ of 472) and 1032 equals 1290 years, corresponding
to the 1290 in Daniel. The forty-five years to 1335 will be
occupied with the wars of Gog.[23]

b. Calculations Based on Astrology.

The eschatology of the philosopher is of unusual interest, because it is steeped in astrology. He employed this
pseudo-science not as a primary source but secondarily,

---

[21]*Ibid.*, pp. 76-77.
[22]*Ibid.*, pp. 89-90.
[23]*Ibid.*, p. 108.

to confirm his Messianic faith and his mathematics based on the Bible. Other rabbis were absorbed in it and had recourse to it in their visionary writings, but none used it so extensively and so freely. Indeed, the revered sage feels compelled to apologize for resorting to this "Gentile science". "The contents of this section", he says, "are refuse and dregs compared to what has been told in previous parts, derived from worthwhile sources, from holy men and holy writings. This part, however, is built on the knowledge of fools, obtained from the absurd arguments of Gentile peoples.[24] If we were firm in our faith we would not require this chapter but be content with what has preceded. The latter is sacred, this is profane." He justifies his wanderings in this astral wonderland on the expedient ground that his book might be perused by those who believe in astrology and desire verification from it. Incidentally, his conclusions will demonstrate the sufficiency of the Torah for every purpose. They will persuade the non-Jew of the correctness of the Bible teaching concerning providence and destiny. The sages themselves approved of astrology, as is obvious from the passage in Moed Katon 28a: "My son, life and sustenance do not depend upon merit, but upon the constellations." The dictum, Sabb. 156a, that Israel has no "mazel", is not a denial of astral influence, but informs us that Israel is not controlled and governed by a star as are other nations. In the case of Israel the power and decisions of the stars can be reversed by righteous men.[25] The conjunction of the two planets, Jupiter and Saturn, "the highest and the lowest of all planets", and also the largest except the sun, reveals all the events of history, Israelitish and universal, since creation. The seventh major conjunction

---

[24]*Ibid.*, p. 11. The entire Chapter V, pp. 111-115, deals with astrology.
[25]*Ibid.*, p. 115. See the illuminating article by A. Marx, "The Correspondence Between the Rabbis of Southern France and Maimonides About Astrology," in H. U. C. Annual, III, 1926, pp. 311-357.

(every 238 years) of the two planets in the earthly trigon, constellation Virgo, began in 3794. It marked the beginning of Israel's tragedy, the appearance of the disciples of Jesus, and the spread of the new faith. With the next major conjunction appeared Constantine the Great, who aided the spreading of the new religion, and Mani, the teacher of dualism and the founder of the Manichaean religion. The major conjunction in the watery trigon, constellation Scorpio, saw the insane Mohammed rise to power in 427. The prince characterizes Mohammed as insane and illiterate, and places him as a man far below the respectable level of Jesus and Mani. Thus he says: "The first ones, although they were absolute rebels, were descendants of royalty and of the renowned of the world, but this rebel was despicable and vile. . . . And because his star was hid from all the stars, his own people testified against him that he was devoid of all wisdom, bereft of understanding, able neither to write nor to read."[26] "One does not find", says the sage, "a system innovated after the establishment of Israel, and after the promulgation of the Torah at Sinai, save these systems which are alluded to in Daniel. They testify against themselves, and astrology testifies against them that they are perverted systems and false and reprehensible religions. Hence the savants of the nations who are absorbed in the science of the stars and in other sciences will be forced to confess that truth and justice are not found among any worldly power except Israel. If one remains obtuse and doubts, let him consider the movements of the stars as we have and see the truthfulness of the matter, and his doubts will depart. For this reason have I expatiated upon the explanation of the planetary movements in every respect, in order that the store of arguments and difficulties and their solutions may be at the disposal of all

---

[26]*Ibid.,* pp. 139-140.

who wish to argue and obstruct, or to clarify and solve.
If this section effected only this much good, it would have
been sufficient; how much more that it harbors other
worthwhile things."[27]

The Torah, which long preceded all other dispensa-
tions, was promulgated in the grand conjunction of Saturn
and Jupiter (every 2859 years) in the watery trigon, constellation Pisces, in the year 2365, which betokens truth
and righteousness. The next grand conjunction will be
in 5224, 1464 C. E. (2365 plus 2859 equals 5224), at which
time the downfall of the Gentile powers and the salvation
of the Hebrew people will take place. The world will
then return to its original state of innocence, and the marvelous things that have been created and concealed at the
beginning of the world will be made manifest.[28]

Lest the influence of the stars negate the power and
providence of God, the prince avers that their good and
evil influence is not absolute. The Almighty controls, and
can nullify their effects upon civilization. "We affirm
concerning each movement that it conduces to such and
such, provided it is desirable before the Infinite to fulfill the design of the stars. If not, He will do His pleasure,
since He is omnipotent."[29]

3—*Resurrection.*

That the doctrine of resurrection was a live question
in these centuries appears from the considerable treatment
pro and con it received by these medieval leaders of
Jewish thought.

It would be seemly, avers R. Abraham, to desist from
investigating the question of resurrection anew, and to
rely upon Saadia Gaon, who so clearly demonstrated from

---

[27] *Ibid.,* p. 145.
[28] *Ibid.,* p. 112.
[29] *Ibid.*

Holy Writ the certainty of the miracle. There are, however, some who deny its possibility. The following passage
vividly sets forth the skeptical attitude toward the doctrine, so prevalent in his days, which made it necessary
for him to re-emphasize it. "But I have seen and heard
of men of our race and generation in Spain and in France,
who declare that the proofs offered by the gaon are not
adequate. Since they are wise and depend upon their own
reason and trust to their knowledge, it is difficult for them
(to understand) that a man should live and return to this
world after death, except possibly at the great day of
judgment. But how a person can live again in this world,
without pain, sickness, and death overtaking him, they
cannot grasp. Their logic does not admit it. It is not the
normal thing. Then they argue that they do not find mention of resurrection in the Torah of our master, Moses, nor
any allusion on which they can rely. And how can they be
expected to trust in that which is not derived from the
Torah? These are false thinkers who interpret the resurrection passages as parables or metaphors that magnify
the final salvation of Israel. Israel, they say, will
revive."[30]

Anyone who construes the text beyond its literal meaning, even if he asserts faith in the eschatological future, is
a heretic. He perverts the plain word of God. However,
there are unambiguous promises which bear no other meaning than resurrection. Such a promise is contained in
Ezek. 37:12-14. This clearly presages the miracle not at
Judgment Day but at the redemption. Dan. 12:2 gives
positive assurance of resurrection. The use of the word
"many", restricting it to Israel, indicates it will occur
at redemption, for if it applied to the great Judgment
Day, all the departed, the good and bad of all nations,
would arise. The most conclusive arguments, however, are

---

[30]*Ibid.*, pp. 48-49.

the historical facts of the dead recalled to life by Elijah and Elisha. One who denies resurrection disbelieves a basic doctrine and excludes himself from the Jewish fold. It betrays a distrust in God to suppose that He who created the world from nothing cannot revive the dead.

The re-existence at redemption will be limited to Israel. All the dead will not be revived simultaneously and in the same place, but they will be raised up in the lands wherein they died. In this way they will come into possession of the entire earth, which will then be called the "Land of Israel". The dispersion took place so that Israel might be scattered over the world, and thus receive dominion everywhere on the day of the resurrection. Concerning the difficulty of restoring the former body of the resurrected one, Abraham bar Hiyya affirms that God can be relied upon to recognize and utilize the corporeal elements of the former body. Although he derides, finally, the absurdity of the belief in the transmigration of souls, he nevertheless sees in it a confirmation of the doctrine of resurrection. For the soul after its many incarnations, will return to the original body.

In accordance with the psychology current in the Middle Ages, inherited from Plato and Aristotle, Abraham b. Hiyya attributed three powers to the soul: the physical, the vital, and the psychical. The immortal part of the human soul, which will merit survival in the world to come, is the psychical, for through it man acquires imperishable wisdom and understanding.

BIBLIOGRAPHY

SOURCES

Bible. J. P. S. translation.

Talmud (especially Sanhedrin 97a-b).

Midrash Rabbah. Chapters and paragraphs acc. to Menorah edition.

Eschatological Midrashim in Jellinek's Bet-ha-Midrash, Leipzig and Vienna, 1853-1877.

Midrashim quoted in Raymond Martini, Pugio Fidei, Leipzig, 1687.

SAADIA—Emunot v'Deot, Bialystok, 1913.
Commentary on the Scriptures.

GABIROL—Shire Kodesh ed. Bialik, Tel. Abib, 1925.
Selected Religious Poems, Davidson-Zangwill, Philadelphia, 1923.

RASHI—Commentary on the Bible.

ABRAHAM b. HIYYA—Megillat ha-Megalleh. Berlin, 1924.

JUDAH HALEVI—Kuzari, Wilna, 1914.
His Poetic Works, ed. by A. Harkavy, Warsaw, 1893.

ABRAHAM IBN EZRA—Commentary on the Bible.
Poetic Works ed. by D. Kahana, Warsaw, 1922.

MAIMONIDES—More Nebukim, Wilna, 1904.
Mishneh Torah, Kobez Teshubot ha-Rambam, Leipzig, 1859, including Iggeret Teman, Maamar Tehiyyat ha-Metim, Iggeret ha-Shemad, Pirke Haslaha.

NAHMANIDES—Commentary on the Pentateuch; Shaar he-Gemul, Warsaw, 1876; Sefer ha-Geulah, ed. Jacob Lipschitz, London, 1909; Wikkuah, ed. M. Steinschneider, Stettin, 1860; Torat Adonai Temimah, ed. Ad. Jellinek, Leipzig, 1853.

CRESCAS—Or Adonai, Vienna, 1860.
Bittul Ikarei ha-Nozrim, written in Spanish and translated into Hebrew by the polemist, Joseph Shem-Tob, 1451.

ALBO—Sefer ha-Ikkarim, Warsaw, 1877.

ISAAC ABRABANEL—Comm. on the Pentateuch, Chernowitz, 1860; Comm. on Later Prophets, Leipzig, 1641; Mashmia Yeshuah, Amsterdam, 1644; Yeshuot Meshiho, Koenigsberg, 1860; Mayene ha-Yeshuah, Amsterdam, 1647; Rosh Amanah, Warsaw, 1881; Ateret Zekenim, Warsaw, 1894; Nahlat Abot, Venice, 1567.

LITERATURE SOURCES

Articles on the Messiah and Eschatology in the Real Encyclopedie of Hamburger, the Jewish Encyclopedia, and Hasting's Dictionary of the Bible.

BECK, JOSEPH—Ueber die Entwickelung u. Darstellung der Messianischen Idee in den heiligen Schriften des alten Bundes, Hannover, 1835.

BERDYCZEWSKI, M. J.—Messias-legenden, Tubingen, 1926.

BERNFELD, S.—Daąt Elohim, Berlin, 1899.

BERTHOLET, ALFRED—Die Israelitischen Vorstellungen vom zustand nach dem Tode, Freiburg, 1899.

BRODY and ALBRECHT—The New Hebrew School of Poets of the Spanish Arabian Epoch, Leipzig, 1906.

BUDDE, K. F. R.—Die sogenannten Ebed-Jahwe Lieder, Giessen, 1900.

CASTELLI, DAVID—Il Messia secondo gli Ebrei, Firense, 1874.

CHARLES, R. H.—Eschatology, Hebrew, Jewish and Christian, London, 1899.

DALMAN, G. H.—Der Leidende und sterbende Messias der Synagoge, Berlin, 1888.

DRUMMOND, JAMES—The Jewish Messiah, London, 1877.

ELBOGEN, ISMAR—Die Messianische Idee in den alten judischen Gebeten, Berlin, 1912.

ELIAKIM b. ABRAHAM—Maamar Binah l'Ittim, London, 1795.

FRAIDL—Die Exegese der Siebzig Wochen Daniels in der alten und Mittlern Zeit, 1883.

FRIEDLANDER, I.—Past and Present, Cincinnati, 1919.

FRIEDLANDER, J.—Standard Book of Jewish Verse, N. Y., 1917.

GINZBERG, L.—Eine Unbekannte Sekte, Ch. on Messiology, N. Y., 1922.

GREENSTONE, J. H.—The Messiah Idea in Jewish History, Philadelphia, 1906.

GRESSMAN, HUGO—Der Messias, Göttingen, 1929.

GRESSMAN, HUGO—The Sources of Israel's Messianic Hope, American Journal of Theology, Chicago, 1913, vol. 17, pp. 173-194.

GUEDEMANN, M.—Juedische Apologetik, Glogau, 1906.

HOCK, C. H.—Gründe für die Enstehung der Messianische Weissagung in Israel, N. Y., 1902.

KLAUSNER, JOSEPH—The Messianic Idea in Israel in the Period of the Prophets (in Hebrew), Cracow, 1908; Die Messianischen Vorstellungen des Judischen Volkes in Zeitalter der Tannaiten, Berlin, 1904.

KOENIG EDUARD—Die Messianischen Weissagungen des alten Testaments, Stuttgart, 1925.

KOHLER, K.—Jewish Theology, Ch. 52, 53, 54, 57, N. Y., 1918.

KOPLOWITZ, ISIDORE—Mosheach or Messiah, Athens, Ga., 1907.

LAGRANGE, MARIE JOSEPH—Le Messianisme ches les Juifs, Paris, 1909.

MOORE, G. F.—Judaism, Vol. 11, pt. 7, Ch. 1, 3, Cambridge, 1927.

NEUBAUER, A.—Jewish Controversy, in Expositor, Vol. VII, third series.

NEUBAUER and DRIVER—The Fifty-third Chapter of Isaiah according to Jewish Interpreters, Oxford and London, 1876-1877.

OESTERLY, W. O. E.—The Evolution of the Messianic Idea, N. Y., Dutton, 1909.

POSNANSKI, A.—Schiloh, Leipzig, 1904.

RABINSOHN, MARCUS—Le Messianisme dans la Talmud et les Midraschim, Paris, 1907.

SCHECHTER, S.—Studies in Judaism, First Series, Essays, 4, 6, Philadelphia, 1911.

SCHWARTZ, SAMUEL—Die Messias-zeit, Vienna, 1860.

SELLIN, ERNST—Die Israelitisch-Juedische Heilandserwartung, Berlin, 1909.

SILVER, A. H.—Messianic Speculation in Israel, New York, 1927.

SUSMAN, MARGARETE—Die Messianische Idee als Friedensidee, Berlin, 1929.

TEMPLER, B.—Die Unsterblickleitslehre bei den Juedischen Philosophen des Mittelalter, Vienna, 1895.

TYDINGS, JOSEPH M.—The Messiah of the Targums, Talmuds and Rabbinical Writers, Louisville, 1912.

WASSERZUG, D.—The Messianic Idea, London, 1913.

WUENSCHE, AUGUST—Die Leiden des Messias, Leipzig, 1870.

ZACUTO, ABRAHAM—Motuk l'Nefesh (on Eschatology), Venice, 1607.

The Subject of "ends", when the Messiah might be expected, is treated by the following scholars:

Azariah di Rossi in Meor Enayim, Ch. 43.

A. Marx, Hazofeh, Vol. 5, Budapest, 1921, pp. 194-202, publication of text on Messiah dates.

D. Holub, in his edition of Iggeret Teman, 1875, pp. 53-66.

L. Zunz, Gesammelte Schriften, Vol. III, pp. 224-231.

H. Malter, on Saadia's Mess. calculation in the Journal of Jewish Lore and Philosophy, Vol. 1, pp. 45-59.

INDEX

Abrabanel—see Isaac Abrabanel.

Abraham bar Hiyya—313ff. interprets creation mystically 315-7, eschatology 319, "End" 320-3, astrology 325, resurrection 326-8.

Abraham Ibn Ezra—104ff. comm. on Daniel 78, personal characteristics 104, plaint-poems of poverty 105, enormous influence 105, wit and humor 106, and Isaiah, Ezekiel and Daniel 111, method of exegesis 112-3.

Advent—Ibn Ezra on 112, degeneration before 259. See End of Days.

Akiba—Fall of Rome 12, and non-miraculous Mess. 148, Abrabanel contradicts 266, and Bar Kochba 17.

Albo—see Joseph Albo.

Almohades—excesses 107.

Apocalypse—prophetic 7, Ezekiel, Daniel 8.

Apostasy—Maimonides on 140-2.

Appendix—Abraham bar Hiyya 315.

Aristotle, Opposed by Halevi 81.

Armilus, Saadia mentions first 43.

Astrology—differences on 301-2, and Abr. bar Hiyya 324-5.

Ateret Zekenim—by Abrabanel 227-8.

Avicebron—a Jew 66.

Bahya—emphasizes Judaism 27.

Bar Kochba—the deliverer 12, military measures 17.

Bialik—edits Gabirol 67.

Bible—see Scripture.

Book of Principles—by Albo 210, 211.

Cabalists—and Mess. 148, Maimon. disputes 160, Nahmanides 162-3, Abrabanel 231, 262.

Canticles—Mess. Ibn Ezra 124-5.

Christianity—Mess. idea 15, Rashi opposes 53, 60, Gabirol on 66, comp. with Islam 69, disputed by Maimon. 136, Mess. pivotal for 177-8, and Crescas 197ff., opp. by Albo 210, 211, opp. by Abrabanel 229, 230, and fulfilment 251-3, borrowed Anti-Christ 263, idea of Mess. opposed 272-3, in final war 280-2, providential 310.

Converts—to be servants 49.

Creation—mystical interp. 315-7.

Crescas—see Hasdai Crescas.

Daniel—Biblical apocalypse 8, Saadia interp. 36-7, Saadia explains "End" 39-41, on resurrection 46, Rashi cites 56-9, 60, refers to Cyrus 61, expl. by Gabirol 68, and Ibn Ezra 111, 118-9, 120, cited by Maimon. 137, and resurrection 154, not Christological,

Hiyya—see Abr. bar Hiyya.

Hosea—Messianic 117.

Human Nature—in Mess. State 152.

Ibn Daud—describes Gabirol 65.

Ibn Ezra—see Abraham Ibn Ezra.

Ibn Gabirol—see Solomon Ibn Gabirol.

Ingathering—see Restoration.

Isaac Abrabanel—biog. 225, expulsion of Jews 225, science and script. 226, denounced Albo and Crescas 226, opp. Maimon. 227, Mess. 227, works of 227ff., aims 229, Christology 229-30, against rationalizers 231, anti-Cabalist 232, Script. exegesis 232, Minor prophets 237, Dan. 237, Psalms 237, Redemption 237, Repentance 239, End 242ff., use of Dan. 246ff., controversial 248, on Is. 53—252-3, on Jesus 253ff., on visions of Dan. 257-8, and Advent 259, Talmud 260ff., Cabalism 262, Mess. b. Joseph 262-3, Redemption 264-5, Restoration 265-6, Mess. necessary 267-8, functions of Mess. 269-70, pre-existed 270, character 271, explains 275-6, fate of Israel 280ff., Mess. Age 283ff., criticizes Maimon. 284, resurrection 285ff., differs from Maimon. 289, regeneration of man 289ff., differs from Rashi 292, and New Temple 293-4, restoration of polit. life 295-6, sovereignty of Israel 297-8, earlier gaonic views VII.

Isaiah—miraculous redemption 5, forecasts return 33, Hezekiah the Mess. 11, predicts disarmament 6, apocalyptic 9, resurrection 46, Saadia app. to Mess. Age 50, describes Mess. 58, Rashi interprets 60-1, and Millen. 62-4, and Ibn Ezra 111-17, Maimon. explains 152, redemption in 170-1, in Nahmanides debate 181-4, opp. to Matt. 211, consummated 215, Return 217, refers to Israel 220, to poor 221, rich in Mess. ideas 234-6, Ch. 53 Abrabanel 252-6, Abrabanel cites 273-5, and suff. Mess. 277-8, contradictions expl. 285, and Church 308-9.

Islam—see Mohammedanism.

Israel—sins cause of suffering 31, basis of Mess. belief 33, to be saved 36, must suffer, Saadia 42, enemies of 44, to gather 48, Rashi's prayer 53-4, suffering 55, to be freed 63, cry of, Gabirol 66, enslaved Gabirol 71, "wounded dove" Gabirol 72, confidence sustained 73-4, must hope 76, dispersion Halevi 83, preparing for glory 85, in dispersion Halevi 90, 91, Seen as bride, Halevi 92, unique rel. to God 94, dove of god, 97, internal life 107, dove of Ibn Ezra 108, opp. by Gentiles 109, and redemption 164, eternity of 215-6, redemption 238, to be emancipated 241, fate of 280, to dominate 285, her felicity 295-6, to be sovereign 297-8, legend of rule 298, sins and dispersion 305, final salvation 327.

Jeremiah—says Israel is eternal 6, and End 64, redemption in 171, Mess. sections 236.

Jerusalem—in Mess. Age 21, home of righteous 63, enlarged 64.

Jesus—as Mess. 15, not fulfilment to Saadia 34, Saadia refutes Christ, args. 36, too late, Rashi 60-1, false prohpet 137, in Nahmanides debate 178-80, not Mess. Abrabanel 230, and atonement 254.

Jewish Dogmas—and Crescas 194-5, Albo 211-2.

Job—not opposed to resurrection 46.

Joel—and Millennium 62.

Johanan b. Zakkai—redemption imminent 11.

Joseph Albo—209ff. and Geronimo 209, explains doctrines of Jud. 211, opp. Maimon. 211-3, Crescas 212-6, three central principles 212,

129, Maimon.'s picture 130, motive of hope 130-1, Maimon. doctrine 133, and Script. 134, prefigured 135, soon to come 139-40, prophecy to prepare for 145, def. by Maimon. 146-7, non-miraculous, 148, Cabalist idea 148, state 149, era 150, duration of 151, miracles 151, human nature of 152, and Future World 156, not pivotal to Judaism 177-8, legend in debate 182-6, Nahmanides 163, divinity of 184, Crescas' theory 196, diff. concerning 198-9, calculation opp. 199, doctrine to Albo 211-2, based on Torah 214, 219, and Gog 220, theme variously handled 300, similarities 301, Maimon. theory 302-3, great legacy to Med. Jewry 303-4, son of David 304-5, mathematics 306, apologet. 307-8, not fascinating to mod. Jews 310, virile heart still expects 311-2, ideas of Megillat-ha-Megalleh 313ff., in Minor prophets 237, Psalms 237, Dan. 237, must appear 240, not yet come 248, doctrine of Jud. 227, in Abrabanel 227ff., future program 233-4, Isaiah 235, Jer. 236, Ezek. 236, and Sanhedrin 249-50, and Jesus 253ff., replica of Moses 267, necessary to redemption 267-8, functions of 289-70, preexistence 270, human 271, Isaiah cited 273-5, suffering of 277-8, age, type and devotion 283.

Messiah son of Joseph—9, and Elijah 15, forerunner, Saadia, 43, figment of imagination 16, lacking 68, in Malachi 118, Maimon. omits 149, in Canticles 124, to appear 175-6, Crescas' idea 197, and Anti-Christ 262-3, in Midrash 279, agreement on 309.

Micah—redemption idea 5, cited as foreteller 33, Rashi explains 57, Halevi cites 86, Mess. 117.

Midrash—and Armilus 43, and Rashi 52, Ibn Ezra 113, on Mess. 276-7.

Millennium—Rashi names 54, his idea of 62.

Miracles—to occur in Mess. Age 33, 35, at the last 63, in Mess. State 151.

Mohammedan Oppression—Halevi 99, worse than Christian 69, condemned by Gabirol 70, persecution, Maimon. 127, Maimon. disputes 136, in final war 280-2.

Nahlat Abot—comm. on Ethics of the Fathers 285-6.

Nahmanides (Moses b. Nahman)—162ff., opponent of Maimon. 162, mystic 162, Mess. 163-4, redemption 166ff., on Dan. 172-3, End 173-4, disputation 176ff., eschatology 187-8, Maimon. 189-90, his suavity 34, defends Maimon. 158.

Nahum—vision of deliverance 11.

Neo-Platonism—of Gabirol 65.

Obadiah—Mess. 117.

Pablo Christiani—and Nahmanides 176ff.

Palestine, hub of Halevi's thought 86, and resurrection 24, Halevi on 89, his attachment to 101-2, incentive 132-3.

Paradise—see World to Come.

Pharisees—resurrection 22.

Poetry—Gabirol 65, Ibn Ezra 105.

Prayers, for Mess. 31.

Prophets, present Mess. idea 5, and rabbis 14, Malachi's vision 11, reveal God's will 32, and apocalypse 8, ignore Mess. b. Jos. 9, Nahum's vision 11, conditions of redemption 36, Rashi interprets 52, true acc. Maimon. 139, to precede Mess. 145, redemption in 170-2, cited by Abr. bar Hiyya 327.

Providence, explained by Saadia 38.

Psalms—Rashi cites 54-5, refers to Rome 57, Rashi Interp. 62, and Millennium 62, and Paradise 64, Mess. 121-4, in Nahmanides debate 186, explained 275-6.

Rabbi Akiba—see Akiba.

Rabbinic Ideas—9. see Talmud.

Rashi—51ff., commentaries 51, Mess. Exegesis 53, Calculates the End 59, cited by Abrabanel 292.

Redemption—preparation for 41, authority for 164-6, in Abrabanel 237, Character of 264-5, war and final 282.

"Refutation of Christian Principles", Crescas 197ff.

Regeneration of man—Abrabanel 289ff.

Repentance—to precede redemption 41-2, and redemption 239.

Restoration of Israel—and Mess. 6, in Mess. Age 18, dispersed to gather 48, Gabirol's theory 75, and Mess Doctrine 77, Halevi on 84, 97, Crescas 196, feature of redemption 265-6, of relig. life 290, of political 295-6.

Resurrection—part of Mess. Idea 22, miracle of 24, Saadia in Emunot 44, not illogical 45, as Saadia conceives 46, his details 47, in Mill. 64, and Isaiah 115, and righteous, Ibn Ezra 120, 125, Maimon's dogma 153, essay on 153, difficulties 154, and Dan. 154, and Torah 155, acc. to Nahmanides 191, Crescas 201-3, purpose of 204, possibility 205, life in 207, grounds for belief 220-1, is possible 221-2, universal 223, and body 223, Abrabanel explains 285ff., cardinal principle 286, Maimon.'s theory 303, diff. theories 307, of Abr. bar Hiyya 326-8.

Revelation—Halevi's concept 82.

Revenge—as motive 132.

Rome and Roman—related to Mess. 9, in Mess. Age 19, 20, oppression 56-7, end of rule 143-4, degeneracy 260, in final war 281.

Saadia Gaon—27ff, trans. script. into Arabic 28, defends trad. 29, book of Doctrines and Beliefs 26, prayers for Mess. 31, refutes Karaites 28, expands Jud. 27, presents Midrashic school VII, Jesus did not fulfill 34, polemist 34, refutes Christ. args. 36, interprets Dan. 36-7, Expl. providence 38, on repentance 41-2, theory of Mess. b. Jos. 43, resurrection 44, on Ps. 73:39, Job 14:12—46, details of resurrection 47, Isaiah 51, date of End past 60, theologian of Mess. 67, and Maimon., future world 156.

Sadducees—resurrection 22.

Sanhedrin—and Mess. 249.

Schechter—on Abrabanel 227.

Scripture—on resurrection 22, trans. into Arabic 28, basis of Mess. 29, 5 proofs of redemption 35, and resurrection 45, Ibn Ezra's exegesis 113, his Mess. interp. 114, Maimon. interprets 130, value acc. to him 132, sanctions Mess. hope 134, no ref. to Jesus or Mohammed 137-8, redemption from 166-9, and science 226, Abrabanel's use 226, not fulfilled 230-1, exegesis of Abrabanel 232.

Second Commonwealth—not up to Mess. Idea 35.

Seder Olam—semi-historical book 16.

Shekina, in Palestine 87.

Shiloh—explained by Saadia 37.

Solomon Ibn Gabirol—65ff., philosophic 27, 1st poet of redemption 65, original philosopher 65, true to trad. 67, suffering under Islam 69, optimism of 76, astrological calculation 78.

Spain—auto-da-fes in 192-3, expulsion of Jews 225.

Spiritual State—Maimon. 158-9.

Suffering—and innocent 38.